ORGANIZATIONAL AND PROCEDURAL ISSUES IN GOVERNMENT

L.P. Singh 1912-1998

ORGANIZATIONAL AND PROCEDURAL ISSUES IN GOVERNMENT

Editors
Ramesh Kumar Tiwari
Sujata Singh

INDIAN INSTITUTE OF PUBLIC ADMINISTRATION

GYAN

Organizational and Procedural Issues in Government

ISBN : 978-81-212-1148-2

Published in 2012 in India by
Gyan Publishing House
23, Main Ansari Road, Daryaganj,
New Delhi - 110002
Phones : 23282060, 23261060
Fax : (011) 23285914
E-mail: books@gyanbooks.com
website: gyanbooks.com

Laser Type Setting : Rajender Vashist, Delhi
Printed at : Chawla Offset Printers, Delhi

This book is dedicated with gratitude
to the memory of
Shri L.P. Singh
1912-1998
Governor, Assam, Manipur, Meghalaya,
Nagaland and Tripura
1973-1981
Editor, *Indian Journal of Public Administration*
1958-1970

Contents

PART II
SELECTED ADDRESSES OF L.P. SINGH

PART III
EXTRACTS FROM GOVERNMENT REPORTS

Foreword

The machinery of the Government of India and its procedures of work has been a subject frequently analyzed and debated since Independence. The Gopalaswami Ayyangar Committee (1949), Estimates Committee of Parliament (1951), A.D. Gorwala Report on Public Administration (1951), and the First Five Year Plan (1952), emphasized the need for reorganization of the machinery of the Government of India and its procedures of work. This was further strengthened by Paul H. Appleby's Report on Public Administration in India (1953).

However, it was Pandit Jawaharlal Nehru, the first Prime Minister of India, more than anyone else, who was keen to bring about change in the administrative system. His whole emphasis was on how to adapt the administrative system to the temper of democratic government. He was critical of the existing administrative system in terms of structure, procedures and outlook. On these issues, he gave vent to his feelings, primarily in his 'Letters to Chief Ministers'. These fortnightly letters reflect his views on many contemporary problems. Most of them are still with us. But from the perspective of public administration, these letters reflect the importance he attached to it. In the contemporary literature on administrative reform, this important source rarely finds mention. In a letter addressed to Chief Ministers as early as May 1948, Nehru observed "the question of overhauling the administrative machinery of government is very much before us. My experience here has led me to the conclusion that our present machinery is to some extent archaic and certainly not conducive to rapid and efficient handling of matters. There is a great deal of lack of coordination and red tape and unnecessary noting" (*Letters to Chief Ministers, 1947-49*, Volume I, p.122). He wanted to give the administration of the country a different set of objectives and change its entire tone and tenor. Nehru was aware of the fact that the government departments work without "organic unity" of purpose. He was of the view that the administrative machinery does not permit the people to feel that they are partners in running the state machine. He was keen that the administrative machinery should fit in with democratic and developmental processes.

Besides, as Prime Minister, Nehru was from the very beginning critical of the rules and procedures which were framed during colonial times. He questioned their applicability and relevance and pleaded that they should be changed to keep them in tune with the changing times. Nehru particularly emphasized the need for change in the civil services classification rules, central appeal rules, fundamental rules, supplementary rules and the financial rules. He attached the greatest importance to the change in procedures, because he felt that even the best policies could slow down and be made less effective if the "procedures are cumbersome and result in diluting the policies." These procedures often result in delay and this leads to corruption making the administration rather "irresponsible." He agreed with Paul H. Appleby on the problems relating to procedures, rules of business, lack of administrative delegation, diffusion of responsibility and class character of the services.

'Measures for Strengthening of Administration' (1961) was an important initiative by the Prime Minister towards strengthening the administration. These measures provide the essence of Nehru's thinking on the administrative problems so as to make the system responsive, accountable and transparent. These measures suggest: individuals and organizations should be judged strictly by the test of results; itemized examination of financial proposals should be confined only to vital matters; additional powers to the head of department to accomplish the implementation of programmes; simplification of procedures and attention to relations with the public, etc.

However, despite a number of committees recommending changes in these areas, a feeling persists nothing substantial has been done as regards their implementation in true spirit. As a consequence, nothing much has happened in the direction of rationalization of organizational restructuring and work ethos. Organizational restructuring and improvement in procedures continue to be important. Organizational restructuring is the primary step towards a meaningful administrative reform.

I am very happy that we are bringing out under the Golden Jubilee series, a publication devoted to organizational and procedural issues in government. This collection includes not only some important essays on the subject published in the *Indian Journal of Public Administration* from 1955 to 2008, but also the paper dealing with the Measures for Strengthening of Administration, digest of Report of the First Administrative Reforms Commission on the Machinery of the Government of India and its Procedures of Work, as well as Extracts from the Report of the two Administrative Reforms Commissions, Report of the Fifth Pay Commission and significant excerpts from the Report of the Second Administrative Reforms Commission on Organizational Structure of Government of India. Much of this material is not easily available to students and scholars of administration. These extracts in a way update the thinking on these issues. I congratulate Prof. Ramesh Kumar Tiwari and Prof. Sujata Singh for providing an overview of administrative reorganization and procedures as well as effectively summing-up the basic theme of the valuable material that constitutes the volume.

T.N. Chaturvedi

Chairman,

Indian Institute of Public Administration

Former Governor of Karnataka and Kerala

Preface

Research and publication on issues relating to the machinery of the government has been one of the important objectives of the Institute. In its formative years, studies were undertaken in this direction. In this context, *The Organization of the Government of India* (1958) was one of the important publications of the Institute. Besides, the Institute contributed immensely to the Administrative Reforms Commission's Reports on the 'Machinery of the Government of India and its Procedures of Work' (1968).

This Golden Jubilee volume (whose publication unfortunately got delayed) devoted to the organizational and procedural issues in government is a step forward in the same direction. It contains articles which deal broadly with the concept of productivity in administration, organizational effectiveness, work study, efficiency in development administration, organizational goals, reform in the system of filing and noting and of inter-departmental references, improving state administration, and reform of administrative procedures, etc. It also contains two very important documents: Prime Minister Nehru's Measures for Strengthening of Administration (1961); and a Digest of Report on the Machinery of the Government of India and its Procedures of Work (1968). Besides, to bring the volume more upto-date and to show how thinking evolved, effort has also been put in to provide extracts from the Fifth Pay Commission (1997), the Expenditure Reforms Commission Reports (2000), and from the Report of the Second Administrative Reforms Commission on Organizational Structure of Government of India (2009) having bearing on these questions.

This volume compliments the earlier volumes brought out on the occasion of the silver jubilee of the Institute on various aspects of public administration such as: district administration, union-state relations, panchayati raj, administrative theory, comparative public administration, local institutions, urban development, police administration, planning and its implementation, public enterprises, administrative reforms, development administration, and local government, as well as more recent books of selected articles from the *Indian Journal of Public Administration* on the role of the district collector, multi-level planning, natural resources and public administration, and fifty years of panchayati raj and development.

Professors Ramesh Kumar Tiwari and Sujata Singh have worked hard at putting together this volume which is dedicated to the memory of Shri L.P. Singh who in addition to being a distinguished civil servant was closely associated with the development of the Institute since its inception. He edited the *Indian Journal of Public Administration (IJPA)* from 1958 to 1970. Under his editorship, the IJPA received international recognition which is evident from the fact that distinguished scholars from all over the world contributed to it and it was also very widely quoted. As part of the tribute to Shri L.P. Singh, we have also included some of his significant writings/addresses like: Training of Civil Servants; Morality in Public Affairs; Sardar Patel and the Indian Administration; and Administrative Leadership.

We are grateful to Shri T.N. Chaturvedi, Chairman, Indian Institute of Public Administration, for writing a tribute to Shri L.P. Singh. We are also thankful to Shri Bishan Tandon for specially contributing an article on Shri L.P. Singh.

Dr. Rakesh Hooja
Director,
Indian Institute of Public Administration

Acknowledgements

We are thankful to Kamal Jit Kumar, Chief Librarian, Centre for Policy Research, New Delhi, for providing some publications of Shri L.P. Singh brought out under the aegis of the Centre for Policy Research, New Delhi. We are thankful to Sunita Gulati and Narender Kumar of the IIPA library for providing necessary information and references for this volume. We also sincerely thank Sunil Dutt, Assistant Editor, and other members of IIPA's Publication Section for their painstaking effort in ensuring the quality of this publication. We are thankful to Suparna Das Mukherjee for assisting us in the preparation of a chapter. We are also thankful to Gulshan Arora Senior Personal Secretary to the Director IIPA for providing some important information regarding this volume

We are grateful to H.P. Singh and Ajay Singh Verma who provided excellent secretarial assistance in the completion of this volume. We are also thankful to Taruna Rani for providing all necessary support in the library and computer related work.

Ramesh Kumar Tiwari
Sujata Singh

L.P. Singh: Visionary Administrator

T.N. Chaturvedi

Shri L.P. Singh, during his four and half decades of public service career in the ICS (1935-1981), served in various capacities in the government: Chief Secretary, Bihar; Union Home Secretary; Ambassador to Nepal and Governor of Assam, Manipur, Meghalaya, Nagaland and Tripura. He was associated as Member-Secretary with the Second Pay Commission and also served as member of the Committee on the Prevention of Corruption. All these positions provided him an opportunity to look closely at real political and administrative issues. After his retirement from public life, he devoted his time to reflecting on issues related to ethical standards in public life, electoral reforms, political institutions, national integration and Indian bureaucracy.

Probity in public affairs was not only an issue of abiding interest but also a matter of faith to him. He attributed to Indian politics the decline of public morality. He observed that in Indian politics there is no place for "ideological divisions", and social, political and economic issues are "guided mainly by lust for power." As a consequence, over the years, the high ideals of Indian politics "lost much of its finer features". He pleaded for "courageous action" to contain this problem: a law against defections; measures to check the operations of the black economy; to break the nexus between electoral politics and money; observance of the Code of Conduct for Ministers (embodied in law); and legislation to establish the institution of Lokpal.

Electoral reform was another area which drew his attention. He brought out a full length study on this problem, where he provided a broad perspective on issues relating to the electoral system of the country. This study not only examined the deficiencies in the present electoral system but also suggested partial modification in the system of representation. He was categorical in his views regarding the generation and growth of *black-money* and its link with politics and administration: "The requirement of funds for fighting elections, and to a lesser extent for meeting the needs of political parties for other political activities, legitimate or illegitimate, has led to a heavy, if not exclusive, dependence on those operating the black economy; and these have, at least in the past, received a return in the form of virtual freedom to carry on their unlawful activities, apart from positive favours in the form of governmental decisions". Further, this linkage has resulted in a "general lowering of ethical standards in public and personal life and is at the root of much of the prevailing corruption in politics and administration". He was in favour of the state providing funds to political parties for developing and maintaining their organization. These issues continue to agitate the public mind even today.

Shri L.P. Singh was also deeply concerned with the problem of national integration. He pointed out that totalitarianism, pluralism, and fundamentalism have never been a feature of Indian society and the Indian Constitution is in line with the history and culture of the country. He was of the view that there is a need to have a general civil code which would be applicable also to the Muslim community. He not only advocated horizontal integration to bring about a desired level of national integration, but also felt the need for vertical integration to uplift the poor and the downtrodden to the mainstream of national life.

In a paper on the role of the Rajya Sabha in the Indian federal system, he was critical of the fact that political considerations were playing an important role in the nominations of the nominated members. He also observed that this situation did not evoke public criticism and protest due to the "dulling of constitutional and ethical sensibilities...." He suggested that the provision for nominations be deleted, and instead, nominations be made from a panel approved by the Inter-State Council. This is certainly an insightful suggestion and gives meaning to the significance to the rationale of the Rajya Sabha.

Shri L.P. Singh had deep insights into and understanding of the problems of the Indian bureaucracy. He was of the view that the field level bureaucracy was too "pliable", and that civil servants in India, by and large, "function in a mechanical way". Besides, there was not enough sense of vocation and far too much of "careerism". Regarding the commitment of civil servants, he observed that a civil servant in India took an oath of loyalty to the Constitution, and, therefore, he "commits himself to the Preamble, the Fundamental Rights and the Directive Principles, among other provisions of the Constitution". A good civil servant "subordinates his personal beliefs and the interests of the social group to which he belongs to his professional loyalty to the Government he is serving". He was of the view that a "strong sense of professional obligation will make them conform in their work to the social ideas and values of their Government".

He felt that a generalist administrator should possess specialization in some field as he went along. For the highest level posts, he was of the view that "the net has to be cast wide to get from the specialized groups men with conspicuous managerial ability and wide understanding of problems". The answer lay in training particular groups for specialization. For a rapidly changing technological and social environment, training had to match "the job requirements of today and those of tomorrow and perhaps the day after should be blended".

During his tenure as the Union Home Secretary (1966-70), he initiated a number of measures for the modernization of the police force in the country, particularly in establishing the Border Security Force, Central Industrial Security Force; Bureau of Police Research and Development, and Research and Policy Division (Ministry of Home Affairs). He also took the initiative in setting up a Committee on police training for the purpose of reorganizing the police force in a manner appropriate to a democratic and secular country. Besides, he also tackled some complex and sensitive problems like language problem in Assam, and the Hazratbal episode, in Srinagar etc.

Shri L.P. Singh was closely associated with the Indian Institute of Public Administration since its inception. He was a Member of the Institute's Executive Council in its formative years, Vice-President of the Institute in the late 1980s and Editor of the *Indian Journal of Public Administration* (1958-1970). As editor, he was of the view that there should be "fundamental rethinking on the basic problems of public administration". Due to his dedication and scholarship, the journal became a leader in the field of public administration. He also started the practice of bringing out special issues on contemporary problems: Panchayati Raj, Administrative Reforms, Public Enterprises, the role of Collector, Food Production, Urbanization etc. At the suggestion of Bertrand De *Jouvenel*, a distinguished *French* political philosopher, he started *Perspectives* series of studies in social, political and economic forecasting. The objective was to understand the process of change taking place in Indian life. He was instrumental in setting up at the IIPA, "The Indian Council for the Future", (1963) for the promotion of such studies in India. He was also a founder member of the Governing Board of the Centre for Policy Research, New Delhi.

I had the opportunity to have known him from the late 1950s. As a young officer from Rajasthan, along with my senior colleague Shri Mohan Mukerji, I met him first when the State Government of Rajasthan wanted to set up an Officer's Training School (now H.C. Mathur Institute of Public Administration) and we wanted to seek his views and guidance in the matter. He gave us a masterly analysis of the situation and the problem which enabled us to submit our Report. I happened to be in the U.S.A. when he was for a year invited to Harvard University on a fellowship. He was highly regarded by his peers and particularly the distinguished members of the faculty. I saw the same consideration and respect accorded to him when he visited the World Bank. He took great interest in the training of civil servants. It was his sweet persuasiveness which made me join as Joint Director, National Academy of Administration (now named after Prime Minister Shri Lal Bahadur Shastri). He took very keen interest in the training of civil servants and various aspects of administrative reforms. He visited the Academy, addressed the probationers and interacted with them. He asked me to write a paper about the so-called 'sandwich pattern of training' and submit it to the Ministry, which adopted it with modifications. It was at his initiative that a Conference of Central Vigilance Commissioners was organized to discuss about the implementation of the Santhanam Committee Report. The then Chief Central Vigilance Commissioner, the late Subimal Dutt, was also present. It became for the next few years an annual feature at the Academy. Besides, I recall my continuing contact and interaction with Shri. L.P. Singh, when I was Secretary of the Ministry of Education and Culture and later on Union Home Secretary on issues relating to state governments and people in the sensitive border states in the North East.

Shri L.P. Singh was a man of ideas and action. He combined in himself both idealism and realism. This enabled him to suggest ways and means to resolve complicated matters. He always gave strong support to the young and upright officers with potential. A man of principles, he had courage of conviction. He could speak Truth to Power. He also stood by an officer if he smelt any victimization or unfair treatment. He had unparalleled familiarity with the world of administration and his effort was to simulate research in quest of better performance in the service of the people in our democratic set-up. I pay my homage to the memory of this great public servant.

L.P. Singh: A Tribute

Bishan Tandon

I first met L.P. Singh in September 1956 when he came to the Ministry of Home Affairs as an Officer on Special Duty. I was then working as an Under Secretary there. But I had become familiar with his name in the University of Allahabad in the early forties. He was remembered in the Department of English, as also in his hostel the famous Muir Hostel (now renamed after the legendry Vice-Chancellor of that University, Dr. Amarnatha Jha), as an outstanding student. He was in fact offered a post of Lecturer there when he passed the M.A. Examination. But he had made up his mind to compete for the Indian Civil Service and so when he missed it by one position in India he went away to London where he succeeded at the next competitive examination. After his probationary training for a year, he started his life as a public servant at Gaya in 1936. He served in Bihar and Orissa for the next twenty years. Even before he completed twelve years of service he was appointed Chief Secretary to the Government of Bihar in May 1948 and remained in that position till he was called to New Delhi in September 1956.

He had a distinguished career at the center also. Between 1956 and 1970 he worked mostly in the Ministry of Home Affairs (including a spell as Member Secretary of the Second Pay Commission), with a year's interlude as a Fellow at the Center for International Affairs, Harvard University. In 1964 he was appointed as Home Secretary and served in that capacity for more than six years, a record still not surpassed. After retirement from the ICS, which was taken before it was actually due, he was persuaded to become India's Ambassador to Nepal (1971-73) and was subsequently appointed Governor of Assam and the other four states in the north-east and remained there for eight years.

This article was specially written for this volume.

His coming to the Central Government in September 1956 as an OSD (in the rank of a Joint Secretary) has a very significant background. Replying to the debate on the demand of grants for the Ministry of Home Affairs in April-May that year the Home Minister, Pandit G.B. Pant announced that he was soon going to take action regarding administrative reforms. The general expectation was that a commission would be appointed for the purpose. But the Home Minister decided to appoint a single officer to go into the various aspects of administration and recommend appropriate measures for action. Obviously the Home Minister thought that the worthwhile changes and invocations in administration and management of services could be brought about from within the civil services. Bureaucracy has, at all times, been accused to be inert and unduly bound by tradition but the superb administrator in the Home Ministry would have thought that since the institution has by and large done reasonably well, it must be having within it perceptive and socially conscious far-sighted persons who could recognize the future needs and requirements of the administrative structure and functioning and could devise remedial measures. After all it was then becoming known that most of the important recommendations of the Hoover Commission in the USA had come from within the civil services. L.P. Singh was thus the personal choice of Pandit G.B. Pant for this assignment.

It is unfortunate that L.P. Singh worked in this post only for less than a year. In September 1957 when the Second Pay Commission was set up by the Central Government he was appointed its Member-Secretary. The work he was doing in the field of administrative reforms came to a premature end. But even during this short span of about a year he was able to do considerable work on certain important aspects of the civil services, including probation, recruitment, training etc. In brief, the setting up of a National Academy of Administration, training institutes for a number of professional services, framing of a foundational course for most of the superior services and related matters owe much to the recommendations made by him in this assignment. It is however not widely known now that he was very disappointed when against his advise the National Academy of Administration was located, for political reasons, at Mussoorie and the grand building built up for it in New Delhi had to be transferred to the Jawarharlal Nehru University.

A special mention must be made of the two recommendations made by him and implemented without undue delay. The first one related to the emphasis given to the interview in the scheme of competitive examination held by the Union Public Service Commission for recruitment to the IAS and other superior services. The Commission insisted that unless a candidate secured at least 35% marks in the interview he would not be considered as qualified for any superior service irrespective of his/her marks in the written papers. What was worse—there was patently a great degree of arbitrariness in the marks given by the interview board to various candidates. There was considerable agitation among a sizable section of candidates on the system as it was being operated and a large number of representations were received against it by the Ministry of Home Affairs. These were referred to the OSD for examination. L.P. Singh made a very systematic study of this question with the help of the mark sheets of the examinations held since 1947. He came to the conclusion that there was substance in the complaint which required rectification. He wanted a discussion with the Chairman of the Commission but, to begin with, was invited to a session of the interview board which was holding its meetings in New Delhi those days. What L.P. Singh experienced at that session clinched the ultimate decision in the matter. After the interview of a candidate was over the board wanted to disqualify him. L.P. Singh considered it necessary to intervene on being told that the candidate lacked personality and his expression was somewhat poor. In reply to a query by L.P. Singh the board accepted that the intellectual content of the candidate's replies was satisfactory. L.P. Singh then retorted that he would like to suggest to the members to look at their photographs and record how they themselves spoke before they went to London to take the ICS examination or were at the closing stage of their university education. The candidate was saved from being disqualified. It may be interesting to know that this candidate had a remarkable career in service culminating in his serving as Secretary to the Prime Minister. Anyway, this entire exercise resulted in the abolition of the rule relating to the qualifying marks.

The other matter related to the increasing requirements of the IAS officers for the developing administration. The existing cadres were proving to be inadequate and it was feared that in the coming years the difficulty would be accentuated. At the time of the Partition (1947) the ICS cadres were seriously depleted by the termination of the covenants of the British officers (including 4 Indians) and departure of a number of Muslim officers to Pakistan. An emergency recruitment was inevitable (1948-1951) to tide over the difficulty. But another special recruitment had to be planned in 1957-58. L.P. Singh was not at all enthusiastic about the continuance of such ad hoc recruitments from time to time. On the basis of two very detailed studies–one on the contribution of Indian universities to the IAS during 1947-56 (in which he was very excited to find that his alma mater's performance was the best) and the other on what should be the annual intake keeping in view the anticipated requirements of the central and state governments during the next fifteen years or so he worked out a broad plan of substantially increased annual recruitment. This study also showed that compared with the recruitment of Indians to the ICS, both from the London and the Indian examinations, during 1920-36, the increased recruitment would not affect the general quality of the new entrants to the IAS. The states generally agreed with the proposed plan of action. The ministries and departments controlling other superior services were advised to consider similar proposals.

Subsequently it was discovered in the old records that in 1945 the then home department had invited F.G. Rowlands, a retired ICS officer, from England to study the long-term problem of reorganization of the services to suit post war conditions. The report submitted in June 1945 had worked the requirement of ICS/ IP officers up to 1985-but mainly on considerations different from those examined by L.P. Singh.

L.P. Singh was an outstanding civil servant mainly because he had a deep understanding of the society, the welfare of human beings, the political leadership and the administration, which was the main instrument through which the political will was executed. As he said in one of his talks "In the ultimate analysis, it is the norms and values of a society and the goals it seeks to achieve, that shape the character of its government and determine the performance of its administration. And in a democracy the sort of individuals the citizens elect to the legislatures are of fundamental importance". He considered the political leadership to be of the highest important and since its will, as stated earlier, was executed by the administration, the administrative leadership was 'an essential complement of political leadership'. A harmonious relationship between the two was therefore absolutely necessary. In our conditions this would be possible if a civil servant has firm faith in the Constitution, in the fundamental rights and the directive principles and above all in freedom, democracy and the rule of law. He should have an understanding of human beings and a genuine interest in their welfare. This would require an academic purposefulness in him with devotion to 'acquisition and communication of knowledge' to sharpen his intellectual equipment which, according to Singh was essential in a good civil servant.

It was not a mere preaching. L.P. Singh himself was all the time engaged in academic work also. At the Center for International Affairs, Harvard University (1959-60) he was engaged in a study of parliamentary control over public undertakings. He was intimately associated with the IIPA and was the editor of its journal for many years. He was on the governing bodies of the IIM, Ahmedabad and ICSSR, New Delhi. He was a founder member of the Center for Policy Research, New Delhi and remained active in its academic work for many years. Above all his idealism whetted these qualities. This enabled him to make significant contribution in building institutions to strengthen administration. He believed that institutions were as important, if not more, as individuals in public administration.

With these basic qualities, in the day-to-day work our system requires a civil servant to remain detached from partisan politics. He has no doubt to carry out faithfully the policies and lawful orders of the government he is serving. But, as Paul Appleby, a public administration expert invited to India by our Prime Minister in the nineteen-fifties, warned that this loyalty to policies and administrative discipline must not be extended to identification with the political party running the government (or, it may be added, to any political party). L.P. Singh's contribution to administration was highly appreciated by all the ministers with whom he worked and consequently became close to them. But he kept his aloofness in matters purely of a political nature. In 1962, elections Sukhadia failed to get a majority in the Rajasthan assembly and political bargainings were reportedly rampant. Shastriji, the Home Minister, wanted L.P. Singh to talk to Sukhadia and some others to find out what was happening. He declined to do so saying that if he did that he would be accused of meddling in politics to help the Congress Party. He would, he added, certainly request the Chief Secretary to keep the Home Ministry informed of the developments so that it should remain in readiness in case it became necessary to arrange for the imposition of the President's rule, which was essentially an administrative function.

But when it came to official work he would express his views and advise without 'any fear that it would displease' the political bosses. In fact, that was his nature. Just one example. In 1970 the government's proposal to abolish the privy purses of the rulers of the erstwhile Indian states was defeated, thanks to a member of the ruling party itself, in Parliament by a fraction of a vote. The Prime Minister was not inclined to let the matter rest at that. She decided to recommend to the President that he should derecognize each and every prince individually. The Home Secretary (L.P. Singh) was summoned after the decision had been taken; all others had left. To put it briefly, L.P. Singh, speaking with a candour advised that the matter required to be considered further before a final decision was taken. But the decision had already been taken. At the same time, L.P. Singh fully recognized where such candid speaking had to be restrained – and often completely. When in respect of the publication by the New York Times the report on the receipt of foreign money by the political parties and other organizations Bhupesh Gupta in a speech in the Rajya Sabha, held L.P. Singh responsible for the leakage he maintained his silence though he had come to know how that had happened. He considered that such allegations were professional hazard and that it was for the government and/or ministers concerned to defend the officer concerned as considered appropriate.

L.P. Singh worked mostly in 'a period of relatively clean politics and administration'. But by the time he formally quit the service in the seventies he had seen the coming decline, which was corroding the early idealism and creating an atmosphere of cynicism. This was due to substantial dilution of moral standards in public life, widespread corruption, 'intrusion of political factors' and personal influences' in service matters and the fast growth of the black economy. An administrator like L.P. Singh was deeply affected by this deterioration and could not remain silent. His anguish and unhappiness is writ large in a number of his public addresses at the universities and other organizations of higher learning. His Dr. Amarnatha Jha memorial lectures three in number delivered at the Darbhanga University in February 1983 have got converted into a remarkable document of our attachment to values and the moral decline. Only L.P. Singh, with his abilities, wide learning and personal qualities, could have painted this picture in a superbly objective manner. The administration today is certainly missing such a stalwart.

Introduction

Ramesh Kumar Tiwari and *Sujata Singh*

After independence, we could give for the governance of the country, a Constitution. We could also provide an approach to development through the mechanism of the Five Year Plans. The new responsibilities and the compulsions of development and democracy required a different organizational structure, procedures and practices and different outlook. However, we could not provide to the administration of the country, a new set-up and approach to fulfill the responsibilities in the spirit of the Constitution as well as the requirements of planning. As a consequence, we started to face administrative problems since the very beginning.

Various committees including those of Parliament have commented on the defective methods and procedures of work in the Ministries and Departments of Government of India. Some of the common defects noticed are: unnecessary and excessive noting; inadequate attention to problems and vital issues; lack of a proper system of information and control; draw-backs in the system of inter-ministry consultation; lack of scientific problem solving approach, etc. It was also realized that administrative machinery can never run satisfactorily unless the Cabinet functions with a rational combination of subjects. The dilatory procedures of decision-making, inadequate methods of financial and administrative control and absence of rational arrangements for coordination between closely related functions have all been responsible for these deficiencies. The multiplicity of agencies in a single area working without any effective coordination, has been repeatedly highlighted as yet another of the key factors responsible for the inadequate performance in almost all the development programmes. It was felt that in order to create greater confidence in and to generate popular support in the system of planning and development, the administration has to be made a more effective instrument for carrying out the national policies with utmost efficiency.

The cataloguing of the problems of administration since 1947 clearly showed the need for a new approach. It was also realized that reform in public administration has to be based on modifying the system rather than bringing radical changes in it.

It is against this background the question of reorganization of the machinery of government and procedures of work was engaging the attention of the Government of India. To address this issue, the Government of India, appointed N. Gopalaswami Ayyanger, who in November 1949, submitted the Report on "Reorganization of the Machinery of Government".[1] The report emphasized the need to carry out changes in the machinery of government due to insufficient coordination in the framing of policies and plans and inadequate speed and efficiency in their implementation. Ayyanger also mentioned that these defects are serious as far as handling of economic situation and the planning and implementation of development works are concerned. He pointed out that along with these defects there are some other factors which are also of decisive importance: increase in the volume and variety of work; complexity of problems; depletion of experienced personnel; the untrained lower staff and inexperience at the political level. Ayyanger Committee while formulating the proposals for the reorganization of the machinery of the government, outlined the future structure of the Council of Ministers and defined the responsibilities and status of the three categories of ministers. It suggested the constitution of committees of the Cabinet for ensuring coordination and speedy decisions on vital questions of political and economic significance. The Committee also suggested that allied departments should be brought together in a relatively small number of stable groups for financial and administrative coordination and for bringing about coordination of policies and plans. It recommended the strengthening of the Cabinet Secretariat and pleaded for redefining the status and functions of the Cabinet Secretary.

The Estimates Committee's, Second Report on "Reorganization of the Secretariat and Departments of the Government"[2] (1951), recommended reorganization of the work of the secretariat to secure better coordination and unified control over allied subjects. It pleaded for amalgamation of related ministries and departments. Besides, it recommended that the system of drafting, noting and inter-departmental references should be simplified; greater financial powers devolved to the ministries and departments so as to avoid unnecessary delay. It also recommended the revision of the method of disposal of work in the secretariat. A.D. Gorwala in his 'Report on Public Administration'[3] (1951), also stressed on administrative reorganization. This report contains a full chapter on the problem of 'Reform and Reorganization'. Some of the suggestions made by Gorwala relate to: relationship between the ministry and the head of the department; relationship between the administrative ministries and the finance ministry; cabinet rules of business and measures to minimize delay in the disposal of business, etc.

The First Five Year Plan (1952-57)[4] document, highlighted the urgency for the reform of public administration and pointed out the need for changes in the methods of work and organization. It recommended the setting up of Organization and Methods Division to review organization and methods of each ministry. It was felt that this can lead to greater economy and efficiency. The plan document also pointed out the problems relating to simplifying office procedures, elimination of delays, improvement in the system of record management, the movement of files etc. It suggested delegation of responsibilities; relations between the planning units and the executive and administrative sections; and improving the working conditions of the lower grade employees, etc.

Paul H. Appleby's Public Administration: Report of a Survey pointed out the need for change in the administrative structure in the context of democracy. Regarding the structure of administration, Appleby was of the view that it was not tuned to the popular sentiments and needs. He observed that there are too many administrative procedures and there is a need for "vigorous overhauling", primarily from the perspective of the hierarchical movement of paper and the filing system. He pointed out the Rules of Business, Secretariat instructions and Office Manuals are "too didactic and confining, too detailed and unimaginative".[5] As a consequence, there is diffusion of responsibility and clearance is slow. Appleby recommended establishment of a central office to provide leadership role in respect to management and procedures. This office could give attention to work management, work flow, office management, filing systems, space arrangements etc. Appleby also suggested that another important function of this office would be "enhancement of democratic manner and method within the bureaucracy and between the bureaucracy and the public".[6]

The Third Five Year Plan in the context of administrative restructuring, pointed out that the "administrative machinery has been strained at many points".[7] It identified slow pace of execution in the planning, construction and operation of large projects resulting in costs and non-adherence to time schedules as well as lacking in coordination in related sectors.

'Measures For Strengthening of Administration'[8] (1961) laid down by the Prime Minister in the Parliament, contained an approach to significantly reorganize the structure and methods of work: ministries need not conform to a standard pattern of organization; executive agencies should be made stronger and given greater responsibility; greater devolution of responsibility for financial management on the ministries and the executive agencies; and studies to simplify and improve procedures. A Committee on Administration was also established at the Centre headed by the Cabinet Secretary to look into the progress of these decisions and to report periodically to the Cabinet.

The subject of "reorganization" and "procedure of work" was considered so important that it was the first subject which was referred to the Administrative Reforms Commission for their examination. The "Machinery of Government of India and its Procedures of Work"[9] (1968), reviewed the functions of the Council of Ministers, examined the relationship between Ministers, Civil Servants and Parliament; and administrative set-up and methods of work in the Ministries and Departments. The report observed that the administrative machinery of the Government of India, is important as "it sets the pace for efficiency in the entire organization". It recommended a compact cabinet of sixteen ministers so as to ensure homogeneity, speed and purposeful functioning. The size of the Council of Ministers should normally be forty. It also recommended that every department in the Government of India, should be under one Cabinet Minister or the other. The practice of some departments being independently under a junior Minister is not conducive both for policy formulation and decision-making by the Cabinet. The report suggested a rational combination of subjects into portfolios distributed among 16 Cabinet Ministers. It also recommended a Cabinet Committee on Administration to deal with the implementation of the recommendations of the Administrative Reforms Commission. Another important recommendation of the Commission was the setting up of Department of Personnel, to formulate personnel policies and review their implementation. It recommended that the Department of Personnel should be in-charge of the Prime Minister. However, the Department of Administrative Reforms should be retained and be placed directly under the Deputy Prime Minister. The intra-ministerial coordination and the committee system of government should speed up decisions on vital questions of political and economic significance. It also recommended enhanced responsibilities to the Cabinet Secretary. This includes his role as a general coordinator and Principal Advisor to the

Prime Minister, the Cabinet and the Cabinet Committees. Besides, the Cabinet Secretary should be associated in the determination of overall policies and actions concerning the selection and career development of all senior management personnel.

"Economic Administration Reforms Commission" (1983)[10], under the Chairmanship of L.K. Jha, also examined the methods of working in government offices. It pointed out that the present methods of working in government offices reinforce a 'pyramidal structure' which is not conducive to the economy. It was suggested by the Committee that a change in the organizational structure of government offices is necessary.

The Fifth Central Pay Commission[11] (1997) though basically dealt with issues regarding pay and allowances and conditions of service, promotion policies, etc. also examined the role of public services, the work methods and work environment, to suggest rationalization and simplification with a view to promoting efficiency in administration, and optimizing size of the government machinery. The Commission recommended a step-by-step approach to public service reform. The Commission outlined certain broad directions regarding number of ministers, merger of department, size of a ministry, organizations attached to ministries, etc. It discussed the role of the coordinating agencies like Planning Commission, the Prime Minister's Office, Cabinet Secretariat, Department of Programme Implementation etc. This report also recommended reduction of paper work, streamlining file movement, reorganizing Staff Inspection Unit (SIU), Internal Works Study Unit (IWSU), reducing the supervisory levels, etc.

The Expenditure Reforms Commission was set up in February 2000[12]. The Commission submitted ten reports. It recommended a total ban on creation of new posts for two years and a freeze on direct recruitment in all cadres for five years. The focus was on downsizing. The staff declared surplus was to be transferred to the Surplus Cell, re-designated as Division of Retraining and Deployment. It further suggested setting up of a screening committee consisting of the secretary of the concerned ministry, a representative of DOP&T and a representative of Department of Expenditure to prepare annual direct recruitment plan for all cadres.

The Expenditure Reforms Commission observed a substantial increase in the police forces and in some ministries like Information & Broadcasting, on account of a vast expansion in the field network. However, given the extent of automation that has been introduced in most offices with the information technology revolution, the workload in large areas of governmental activities had dramatically reduced, it observed. The Commission also noted the creation of a large number of autonomous bodies, which have experienced a substantial increase in their staff strength. At the same time the financial allocations to most of these organizations were found to figure in the budget under a single entry – "grants".

It found enormous scope for abolishing/reducing functions and activities in government organisations. It suggested a drastic downsizing of the government staff strength to check the burgeoning salary bill so that scarce resources could be utilized in areas such as poverty alleviation, infrastructure and human resource development. The Commission recommended a total ban on creation of new posts for two years and a freeze on direct recruitment in all cadres for five years. It emphasized the need for monitoring and regulating direct recruitment in each department to check the growth of government work force. In addition to the 10 per cent cut already imposed by the government, the Expenditure Reforms Commission recommended a further 10 per cent cut in the sanctioned strength of staff as on 1.1.2000. This was to be carried out by each ministry/department by the year 2004-05. It further suggested setting up of a screening committee consisting of the secretary of the concerned ministry, a representative of DOP&T and a representative from the Department of Expenditure, to prepare annual direct recruitment plan for all cadres. In the case of Group 'A' Services the annual recruitment plan was to be cleared by the Committee headed by the Cabinet Secretary with Secretary of the Department concerned, Secretary (DOPT) and Secretary (Expenditure) as members. The staff declared surplus was to be transferred to the Surplus Cell, re-designated as Division of Retraining and Deployment. Rationalizing the organizational structure of the Government of India was accorded the top priority by the Expenditure Reforms Commission.

Nearly four decades after the First Administrative Reforms Commission(ARC) the Second ARC was set up in August 2005[13]. The six member commission was headed by Shri Veerappa Moily. Its terms of reference included: Organizational structure of the Government of India; Ethics in Governance; Refurbishing of Personnel Administration; Strengthening of Financial Management Systems; Steps to ensure effective administration at the State level; Steps to ensure effective District Administration; Local Self-Government/Panchayati Raj Institutions; Social Capital, Trust and Participative public service delivery; Citizen-centric administration; Promoting e-governance; Issues of Federal Polity; Crisis Management; and Public Order.

The Commission submitted 16 reports. The 13th report of the Second Administrative Reforms Commission focuses on the organizational structure of Government of India. The report examines the issue of reorganization of ministries and departments by revisiting and redefining the role of ministries and departments in view of the evolving role of governance. It also examined the framework for areas wherein there is a need for governmental regulation and the role of regulators therein.

The Report highlighted the weaknesses in the existing structure which include: (a) Undue emphasis on routine functions instead of policy analysis and policy making functions; (b) Proliferation of Ministries/Departments resulting in illogical division of work as also lack of an integrated approach; (c) Too many levels in the hierarchy which do not contribute to the decision-making process; (d) Tendency towards risk avoidance; (e) Rigid hierarchical structure hampering team work; (f) In-efficient delivery of services on account of fragmentation of functions; and (g) Considerable weakening of the autonomy of committees and boards.

So far as the rationalization of the functions of the government was concerned, it emphasized on the need for Government of India to focus primarily on the core functions such as: Defence, International Relations, Public Order, Justice and rule of law; Human development through access to good quality education and healthcare to every citizen; Infrastructure and sustained natural resource development; Social security and social justice; Macro-economic management and economic policy; National policies in other sectors.

Its other important suggestions are: (i) Grouping together departments performing closely related functions under one Ministry to be headed by a First or Coordinating Minister which would thus result in a sharp reduction of Ministries in the Government of India; (ii) Each Department to focus on policy evaluation to be carried out at the end of prescribed periods; (iii) The number of levels through which a file passes for a decision not to exceed three; and (iv) Creating an effective Regulatory framework wherein each Ministry/Department should evolve a 'Management Statement' spelling out the objectives and role of each regulator as also guidelines governing their interaction with the government.

It is evident from the foregoing analysis that almost all committees/commissions appointed by the Government of India to reform public administration, since independence, highlighted the need for change in the administrative structure as well as procedures of works. It is also evident that their recommendations were uniform in approach to the problem of restructuring and procedures. However, nothing much happened in both these areas. It has been rightly pointed out that "organizational reforms have tended to be more in the form than in real substance, leaving little impact on the efficiency of the system. What has been lacking is congruence between strategy, structure and substance. Indian experiments with reforms do not get institutionalized, they often fade away with the personalities who introduced them"[14].

These concerns are echoed in the essays included in this volume. S.N. Sadasivan in his essay on "The Concept of Productivity: Its Application to Administration" debates the implications of the concept of productivity in the context of politics and public administration. He discusses the role of administration. Whereas earlier its role was confined to regulating economic activities, however, now its responsibility is for social development and economic progress. From this perspective, Sadasivan elaborates on the administrative system and the need to reorganize it, so as to make it responsive to the demands of the citizens. Within this framework, the author discusses the monitoring role of administration to achieve the social objectives. He also advocates the need for restructuring of organization and management in each sphere of production. He is of the view that the administrative productivity sustains and promotes economic productivity. But both these have to rely heavily on political productivity. The author warns that political productivity and democracy will decline, if "expediency, personal ambition, family image, temptations, falsifications, craft, cunning and violence" play a role too frequently in the running of government.

The essay on "Organizational Effectiveness: Some Issues" by Anil Chaturvedi focuses on the various approaches to effectiveness and examines criteria for the measurement of effectiveness. The author differentiates between the goal-oriented approaches and the system-oriented approaches.

This essay clearly demonstrates that the literature on organizational effectiveness represents a diverse set of approaches and models. Besides, each set of approaches, models has its strengthens as well as limitations. The author concludes that it is difficult to have a universally accepted definition of effectiveness, as this problem is closely linked with value-laden problem of purpose. Values play an important role in any approach to effectiveness. It is also true that most theorists do not explicitly state their values. The author concedes that the study of effectiveness can provide the much needed frame around which to integrate organization theory.

Indrajit Singh and K.N. Butani's essay on "Work Study in Government Organizations", deals with the experience of the Special Reorganization Unit regarding work study of government organizations. This theme has been analysed in the context of tools of analysis, works simplification, assessment of staff, and organizational matters. The authors describe within the broad framework of tools of analysis: organizational charts, duty lists, job description sheets, process charts and flow charts. These activities provide the nature of duties and also help as a basis for work measurement studies. The second aspect in this essay, deals with work simplification, the whole objective is to suggest simplification in the performance of the various jobs in the organization. The study for this purpose is always undertaken in collaboration with the persons who are engaged in the performance of various jobs. Another important aspect of work study in government organizations deals with work measurement. The authors have cautioned that work measurement exercise requires "considerable education of the organization on the manner in which these studies should be carried out". It has been observed by the authors that whatever method is adopted, a large number of case studies of the past performance, need to be made, if the method has to carry conviction. It has also been pointed out by the authors that the staffing needs of the organization are worked out by multiplying the standards of performance with total amount of work. Similarly, the authors have also pointed out that it is more profitable to make an analysis of the organizational structure only after the methods of work have been "carefully planned out and simplified". The people who are engaged in work study need to be fully trained in "the art of analysis and has to have patience and persuasiveness".

"Speed and Efficiency in Development Administration" by Tarlok Singh deals in the context of development with suggestions like: raising administrative efficiency and standards; simplifying procedures and securing better management. The author also discusses measures for speeding implementation. This depends on: quality of personnel, the extent of their training, supervision, delegation of responsibilities, etc. Within this framework, the author points out the following: need to fix responsibility; procedures relating to financial control; administration of secretariat services and references to the Union Public Service Commission. The author believes that changes in organization and procedures will remove to some extent, the causes for delay. To bring action orientation in administration, the author suggests four essential conditions: policy directives, responsibility for execution, test of performance, and personnel policies. Tarlok Singh emphasizes the need for "procedures which will make for radical re-orientation in attitudes both at the level of policies and of execution". He also discusses administrative problems in the states and the need to ensure right public relations and co-operation from and with the public. He elaborates on the need for reduction of references to the Planning Commission and suggests methods to minimize them.

The essay "Concept of Efficiency in Administration: From Curzon Onward" by S.K. Pachauri, traces the concern for efficiency in Indian administration. He describes the contributions made by Lord Curzon towards: reforming the bureaucracy; simplification of procedures; and introduction of scientific principles in the management of government. He identifies the creation of All India Services; and demarcation of responsibilities under the federal system as some of the major approaches to bring efficiency after independence. He also analyzes the reports of the Administrative Reforms Commission which provided a number of recommendations to make the system efficient such as: creation of more All-India Services; and limiting the role of the IAS etc. Besides, the report of Sarkaria Commission on 'Centre-State Relations' in (1988) also pleaded for more decentralization of power to state governments. The author describes the 73rd Constitutional Amendment (1992) which devolved power to local bodies and discusses in detail the compulsions of liberalization and the need for reform of structures, systems, personnel policies and outlook towards development. In this context, the author mentions the report of Fifth Pay Commission which recommended some significant changes with regard to the restructuring of government in order to enhance the efficiency of government. The author also refers to a report of the Parliamentary Committee which suggested holding mid-career exams for civil servants in order to improve performance and ability. Besides, emphasis has also been given to the introduction of information technology in administration and need for a closer look at policy of transfers and postings.

The purpose of the essay "Understanding Organizations Through Perceptions of Organizational Goals" by Raj Nandy, is to understand organizations through the goals it pursues. For this purpose, the author studies the traffic police department in a metropolitan city. On the basis of an empirical study, the author concludes that a large percentage of officers are not clear about the goals of their organization; "undisciplined and ill-behaved public"; and lack of commitment on the part of the personnel to the organizational goals. The author pleads for the need for indoctrination of traffic police personnel at all levels. The author concludes by stating that it is possible to bring about considerable change in the organizational behavior of the officers "once goals are clarified, understood and internalized."

A.P. Saxena's essay on "Improving State Administration: Search for Directions", deals with the complexity which has come in the state administration after independence. This complexity is a result of the enlarged purpose, functions and scope of state government activities. The author has highlighted that administrative reorganization and procedure are important variables in this task. He points out the need for introduction of new technology and planned organizational change to bring about some kind of transformation in the state administration. The author also discussed the use of management techniques in a planned manner for improving state administration. He believes, this use will facilitate in generating creativity and innovation in the administration. The author has also emphasized the need of training for upgrading the levels of performance of employees. However, this training must begin with identification of training needs and need based plans for the training of public personnel.

Arthur J. Naftalin's essay on "The Reform of Administrative Procedures", deals with the problem of procedural improvement. He first deals with the essential requirements of any effective administrative system. He believes that simplicity and clarity is the first requirement of any effective administrative system. The second aspect of effective administrative system is the flexibility to respond to change and adapt to new needs and new circumstances. There is a need to re-evaluate all administrative operations so that procedures can be related to their proper objectives. Another aspect of effective administration is definitiveness and uniformity in similar operations in different agencies. The author points out that "Procedural improvement in administration...is aimed at achieving internal and external stability, at ensuring flexibility and responsiveness, at overcoming inertia, at smashing bottlenecks, at developing an appropriate division of labour and effective coordination, and at achieving continuous communication in all directions." This requires intensive planning, analysis and programming. The author concludes by stating that for procedural improvements, it is necessary for any government to define its purposes with clarity. However, top level leadership should provide necessary direction, clarity and willingness to make administration a co-operative operation.

The essay on "Reforms in the System of Filing, Noting and Inter-Departmental References" by Lord Curzon is a minute recorded on May 24, 1899, on the system of filing, noting and inter-departmental references in the Government of India. This essay primarily deals with the problem of excessive noting and writing which delays the matter due to its complicated chain of reference and annotation. Lord Curzon first describes the anomalies of the existing system and differences between the Indian system and the practice of English or foreign departments. In this context, he observes that the practice of noting on the file, by the whole hierarchy of officials, leads to the loss of fundamental problem. Lord Curzon prescribes the possible remedies: head of the department should be responsible for the presentation of the case to his superiors; numbers of subordinates who are permitted to note should be determined by their aptitude, etc. Regarding the problem of inter-departmental reference, Lord Curzon suggests that in all these cases "the Secretary of the original Department alone should note upon the papers after they have been returned to his office". He also discusses the problem relating to arrangement of printing and proceedings of notes and suggests that a uniform system should be adopted for this purpose.

Notes

1. India, Planning Commission, The Reorganization of the Machinery of Government (N. Gopalaswami Ayyanger), 1949.
2. India. Parliament: Estimates Committee. Second Report on Reorganization of the Secretariat and Departments of the Government of India (1950-51).
3. India. Planning Commission. Report on Public Administration (A.D. Gorwala). 1951. p. 5.
4. India. Planning Commission. First Five Year Plan. 1952.

5. India. Cabinet Secretariat. Public Administration in India: Report of a Survey (Paul H. Appleby). 1953. p. 18.
6. *Ibid*. p. 59.
7. India, Planning Commission. Third Five Year Plan. p. 277.
8. India, Cabinet Secretariat. Measures for Strengthening of Administration. 1961.
9. Government of India, Administrative Reforms Commission. Report on the Machinery of Government and Its Procedures of Work. 1968.
10. India. Department of Administrative Reforms and Public Grievances. Economic Administration Reforms Commission. Report on Economy in Public Expenditure, 1983, p. 18.
11. India. Ministry of Finance, Report of the Fifth Central Pay Commission. Volume. I, 1997.
12. India. Ministry of Finance, Report of the Expenditure Reforms Commission, Vol. I, 2000.
13. India. Ministry of Personnel, Public Grievances and Pensions, Report of the Second Administrative Reforms Commission on Organizational Structure of Government of India, 2009.
14. India. Ministry of Finance, Report of the Fifth Central Pay Commission, Vol. I, p. 106.

List of Contributors

Anil Chaturvedi, Faculty Member, Administrative Staff College of India, Hyderabad.

A.P. Saxena, Consultant, Indian Institute of Public Administration, New Delhi.

Arthur J. Naftalin, Commissioner of Administration, State of Minnesota, U.S.A. and formerly Budget Consultant on the South Vietnam Project of the Michigan State University.

Bishan Tandon, Retired Senior I.A.S. Officer and Writer.

Indrajit Singh, Joint Secretary, Special Reorganisation Unit, Ministry of Finance and Secretary, Committee on Plan Projects, Planning Commission, Government of India.

K.N. Bhutani, Deputy Secretary, Special Regorganisation Unit, Ministry of Finance, Government of India.

Raj Nandy, Lecturer, Indian Institute of Public Administration, New Delhi.

S.K. Pachauri, Secretary, Liberhan Ayodhya Commission of Inquiry, Ministry of Home Affairs, Government of India, New Delhi.

S.N. Sadasivan, Professor of Public Administration, Indian Institute of Public Administration, New Delhi.

Tarlok Singh, Additional Secretary, Planning Commission, New Delhi.

PART I
ORGANIZATIONAL AND PROCEDURAL ISSUES IN GOVERNMENT

1

The Concept of Productivity: Its Application to Administration

S.N. Sadasivan

Adopted in economics from literature to give expression to a specific capacity and its measurement, the term productivity has gradually found its place and use in almost every social science. As an economic concept, productivity in the first instance is associated with the factors of production and has varied applications.

In a predominantly agrarian society, the produce of land constituted most part of the total output and the natural powers of the soil were the main element that determined and sustained the standard of living of the people. The natural powers of the soil or the productivity of land could be enhanced by improved agricultural methods and efficiency of labour. Where the productive powers of land are limited, the living standard of the people is bound to be low. A concomitant variation could be observed between land productivity and the people's living standard.

With industrialization direct dependency on agriculture is considerably reduced and the emphasis on the productivity of land is shifted to other factors such as capital and labour and their sub-categories. Nevertheless, the productivity of the soil is a fertile element behind industrial prosperity and any conceivable decline in it is bound to retard industrial growth. The significance of soil productivity to national economy, therefore, still remains undiminished although it is not so much highlighted as the productivity of labour. As the total productivity is apportioned in terms of the factors of production, the share that goes to the labour is its productivity. While technological advance may tend to

From *The Indian Journal of Public Administration*, Vol. XXVIII, 1982.

enhance the productivity of labour, malnutrition, ill health and unhygienic living conditions may adversely affect the worker's productive capacity. It is a valid assumption that wages depend on the productivity of labour, and when the reward is fixed according to the unit of work done, the productivity of labour alone will be the determinant of wages. The application of advanced technology and scientific knowledge to capital assets such as plants and installations tends to enhance labour productivity but it also brings about a situation of reduction in labour requirement mainly on account of innovations in terms of labour saving devices. The higher the labour productivity in a country the higher will be the real wages there. Where social conscience permits the continuance of slavery as the bonded labour, the notion of productivity needs a different interpretation in order to establish its relation with wages.

The concept of productivity is applicable to any factor of production and to every productive unit, every machine. The productivity of a sugarcane crusher is not only dependent on the quantity of cane it can crush per day but also the actual number of days it can be put to use. Productivity is the main consideration in the purchase of the crusher and it should be properly balanced against the cost and should fetch a return over and above its cost.

Productivity is said to be normally higher when more is produced with less or when the output is more than the input both in money value and in utility. The demand for the factors of production is largely guided by their capability to produce or their productivity, which can be measured in each individual case.

As the cost of labour forms a significant part of the total value of a manufactured item, the input of labour is more easily assessed than that of others and as information on such matters like employment and man hours is obtainable in needed detail, productivity of labour can more effortlessly be measured, and labour has become the factor most commonly used for measuring productivity. However, for the purposes of measurement, it is the numerical strength of labour that gets more importance than individual skills and capabilities for better performance.

Productivity is better expressed in terms of the ratio between what is produced or the output and what are necessary for its production or the inputs. It has various uses in the economic sphere, especially the industrial sector, where among other things, it is applied for gauging efficiency, both individual and comparative. In fact high productivity invariably signifies high efficiency.

As an economic standard, while productivity is used for determining prices and wages, it is in turn, determined by a number of factors such as the supply of educated and energetic labour, availability of raw material, capital facilities, appropriate technology, entrepreneurship, creative management, manufacturing capabilities, social responses, political behaviour and economic conditions.

Role of the State and Society

An understanding of the primary implications of the concept of productivity in the economic sphere is crucial to its application in other areas, particularly politics and public administration. Although the activities of the state and society intersect at many points, politics in general forms the outermost circle within which are set systemically the circles of all social units and administrative agencies. The primacy of politics over all matters and subjects is primarily due to its direct relation with the state and its apparatus of power which alone can establish order, act as a sovereign safeguard to society and made available justice to the needy promptly and speedily.

The power of the state is superior to all other powers within and the state as an organization is all comprehensive and has its acknowledged supremacy. Politics is the struggle to attain power in order to further diverse interests. In democracy, however, politics is free and competitive and power is not absolute but rationalized by its legitimate distribution for specific objectives. Nevertheless, the very ascendancy of politics confers upon the political leaders, successful in obtaining a majority in the election, the right of controlling the government and utilizing its administration as necessary to effect the desired social change and extend the services due from the state to society. For the existence of a dynamic and progressive society in a representative system, politics must perform what it promises, and produce what democracy seeks to provide.

Political productivity is the ability and resourcefulness of political parties and their leaders to find the inputs necessary for the political system so that it may function in accordance with its cherished principles to render the output as anticipated to the satisfaction of society. If an educated and skilled work force is necessary to take advantage of the technological developments to enhance industrial productivity, political leaders of high integrity, great moral stature and intellectual strength are indispensable to maintain the productivity of the democratic system.

To democracy, its system is more significant than its leaders and, therefore, their disposition to its cause is to be sought in their determination to keep the system in tact permitting room for its healthy growth. As the productivity of a sophisticated and complex machinery depends not only on well-trained and competent workmen but also on their patience, concentration and diligence, so the operation of a highly civilized system as democracy, calls for men of highest refinements who have such attributes as probity, rectitude and self-reliance. Truth, freedom, justice, reason, and toleration are the fundamental values of democracy and unless the leadership is devoted to their promotion, it may degenerate into a corrupt oligarchy.

The productivity of democracy may be measured in terms of the development attained by each individual, contributing to collective welfare or general happiness. When the component groups of society sink their differences and seek identity in a common nationhood to achieve for them harmony and solidarity, the first condition for democratic productivity will be satisfied. Mass and secular education, organization of public health and public hygiene schemes, political and social enlightenment of the masses so as to promote the basic values of democracy, universal extension of the benefits of social welfare – will all go to raise the level of political productivity in democracy. With all these, every effort aimed at augmenting productivity is bound to be thwarted unless law is given the respect it deserves by the rulers and the ruled. Violation of law by the rulers and instrumentalities of the state should be considered as serious as the infraction of law by an average citizen.

Law must be enforced to extend justice not only to the indigent but to every needy member of society. It has become the provocative style and fashion of populist elements or predatory militant groups in some developing countries, to cater for aggressive and unreasonable demands of the so-called poor at the cost of sober and self-respecting citizens who struggle to live a modest life with honest means. Sometimes the law enforcing agencies, due to reasons of their own or under pressure, misguide themselves to the extent of driving such citizens to a state of helplessness, making them vulnerable to rapacious elements instead of promptly affording them the protection they require against the greed and the exploitation of the allegedly exploited. Democracy will be reduced to an unproductive anarchy if law is rendered ridiculously ineffective by its own guardians, and justice is iniquitously distributed.

Political Productivity

The higher the standard of political productivity the greater will be the productivity of administration. The forces of economics can function confidently to produce results only if the quality of politics is high and there is some reasonable guarantee of political stability. The greatest safeguard against political instability is the social harmony emerging from the quality of politics and the allegiance of the people to the state derived from their satisfaction over the rule of law. Political stability is directly relevant to administrative efficiency and economic productivity.

In the post-war world, the role of the state in democracies has changed from that of the agency maintaining the social equilibrium with the aid of its instruments of power to that of the principal institution for social development through a more equitable economic redistribution. The administration of the state which hitherto was a controlling or regulating machine for economic activities, has to take upon itself the responsibility for accelerating the pace of economic progress.

In developing countries like India, planning has become a prime function of the state as under socialism and public sector, investment has increasingly become imperative not as a measure to compete with private capital but as an obliging alternative to fill the existing capital vacuum. Already from the British time, the state in India has the monopoly of managing the public utilities like the railways, posts and telegraphs and telephones and industries associated with defence production. Travancore was the first princely state in India to nationalize road transport and to organize a number of industries like ceramics, rubber, titanium and electricity, not motivated by socialist ambitions but as a matter of socio-economic compulsions.

Political independence has envisaged for India a socialist economy, the responsibility for which, in terms of planning, resource mobilization and implementation, has in the usual course descended on its administration. As a result, a vast transformation of administration has taken place, forcing the old fashioned generalist to acquire knowledge, skills and perspective to re-emerge as a limited multiple specialist to perform his new tasks.

If a state does not want its people to be left to the sweet will and mercy of the private investor for meeting their basic needs, its administrative system should be so reorganized as to be responsive to their demands and should be above the reach of corruption and unwholesome influences. If political adequacy and political competency are two cardinal factors that provide an environment for administrative productivity, honesty and incorruptibility of the individual public servant are essential to keep it up to the desired level. Both politics and administration borrow their values from society and, therefore, unless society has the determination to maintain its ethical fabric, the expectation that politics and administration should preserve higher standards may prove to be fallacious.

Productivity will be poor where politics is the game of moral degenerates and administration is largely inhibited by self-seeking, mediocre bureaucrats indulging in abuse of power. It may register a downward trend where institutional power is personalized and personalized power is directed to debilitate institutions. The void of an intellectual community led by self-denying social philosophers to strengthen social morals and the basic values of the democratic way of life and to caution restraint on the use of power for personal ends may work as an enormous obstruction to the organization of efforts aimed at raising the productivity of a nation.

The Monitoring Role of Administration

Mixed economy is in fact a euphemism for indirect private control over public enterprises unless the state is capable of regulating private capital and production to legitimate public objectives. Similarly, parallel economy builds up illegal and hidden centers of power to break the resolve of a nation for the reduction of economic disparities, and to rear a monstrous parasite upon the national growth and national productivity. Where administration is oppressive or has adopted discriminatory standards in dealing with economic initiative, it may fail to create those essential conditions necessary for the efficient working of the productive forces.

In view of the governmental entry into business in a big way, the difference between public administration and private has ceased to be of any serious consequence except in the sphere of law and order, and their ethos and ethics have become mutually influencing. If public administration is to be of assistance to productivity in other areas, it must, first of all, concentrate on maintaining the level of its own productivity. Its earnestness and efforts to raise its productivity should serve as an example to its own undertakings as well as to private industrial organizations.

Administration alone can formulate national policies for the agricultural front almost entirely left to the private hands, and assume steps to induct there scientific methods and techniques to achieve all round improvement. The enormous resources required for research in the agricultural sphere cannot be found but from the public revenues, especially in a developing country where medieval feudalism stubbornly resistant to ideas of incurring expenditure for agronomical studies, thrives stronger than before despite the conspicuous laws enacted for its elimination.

The productivity of administration, in the present context, is to be assessed not only in terms of its organizational power applied to maintain the social equilibrium as envisaged by the laws but its consistent endeavour to direct its energy and resources to make its undertakings work profitably to their fullest capacity and its success in rationalizing and regulating the private investments to function effectively within the broad frame of the national economy to achieve the social objectives to which it is committed. Administration should demonstrate its determination to remove the cause of waste and create waste-consciousness in the public and in all organizations in regard to the use of water, energy, raw material and such other essential items.

Public undertakings have become centers of recurring losses primarily because of the bureaucratic style of their management and irresponsible trade unionism indulging more in politics than looking after labour welfare. While private business has increasingly introduced modern management techniques to improve its managerial performance, state enterprises have by and large found reasons to adopt an ambivalent attitude to them. The practice of compensating the losses in governmental corporations from the public exchequer should be discontinued lest the generation of the climate for managerial development as required for higher productivity and effecting economy be delayed. Motivated by the welfare philosophy or other considerations, public corporations incur burdensome overheads at their inceptive stage which, although in course of time may prove to be advantageous, on the whole, tend to be a drag on their productivity for a long time. If administration can put its house in order or maintain its level of productivity in every sphere, including public relations, it can justifiably claim the moral authority to extend the necessary counsel or monitoring its corporations without diluting their autonomy for augmenting their capacity to produce more at less cost. A political executive developed in the art of statesmanship will be a valuable asset to administration in democratizing its own management in order that the public sector may overcome its inhibition to adopt measures aimed at enhancing the productivity of labour in tune with the time and in consonance with the philosophy of the state.

Administrative Ecology

A labour force which eats on the pavement at the hands of the dirty hawker whose foodstuffs are wrapped in a blanket of flies, dust and soot, and delightfully dwells in filth and squalor will obviously be one of the lowest productivity. In a country where even the leading institutions are negligent of maintaining public hygiene and the elite has no personal insistence on cleanliness, administration should assume vigorous steps to maintain the standard of hygiene and sanitation both environmental and institutional which is of foremost relevance to productivity. Industrial effluents untreated to be innocuous are a major threat to public health and productivity. Ideal labour management relation presupposes an environment of health and hygiene not as a co-efficient but as an essential component of productivity which should be the contribution of administration. A management compromising with its absence is ostensibly callous to the basic requirements of productivity.

Administration should evolve its agricultural and industrial policies on the principle of fairness both to labour and management so that disputes and strikes can be reduced to the minimum to save the maximum mandays. Increasing productivity calls for inventive and creative talents which can develop only in an atmosphere of fearlessness and personal security arising from the guarantee of individual and collective freedoms.

Periodic changes as necessary in the structure of organization and management of each sphere of production, industry, plant or unit should be carried out. An administration which is amenable to reform has the will to create the climate of change necessary for producing organizations, whether private or public, and to adopt suitable measures required for regularizing the changes introduced.

A country's administration is the model as well as the pivot of its productivity. Every department, every branch, every unit of the administration should turn out the maximum volume of work that conforms to the prescribed qualitative standards with the maximum efficiency for the maximum satisfaction of its clientele. It is an administration, conscious of its responsibility for social development, that engages itself honestly and zealously in the task of building up the environment essential for productivity and its steady enhancement. In recent years ecology has gained a new dimension in the context of productivity. It is the administrative productivity that sustains and promotes the economic productivity but both, however, have to rely heavily on political productivity. Expediency, pragmatism, personal ambition, family image, temptations, falsification, craft, cunning and violence have their appearances in politics but if they are allowed to have their roles too frequently, political productivity in democracy will face its decline, inviting social decay and economic chaos.

2

Organisational Effectiveness: Some Issues

Anil Chaturvedi

If there is one thing that can be said with any degree of certainty about organizational effectiveness, it is that there are as many models, approaches, and criteria of effectiveness as there are people attempting to explain it. Yet "there is only a rudimentary understanding of what is actually involved in or constitutes the concept" (Steers 1975:546). Such protestations are not new; they have been continually voiced in the past three decades.* This is hardly surprising in view of the turmoils organization theory has undergone. Every new development in organization theory has led to a reassessment, often verging on a complete rejection of previously held view points. With respect to effectiveness, this is epitomized by the verbal broadside by Katz and Kahn who state that "what has been written on the meaning of these (effectiveness) criteria and on their interrelatedness, however, is judgemental and open to question. What is worse, it is filled with advice that seems sagacious but is tautological and contradictory" (Katz and Kahn 1966: 149). Of course, one can question whether the same thing can be both tautological and contradictory. However, the statement by Katz and Kahn does underline seemingly sharp differences in approaches to effectiveness.

This paper focuses on the various approaches to effectiveness and the conceptual differences underlining them, and examines the criteria suggested for the measurement of effectiveness in terms of their practicability, generalisability, and their utility.

From *The Indian Journal of Public Administration*, Vol. 26, 1980.

**See* Friedlander and Pickle (1968): Yuchtman and Seashore (1968); Georgopoulos and Tannenbaum (1957); Etzioni (1960); and Bass (1952).

Approaches to Effectiveness

The various approaches to effectiveness have generally been categorized into two: the goal-oriented approach and the natural-systems approach. The goal-oriented approaches define effectiveness in terms of the goal attainment of an organization. Thus, for example, Barnard conceives organizations as 'co-operative' systems and contends that "What we mean by 'effectiveness' of a cooperation is the accomplishment of the recognized objectives of co-operative action. The degree of accomplishment indicates the degree of effectiveness" (Barnard 1938: 55).

On such a definition, since effectiveness consists only in the degree of achievement of goals, the nature and the quality of goals is not seen to contribute to the effectiveness of an organization. Thus, for example, if there are two organizations one of which has less ambitious goals than the other and both of them achieve their goals then both of them would be considered equally effective.

The natural-systems approach, on the other hand, assumes that "if an organization is of any size at all, the demands on it are so dynamic and so complex that it is not possible to define a small number of organizational goals in any way that is meaningful" (Campbell 1976: 31). The systems-oriented theorists, therefore, in defining the effectiveness of an organization would "have some a priori notions of what the characteristics of a strong system are, and he would center his questioning around those" (Campbell 1976: 32).

The definitions of effectiveness given by various theorists reveal that there are significant differences in what constitutes a strong system. Mott (1972) sees the strengths of an organization in its productivity, adaptability, and flexibility, and accordingly defines effectiveness as "the relative ability of the members of an organization to mobilize their centers of power to produce, adapt, and handle temporally unpredictable overloads of work" (Mott 1972: 178). Georgopoulos and Tannenbaum, agree with the criteria suggested by Mott but believe that the degree of 'organizational strain' also reflects on an organistion's strength. Consequently, according to them, effectiveness of an Organisation is "the extent to which an organization as a social system, given certain resources and means, fulfills its objectives without placing undue strain upon its members" (Georgopoulos and Tannenbaum 1957: 180).

Bennis (1962) views effectiveness in terms of organizational 'health' which is characterized by an organization's adaptability, sense of identity, and capacity to test reality. Katz and Kahn, on the other hand, emphasise the ability of an organisation to control its environment rather than adaptability alone and define effectiveness as "the maximization of return to the organization by economic and technical means (efficiency), and by political means" (Katz and Kahn 1966: 67). Yuchtman and Seashore also stress the ability of the organization to control its environment but, unlike Katz and Kahn, they lay greater emphasis on the political power of the organization. They define effectiveness in terms of the organisation's "bargaining position, as reflected in the ability of the organisastion, in either absolute or relative terms, to exploit its environment in the acquisition of scarce and valued resources" (Yuchtman and Seashore 1967: 154). Finally, Evan (1976: 21) defines effectiveness in terms of the efficiency of the organisation's four systematic processes, namely, inputs, transformations, outputs, and feedback.

As a multidimensional concept, organization effectiveness may be defined as the capacity of an organization to cope with all four systematic processes relative to its goal seeking behaviour – however explicit or implicit this may be.

These differences between the goal-oriented approaches and the system-oriented approaches, on the one hand, and among the systemic models, on the other, have been explained on the basis of their concept of 'organisation' (rational versus natural system); the extent to which the organization is viewed as an open or closed-system; and upon whether the frame of reference in the approach to effectiveness has been organizational or societal.

Rational Versus Natural-System Concept

The goal-oriented approach, taking its lead from the ideal type descriptions of the bureaucratic structure by Max Weber (1974), the scientific management school and the theories of general administration by Fayol, Mooney, Gulick, and others, views organizations as "an instrument – that is, a rationally conceived means of the realization of expressly announced group goals" (Gouldner 1971: 12). Organisations are seen to be characterized by a network of roles, by a division of labour, and a set of hierarchies that define the relationships expected to exist between each activity and function and the overall goals of the organization. The extent to which the relationships are in consonance with the goals would define the degree of rationality present in the organization. In adopting this rational view of the organizations, the goal-approach makes a "reasonably explicit assumption that the organization is in the hands of a rational set of decision-makers who have in mind a set of goals which they wish to pursue. Further, that these goals are few enough in number to be manageable and defined well enough to be understood. Given that goals can thus be identified, it should be possible to plan the best management strategies for attaining them" (Campbell 1976: 31). Hence, the effectiveness of organizations can be represented by the extent to which they attain their goals.

The rational approach to organizations has been extensively criticised by the natural-system theorists. The major criticisms centre around the assumption of rationality in the setting and achievement of goals. The critics point out that organizational decisions are seldom based on a coolly calculated assessment of needs and information; rather they are the product of complex and dynamic processes. Cyert and March (1963) have pointed out that goal setting in organizations is essentially a conflict ridden process and the goals are more a product of a bargaining process. Consequently, goals are not always developed from a perspective of what is best for the organization.

The assumption that organizations can rationally develop optimum strategies for achieving their goals is also challenged by theorists. In order that the best strategies be formulated, it is essential that complete information be available; that the organization be able to manipulate data so that it can know the consequences of each of its proposed courses of action, that is, cause and effects are predictable. Such a situation, however, is highly unlikely. Also, the rational model assumption that an organization is capable of optimizing on its goals, can call forth a problem-solving and decision-making process in which a set of consequences is attached to each of many alternatives, is capable of simultaneously comparing the consequences of each alternative and has the criteria for selecting the most preferred course of action, is highly doubtful.

The rational approach has also been criticized for its implied mechanistic view wherein "it views the organization as a structure of manipulated parts, each of which is separately modifiable with a view to enhancing the efficiency of the whole. Individual organizational elements are seen as subject to successful and planned modification, enactable by deliberate decision" (Gouldner 1959: 13). Such a focus leads to the treatment of the organization as a 'black-box' with a total disregard for the unplanned, adaptive, inter-dependent processes within the organization which lead to an energy loss because "all social units, including organizations, are multifunctional units. Therefore, while devoting part of their means directly to goals, social units have to devote another part to other functions, such as, the creation or recruitment of further means to the goals and the maintenance of units performing goals activities and services activities".

In contrast to the rational-model of organization adopted by the goal-oriented approach, the natural-systems view sees organizations as systems which, though created to achieve specific ends, develop their own needs for survival and homoeostatis. Goal attainment becomes only one of the many needs of the organization. Sub-systems may pursue their own sub-goals instead of the total-system goals and the organization may find itself with a set of conflicting goals. Because the natural-system theorists take organizations as open to the environment, they believe that the structure of an organization emerges not out of planned effort but more out of evolutionary, defensive actions aimed at withstanding influences from the environment.

The natural-system theorists tend to regard the organization as a whole as organically 'growing' with a 'natural history' of its own which is planfully modifiable only at great peril, if at all (Gouldner 1959:14).

The natural-system view has been criticized for leading to a major blind spot by ignoring totally the 'rational' and the 'planned' element of an organization. As Gouldner remarks:

Modern organizational analysis by sociologists is over-preoccupied with the spontaneous and unplanned responses which organizations make to stress, and too little concerned with patterns of planned and rational administration – Use of the natural-system model tends to focus the analysts concern on the forces that undermine the organization's impersonal principles and subvert its formal ends to 'narrower' interests rather than on those that sustain these and bolster the distinctively bureaucratic structures (Gouldner 1959: 16).

This criticism, however, is a trifle dated as organizational theorists, in general, have accepted the strengths of both the rational and natural-system models and use a more synthesized concept of organizational rationality and its behavioural elements (Evan 1976 : 21; Stewart 1976 : 112). An examination of the organization change strategies, however, presents a different picture. Theorists here approach organizations from either a rational or a natural-system view and accept the other perspective only to the extent that they perceive it as providing constraints to the ideal application of the one they favour. For example, management by objectives sees organizational purpose as the rational development of some concrete, achievable objectives and a rationally identified course of action to achieve them. The degree of rationality would, however, it is admitted, be constrained by behavioural factors, limiting the extent to which the objectives are concrete and achievable and the courses of action being undertaken as charted. The organizational development approach, on the other hand, is essentially a behavioural approach that sees the forces of rationality, prevalent in organizations, as a hinderance to the understanding of the inherent dynamics of the organization. Openness in communication, power-equalisation, empathy, etc., considered to be desirable for organization-health would be constrained in their acceptance and practice by the pressure for rationality under which organizational members labour.

It is apparent that theorists have begun to accept that organization involves not only rational, controllable, and, to some extent, predictable forces but that they also harbour some uncertain, uncontrollable forces. The extent to which the rational or natural-system factors are seen to operate in organizations, in reality often becomes a function of the degree of rationality or natural-system attributes the researcher himself feels comfortable in dealing with.

Open-Versus Closed-System

Approaches to effectiveness differ in the extent to which they treat organization as open-or closed-system. Closed-system theorists assume that the organization maintains natural boundaries, is able to isolate environmental influences, and has rationally developed roles and relationships that are imbued with 'mechanistic', properties (Mott 1972). The open-system approach assumes that the organization has a more dynamic relationship with its environment, and that "systems survive and maintain their characteristic internal order only so as they import from the environment more energy than they expand in the process of transformation and exportation" (Katz and Kahn 1966: 28). This is not to suggest that the closed-system approach does not recognize the environment; they only "tend to discount or to under-emphasize the role of the environment in the affairs of the organization. They seldom actually deny the importance of environment in organizational activity; rather, they simply set it aside to concentrate on internal problems and functions" (Mott 1972: 2).

Approaching the organization as a closed system has some advantages in that, keeping in mind the limitations of research methodology to handle too many complex variables, such an approach helps to render research problems more manageable as the complex set of variables associated with the environment (see Thompson 1967; Dill 1958; Thorelli 1967) can be excluded. As Emery and Trist have stated, "thinking in terms of a 'closed' system – allows most of its problems to be analysed with reference to its internal structure and without reference to its external environment" (Emery and Trist 1965: 281).*

There has been increasing pressure on organizational theorists to use a more open-system approach. As Blau and Scott remark:

It is perhaps a truism to say that organizations will reflect the characteristics of the public they serve. A technical school differs in predictable ways from a college preparatory school, and an upper-middle class church is unlike the mission church of the same denomination in the slums. While such differences seem to be important and pervasive, there has been little attempt to relate client characteristics systematically to organizational structure (quoted in Lefton and Rosengren 1966: 33).

The studies of Burns and Stalker (1961), Dill (1962), and Lawrence and Lorsch (1967) have added to the need for a better understanding of the effects of the environment. However, studies which explicitly attempt to relate the environment to internal factors and processes and attempt to evaluate them are very few. Partly this is the result of the absence of a widely acceptable, empirically tested typology of environments (Jurkovich 1974).

The closed-system perspective of organization, since it emphasizes that organizational outcomes are within the control of

---

*Thus most of the models of motivation except 'equity-theory' (Chung 1977); leadership models such as the Ohio State (Stodgill 1965) and the Michigan University model (Likert 1967); studies and concepts of communication (see, for example, Sutton and Porter 1968; Burgess 1969; Ference 1970; Graves 1972; Wager 1972; O'Reilly and Roberts 1974); all essentially rest on a closed-system perspective of organization. Further more, the classical and neo-classical models of structure included much of the recent work on organization structures has tended to focus on such contextual factors as technology, size, etc. (see Woodword 1958 and 1965; Hall 1962; and 1972; Hall et al 1967; Hage and Aiken 1969; Kimberley 1976) comparing and contrasting the formal properties of the organization with expectations derived from such ideal types as the Weberian model of structure.

the organization, in its models of effectiveness, tends of emphasise organizational outcomes, such as, productivity, turnover, efficiency, growth, absenteeism, etc., as measures of effectiveness. On the other hand, the open-system perspective leads to an emphasis on the development of certain organizational processes and abilities which, it is believed, would help the organization in coping with the dynamism and uncertainty of the environment and, thereby, becoming effective. Such criteria as 'sense of identity' and 'ability to test reality', (Bennis 1962), 'integration' and 'voluntarism' (Caplow 1964), etc., are all based on an essentially open-system approach to organizations. Also, as the focus shifts from closed to open-system, there results a shift from the 'efficiency' criteria as a measure of effectiveness to a more societal perspective of effectiveness. As Dubin remarks:

The boundary of the organization is the very critical point at which the dilemma of efficiency versus social utility is highlighted around the issue of organizational effectiveness. Resolving the issue results in either maintaining or modifying the openness or closedness of the organizational boundary – Movements to open the boundaries of organizations are generally inspired by beliefs that greater social utility will be served (Dubin 1976: 11).

Organisational Versus Societal Approach

Models of effectiveness differ in the extent to which they evaluate organizations from essentially an organizational perspective or a societal perspective. The intention is not to suggest that the models have either a societal or a purely organizational perspective. However, they do differ in their frame of reference in that it is either more organization-oriented, or more societal-oriented.

The societal-oriented models are based on the belief that as organization are created to meet societal needs their effectiveness should be evaluated with these needs as base of reference (Parsons 1956). Bass also proposed that "the worth of the organization to the individual worker and the worth of both individual and organization to society should be used as ultimate criteria of organizational success apart from any consideration of these two criteria on the ultimate criterion of profits, productivity, and self-maintenance" (Bass 1952 : 106). The purpose of complex organizations, according to this view, is primarily "to benefit the society to which they belong, and that society is, therefore, the appropriate frame of reference for the evaluation of organizational effectiveness – Not only must the ultimate goal of the organization be functionally significant in general for that system but, in the case of a conflict of interests between it and the organization, the conflict is always resolved in favour of the superordinate system" (Yuchtman and Seashore 1967: 151).

The organization-oriented models of effectiveness, on the other hand, asset that while society places its demands on organizations, organizations too have their own demands and the extent to which they meet their needs determines their effectiveness. Thus the organization-oriented approach necessarily takes a managerial view of effectiveness, the fundamental question being asked whether the organization is efficiently able to obtain and utilise resources.

In the goal-oriented models of effectiveness, a societal focus leads to evaluation of goal attainment on what Yuchtman and Seashore term as the 'functional approach' wherein "the investigator derives the ultimate goal of the organization from his (functional) theory" (Yuchtman and Seashore 1967: 146). They note two major weaknesses in this approach – one methodological and the other conceptual. First, the goals that the investigator arrives at, based on his belief of societal needs, creates a value-ladden frame of reference that the members of the organization may either not subscribe to, or be completely unaware of, or both. The investigator is quite likely to develop a set of 'ideal' goals for the organization, which it may not attain or even have a desire to do so. Thus this approach is seen to suffer from a major methodological weakness, in that the reference base and the objects being measured against it may not at all be on the same plane. As Etzioni points out, the fact that organizations are not seen as having attained their goals occurs because of the 'mistake committed in comprising objects that are not on the same level of analysis, as for example, when the present state of an organization (a real state) is compared with a goal (an ideal state) as if the goal were also a real state" (Etzioni 1960: 34).

The organization-oriented goal approach (also termed the 'prescribed-goal' or the 'goal' approach by Yuchtman and Seashore) has become a more accepted basis for the measurement of effectiveness for it uses the goals that the organization defines for itself. Such an approach facilitates research particularly because "goal identification is reduced to manageable proportions if the focus of research is on the organizational goals that the major decision-makers actually pursue, and if data are collected about the major decision-makers intentions, and activities" (Price 1972: 6). Further more, this approach has the advantage that it avoids the criticism leveled at the derived-goal approach of allowing the researcher's values to impinge on the evaluation. "Such an approach", Steers states, "reduces our reliance on value premises about what an organization should be doing and relies instead on what it is actually trying to do" (Steers 1975: 555).

The major problem with this approach, however, remains in identifying what the decision-makers and the organization are attempting to do. Feuillette (1971) suggests three distinct sources from which such information can be obtained. The first is the official source, that is the annual reports, broachures, pamphlets, information leaflets, and other formal statements by the spokesmen of the organization. However, Perrow (1961) warns against the blind acceptance of such publicly espoused goals as the real or operative goals of the organization. It is quite likely that such goals may be 'window dressing' to satisfy the various publics of the organization. Organizations may not be engaged in attaining such goals and, therefore, any shortfall in performance cannot be assumed to reflect the effectiveness of the organization. As Webb remarks "the public or official goals fail to be realized not because of poor planning or poor leadership, or any of the other factors that may be related, but because they are not meant to be realized" (Webb 1974: 664). The assessment of organizational goals from its 'charter' or 'memorandum of association' is particularly vulnerable to such risks. Most charters are not expected to be statements of organizational goals as much as legal documents designed to protect the organization. Also the charters of similar organizations tend to be similar. However, the goals they pursue may be entirely different and such differences are not identified by using charters as the source for the identification of goals. Of course, it is also possible that organizations with entirely different charters may be pursuing entirely similar goals. Further more, the use of charters as the source or organizational goals makes an assumption that organizational goals are static and given, an assumption which has, in general, proved fallacious.

The second source of information on objectives is the managers of the organization. The objectives an organization is actually pursuing can be identified by asking the members of the organization what objectives and goals they are attempting to attain. While such a method may eliminate the risk of using publicly espoused but non-operative goals as the frame of reference, it adds the risk of developing a set of members private goals which may not be the total organisation's goals. This is very likely to happen unless the organisation's goals have been explicitly communicated to all members of the organization and clearly understood by them.

A final method of identification of goals being pursued by the organization involves an assessment of the decisions being made by the organization and an inference of the possible goals from such decisions. Such a method, while superior to others in respect of identification of the real goals of the organization, suffers from the major problem of imposition of the evaluator's values on the intentions of the organization.

The systems approach too has its share of theorists who take either an organizational approach to effectiveness or a societal approach. Two of the strongest advocates of the societal approach are Bass (1952) and Davis (1940). While Bass considers effectiveness in terms of the individual worker and the organization to society, Davis too suggests that the criteria of effectiveness should include broad social values. Some of the system theorists, while not directly advocating that an organization be judged to be effective only when it achieves societal goals, do suggest, either explicitly or implicitly, that an organization is evaluated by society and, therefore, if it is to survive it has to meet societal needs (Rhenman 1973; Schein 1970). Others, such as Katz and Kahn (1966) view effectiveness from an organizational perspective and define it in terms of maximization of return to the organization.

Parsons (1956) and Etzioni (1964) conceptualise organizations in terms of a system within a larger system and propose that in attaining their goals organizations also, by the same token, attain societal goals. This approach, in essence, represents an attempt to synthesise both the organizational and the societal approaches to effectiveness.

The goals of the organization are seen as synonymous with the primary societal missions or functions performed by the organization which give it its legitimacy and uniqueness (Webb 1974: 666).

Therefore, from a societal point of view the worth of the organization is determined by the extent to which it contributes to the survival, stability, and growth of the larger system. For an organization, on the other hand, achievement of its goals emerges "as one of the functional requirements which the organization has to meet in order to assure its own survival, stability, and growth" (Webb 1974: 666). On a conceptual level, such an articulation of the congruence of societal and organizational goals appears not only plausible but also necessary. However, the problem still remains of how to operationalise such an approach.

There are significant conflicts in the criteria that have evolved on the basis of organization-oriented and society-oriented frames of reference. Dubin highlights the problem when he says:

There is highly significant fact that a high level of effectiveness from one point of view may not be correlated with a high level of effectiveness from the other point of view. For example, the efficient production of chastity belts may still achieve low marks on organizational effectiveness when measured against the societal benefits of wearing the belts in a sexually permissive society – on the other hand, a welfare benefit distribution system which is internally inefficient may be judged to have high organizational effectiveness if it delivers large welfare payments during periods of economic crisis. To my knowledge, there is no single instance when the dilemma of efficient resource utilization versus social utility is resolved by maximization of both (Dubin 1976: 7-8).

The problem thus remains not only with respect to whose point of view should an organisation's effectiveness be evaluated, but also of the basis of what criteria. As Rhenman (1973) shows, the evaluators used to measure an organisation's effectiveness, even from a societal view point, differ significantly from one stakeholder to another. Can these evaluators be prioritised? Can they be weighted? Of course, the concept of organsations being systems within a larger system as advanced by Parsons and Etzioni is appealing, apart from being theoretically plausible. On the basis of it we can perhaps speculate that in the long run the organizational and societal goals will converge. But for the present the conflict remains. After all General Motors' claim 'what is good for G.M. is good for America' was not unstintingly applauded.

Past-Orientation Versus Future-Orientation

Apart from the differences noted above, the various approaches to effectiveness also differ in whether they are predominantly past-oriented or future-oriented. This difference becomes apparent when we examine the criteria that have been suggested as measures or indicators of effectiveness. The predominant approach has tended to be past-oriented with an emphasis on measures of organization performance such as productivity, efficiency, growth, turnover, etc. (for example, Barnard 1938; Georgopoulos and Tannenbaum 1957; Blake and Mouton 1964; Caplow 1964; Katz and Kahn 1966; Lawrence and Lorsch 1967; Friedlander and Pickle 1968; Price 1968; Pugh and Pheysey 1973; Negandhi and Reimann 1973). In other words, such an approach tends to emphasise whether an organization *has been effective* and therein lies its major limitation for it does not address itself to the issue whether an organization that has been effective will continue to remain so. Of course, the assumption can be made that an organization that has had a history of success and has been effective based on such performance measures as have been indicated before, is quite likely to remain effective. However, such assumptions do not stand the test of experience. There are sufficient examples indicating catastrophic changes in the performance of hitherto successful organizations that have not been able to change with changes in the environment.

A few theorists attempt to approach effectiveness as being the potential of an organization to succeed in the future over a long period of time. Yuchtman and Seashore (1967) partially treat effectiveness in terms of organizational potential by emphasising an organisation's ability to command resources. Bennis (1962) and Sahein (1970) give greater credence to potential for the future rather than past performance in their emphasis on an organization's ability to 'test reality' and cope with the environment. Thus they stress the characteristics necessary for an organization to remain effective in future. However, in any attempt to determine whether an organization is effective or not, that is, whether it is adaptable and able to cope with environment, one would necessarily have to focus on its past performance.

One of the major results of a past-oriented approach to effectiveness is that it leads to the neglect of organizational processes in favour of organizational performance. A future-oriented approach would necessarily emphasise organizational process to cope with the future; an emphasis not only on reaching a certain level of effectiveness but also on maintaining it. Further more, there is a shift from a primarily evaluative orientation towards organizational functioning to a diagnostic orientation, thereby, stressing the need for an adequate, periodic assessment of an organisation's strengths and weaknesses and attempts to build on the former and minimize the impacts of the latter. Even when an organization has been successful in the past, a future orientation would emphasise the need to diagnose and learn from the past. On the other hand, a past oriented approach does not sufficiently emphasise such diagnosis, more so in the case of organizations that have been seen to be successful.

Measurement of Effectiveness

Because of the theorists divergent opinions on what is

'effectiveness', it is not surprising that a multitude of criteria have been suggested. Campbell (1976) developed a list of 30 most popular criteria ranging from such economic measures as profit and profitability, to such diffuse concepts as motivation, morale, adaptation, etc. Steers (1975), in an excellent review of 17 models of effectiveness, identified 'adaptability', 'flexibility', 'productivity', and 'satisfaction' as the criteria that were often mentioned, with adaptability-flexibility being the one that was used in over 50 per cent of the models in the sample. While there are significant overlaps in various criteria, they also differ significantly from each other on such dimensions as measurability, universality, and the way they are related to the effectiveness construct.

Measurability

Criteria of effectiveness strongly differ in the ease with which they are measurable. Such criteria as 'productivity', 'profitability', 'operations-efficiency', 'employee-retention', and 'turnover', are more easily measurable, dependent as they are on 'hard' data. Another set of criteria such as 'satisfaction', 'morale', 'control', 'goal-attainment', 'conflict', 'cohesion', etc., have been difficult to measure, dependent as they are on 'soft' data based on aggregated perceptions of individual members of the organization. Finally, such criteria as 'adapatability', 'efficiency', (total organization efficiency as used by Katz and Kahn 1966), 'capacity to test reality', (Bennis 1962), 'control over environment', (Katz and Kahn 1966, and Yuchtman and Seashore 1967), are not only difficult to measure, but even their loose operationalisation has been difficult to achieve. That many of the popular criteria are difficult to operationalise and measure perhaps indicates the complexity of the effectiveness construct.

Goal-Attainment: The assessment of effectiveness on the basis of goal-attainment, apart from the criticism made earlier, is dependent of the extent to which the goal-statements are measurable. Except for the economic and the technical goals of an organization, most other goals are not easy to measure. How does one evaluate an organisation's development of its human resources? How does one evaluate its contribution to society? Because of the difficulty in developing measures, many organizations do not formally specify or formulate goals that are not easily measurable. Goal specificity is a function of the time horizon of the goal and the extent to which the setters of the goal really desire to attain it. The shorter the time horizon the more specific the goal in terms of what is to be achieved, at what cost, that is, with the expenditure of what resources in what time, and with what benefits accruing from the attainment of the goal. Therefore, the measure of goal-attainment does not end with whether the organization achieved the goal but also has to assess whether the goal was achieved within the constraints of time and resources, and whether the purpose behind the goal was achieved.

Absence of specificity is often an indicator of the absence of an intention to achieve the goal. This is more so in those areas of an organisation's functioning where the setting of goals and their specification has not been a traditional concern as, for example, in the area of human resources. Some indicators of achievement can be built into each goal area, in a descriptive fashion if not in completely quantitative terms. For example, 'management development' as a goal can be described in terms of a certain number of managers being available, with appropriate skills, when the need arises to fill in a vacancy. Other such measures can be developed to fit the particular needs of the organization. They are practicable, serve their purpose, and are able to indicate the extent of goal attainment. Therefore, the specificity of a goal statement, particularly in the non-traditional goal setting areas, is itself an indicator of an effective organization. In the absence of specific goals, measurement become a fruitless task, for it is not clear whether the stated goal is actually the operative goal.

A further problem emerges with multiple goals. No organization has a single goal that functions as an operative goal. Single goals tend to be very long-term, directional goals of intention whose purpose is to constrain the direction of the operative goals. Operative goals are multiple and the issue arises that in the absence of equal achievement on all the goals, as is often the case, how does one discern the effectiveness of the organization. Do we prioritise the goals? On what basis? Or do we consider each goal to be of equal importance and average out the achievement? Should we demand from the organization its priorities and use those for our assessment? Is it not likely that the organization will assign the highest priority to the goals that have been better attained and in that event there is really no need to demand any set of priorities? In other words, the question arises whether, despite the needs for rationality and objectivity, we can at all determine an organisation's effectiveness by attempting to measure its goal-attainment.

Adaptability/Flexibility: Many theorists favour such criteria as 'adaptability/flexibility' as indicators of effectiveness. Few authors have defined the criterion (Mott 1972) and fewer still have indicated how to measure it. For (Bennis 1962) adaptability on the part of an organization is its ability to solve problems and to react with flexibility to changes in environmental demands. The problem with such a definition, particularly when used as an evaluation criterion is that it does not identify the bases on which adaptability can be measured. Does an organization have to recognize all the demands placed on it? Does deliberate ignoring of a demand imply a lack of adaptability? If two similar organisations face similar demands from the environment, prioritise them, and meet the ones which they consider to be of greater priority and if their prioritise are not similar, then are they both being effective or can we identify which of the two is not being effective, or more effective? Does adaptability involve certain norms of adaptation time? Is an organization that adapts earlier than another more effective? Or do we have to take a longitudinal approach and observe the impact of adaptive action before summarising whether the adaptive behaviour of the organization was of a reasonable quality?

Survival and Growth: The goals of 'survival' and 'growth' are equally problematic. Survival, particularly, is of little help. How is 'survival' to be defined? If we take the natural-system approach, then, as long as the internal structures and processes of the system are maintained, it survives. With such a definition the only time when an organization does not survive is when it is deliberately disbanded. However, despite assumptions to the contrary, not all organizations face survival as a goal. Large organizations in particular are seldom allowed to die even in strongly market oriented economies. Such cases as that of Rolls-Royce, British Leyland, Lockheed, Chrysler, etc., indicate that organizations are often bailed out rather than allowed to perish. Thus the larger the organization the less likely it would face the problem of survival. And as effectiveness theories have, in general, been developed with the large organizations as their focus the use of 'survival' as a criterion of effectiveness does not appear to be justified.

'Growth' too, as an ultimate goal of organizations, suffers from similar problems as does 'survival'. What constitutes 'growth' has seldom been clearly specified. The assumption that growth is a natural phenomenon of organizations is not always true. There are organizations that may not wish to grow. Also a number of organizations may not be allowed to grow beyond a particular size and beyond a particular level of influencing ability based on norms beyond organization's control. Thus 'growth' too becomes a dubious indicator of organizational effectiveness.

Efficiency: 'Efficiency' has been one of the more popular criteria of effectiveness so much so that there has been a tendency to use the two words synonymously. Designed as it was for the mechanical sciences, the immense success of efficiency as an evaluator in engineering has proven to be somewhat dysfunctional as there have been repeated attempts to extend the measure to the social sciences. While the measure is appropriate in engineering it does not prove to be equally so in the case of organizational effectiveness. The major constraint inherent in 'efficiency' is that the 'inputs' and 'outputs' of the system amenable to measurement, have to be in the same units. Further more, the reliability of 'efficiency' as a measure of effectiveness is enhanced by having fewer variables at both the input and output ends of the system. In the case of organizations both these constraints are difficult to satisfy. Attempts are made to measure organisational efficiency by assigning monetary values to both the inputs and outputs to reduce them to the same units of measurement. Such a procedure, being highly subjective, only serves to reduce a hitherto strong measure to a weak one.

Katz and Kahn (1966) suggest that organizations be seen as energy exchanging units, drawing energy from the environment, consuming some of it to maintain the system and releasing the rest, after transformation, into the environment. The analogy they draw is that of an electrical transformer. An organisation's effectiveness, then, is the efficiency with which it transforms energy and the extent to which the output energy equals the input energy. But Katz and Kahn's conceptualization suffers from an assumption that all organizations can be treated as electrical transformers. This may not be so always. Some organizations, such as, archives may be better conceptualized as 'reservoirs' wherein environmental energies are stored in the expectation of future use. Some organizations may even be designed as energy dumps, designed to drain off the excess energy from the environment. It is not surprising that societies begin to invest heavily in art galleries, museums, symphony orchestras, etc., generally, when they have energy to spare. Katz and Kahn's analogy then has only a limited use and it may not be too far fetched to suggest that such a conceptualization of organizations may have resulted from a need to fit the organization to the effectiveness criteria than the other way round.

The issue arises how specific should the criteria be in order to be acceptable. Should they be so designed that unless they can be precisely quantified they are unacceptable: or are criteria that may not be amenable to quantification equally acceptable. Pertinent to the above issue is the question of what is the function attributed to the criteria. Are the criteria designed as measures of effectiveness, or as indicators of effectiveness. In the case of the former the demand for quantification is acceptable provided the cost of measurement does not negate the benefits of measurement. The demand for quantifiability, however, is unreasonable in the case of the latter. The contention that objectivity requires quantification is spurious, for even the criteria based on the so called 'hard' data themselves have a subjective element in the absence of universally accepted standards. For example, 'absenteeism' in some organizations includes both authorized and unauthorized absenteeism, while in others it only means the latter. In the absence of such standards for 'hard' data "searching for so called objective measures of effectiveness is a thankless task and virtually preordained to fail in the end. The conventional wisdom says objectivity is good, but perhaps a more accurate wisdom says an objective criterion is a subjective criterion once removed" (Campbell 1976: 39).

Generalisability

Another relevant issue with respect to the effectiveness criteria concerns the extent to which the criteria should be generalisable. Most of the models of effectiveness, whether they are goal-oriented or system-oriented, have attempted to develop criteria that are universal. Price (1972) argues in favour of universal measures because the "existence of general measures promotes measurement standardization; measurement standardization, in turn, furthers the development of theory" (Price 1972: 7). As has been pointed out earlier, the measurability of most criteria of effectiveness is weak. But a more significant fact is that while a number of theorists have developed what they perceive as universal measures, few agree with each other's criteria.

A pertinent question then is whether a search for universal criteria is justified at all. While the goal approach, because of its conceptual framework, can be universally applicable, the criteria that have been developed have only a limited application. Such measures as profitability, productivity, etc., are more easily applicable to business organizations than to non-business organizations, though attempts have been made to reconstruct these criteria with a view to accommodate non-business organizations. However, such attempts as by Katz and Kahn (1966) and Evan (1976) to extend the measures of efficiency to non-business settings have only led to a weakening of the measure. For example, Evan suggests that "number of students graduated" be a measure of goal organization efficiency of a university, and "total number of patients treated" that of a hospital (Evan 1976). Such a generalization of a criterion which leads to its weakening only succeeds in making the relationship of the criteria to the construct suspect. Similarly, any attempt to standardise such general criteria as adaptability, flexibility, etc., will only succeed in making them specific to certain types of organizations.

Further more, Stewart (1970) suggests that the criteria of effectiveness of an organisation are related to its stage of development as the organizational goals at each stage have a different focus. In other words, one can question whether it is possible to generalize criteria even for one organization for all times.

Relationship with the Construct

The different criteria of effectiveness differ in their relationship to the construct. For example, such criteria as productivity, profitability, goal attainment, are seen to be directly determining the effectiveness of an organisation, whilst criteria like efficiency, flexibility, adaptability employee-retention, cooperation, morale, etc., are seen as indirect indicators of effectiveness due to their causal relations to productivity, etc. Thus Marsh and Mannari remark:

The goals of economic organizations are productivity, and sales and, if they are part of a capitalist economy, profits.... To achieve these goals, organisations must also meet ancillary or subsidiary goals; a low rate of absenteeism, suggestions from employees which improve efficiency, and eliciting desire among employees to fulfil production goals (Marsh and Mannari 1976: 91).

Similarly, Srivastava and Salipante observe that

It is our view, supported by empirical research, that increasing and facilitating autonomy in an organisation will lead to increased job satisfaction and increased job performance... it is very likely that in most organizations such increase would lead to increased organizational effectiveness overall (Srivastave and Salipante 1976: 58).

Despite these claims, the extent literature shows that empirical generalizations establishing strong correlations between various variables are still wanting. In the absence of such generalizations, evaluation of effectiveness on the basis of these criteria may not be reliable.

Effectiveness: Theoretical Considerations Vs Practicality

An important issue with regard to effectiveness is what is the purpose of the development of a concept of effectiveness. A review of the literature shows that the study of effectiveness is seen as a means to an integration of organizational theories and, thereby, to a better understanding of the organizations. Schein feels that the study of effectiveness should be done with a systems conception because it "allows us to determine how does an organization cope with its environment? How does it obtain information and process it validly? What mechanisms exist for translating information, particularly about alterations in the environment into change operations? Are their internal operations flexible enough to cope with changes? How can organisations coping efforts be improved?" (Schein 1975: 119). Spray (1976) however, points out that "analysts of organizational performance have been concerned largely with raising and answering the following five distinct but closely interrelated questions:

1. "What alternative ways of evaluating organizational performance are conceivable?
2. "What alternative ways of evaluating organizational performance actually have been utilized?
3. "What are the underlined causes of various levels of organizational performance?
4. "What are the consequences of various levels of organizational performance for other organizational processes?
5. "What advantages and disadvantages are inherent in the various approaches to evaluating organizational performance?" (Spray 1976: 2).

The report on the discussions at the 8th Annual Comparative Administration Research Institute Conference held at Kent State University in April 1975, however, shows that the last three issues have not been much emphasized; rather the dialogue among organisatinal scientists tended to revolve around such concerns as "Shouldn't we pay attention to how the issues of internal organizational efficiency and external social utility get resolved in the public context? How far down an organization do you have to go to obtain a reliable measure of group characteristics such as average job satisfaction? In view of existing studies what per cent of variance in satisfaction is accounted for by level of autonomy? How do we determine the system's need for change and stability at a particular point in time?" (Spray 1976: 167-168). These questions, along with others, mentioned above, reflect an approach which is essentially theoretical.

The needs of practitioners have hardly been seen as being of concern in the development of effectiveness construct and criteria. It is not surprising, therefore, that issues, such as what are the means of improving an organisation's performance, or, who is responsible for this improvement, have been mostly overlooked in the discussions of effectiveness, although from a practitioner's point of view they are of prime significance. Consequently, the crucial role of managers in an organisation's effectiveness has not been explicitly identified, in most models of effectiveness. As Kirchoff points out "Organizational effectiveness emerges as the ultimate outcome of a combination of managerial effectiveness and factors not under organizational control" (Kirchoff 1977: 348). The extent to which organisational effectiveness will depend upon managerial effectiveness is a function of the extent to the manager who controls the organization. Mintzberg has pointed out that "In most large organizations because of their diffuse ownership,... effective control of the organization, rests with the senior mangers and seldom with those who legally 'own' the organization" (Mintzberg 1976).

The political power in the organization, also in general, rests at the top of the hierarchy. Crozier points out that "the power of decision-making within the organization is located exactly at the points where the stability of the internal 'political system' of the organization prevails over the demands to adjust to the external environment. This means, finally, that all decisions that have not been eliminated by the system of rules will have to be made at a level where those who make them will be protected against personal pressure from those who could be affected by them" (Crozier 1973: 223).

Crozier's argument, effectively, is that critical decision-making in an organization would always tend to be centralized at the top of the hierarchy and that the normative value placed in the assumption that decisions are best taken at the location of information proves to be dysfunctional in practice. Consequently, the effectiveness of top management is critical to organizational effectiveness. Such effectiveness "involves more than economic effectiveness; it must include political effectiveness in dealing with the external environment and the interest groups ... At a broader and more objective level, one can view managerial effectiveness in terms of how well management does in both formulating and achieving organizational goals, compared to the management of other similar kinds of organizations, and/or compared to itself overtime... In the long run managerial effectiveness also entails the growth, adaptability, health, and viability of the organisation" (Richman and Farmer 1975: 141-142).

Because of the absence of any explicit recognition of practitioner's needs in the effectiveness models, it is not surprising that there exists a substantial gap between the work of the organizational scientist and its acceptance by the organizational practitioners. At the same conference, mentioned above, Spray recorded a number of comments by businessmen revealing such gap. For example, "Businessmen are too busy with day to day problems to get deeply involved with fundamentals. I think it is useful to generate a body of knowledge about organizational problems around how you apply this knowledge to business needs", "...What people have talked about at this conference has a long way to go in terms of being translatable into something we can use. I do not mean that the work is not excellent; I just mean that it is hard to understand and make practical" (Spray 1976: 71-72).

While such statements, as quoted above, only reflect a concern at the gap between theory and practice as expressed by managers themselves, a study by Feullette (1971) is indicative of the extent of gap. Feullette (1971) notes that in business organizations in France, Germany, and the USA, the concepts and doctrines of the classical and neo-classical schools are more widely accepted than are the modern organizational theories. By this estimate only 10 per cent or fewer managers are inspired by the current theories. However rough this estimate may be, it is significant enough to indicate that a large gap does exist between the organizational theorists on the one hand and the organizational practitioner on the other.

Concluding Remarks

The above discussion shows clearly that the literature on organizational effectiveness represents a diverse set of approaches and models. The difference are based on a number of factors: the extent to which the theorist has taken a rational-model or a natural-system view of the organization; whether the organization has been seen as an open or closed-system; whether an organizational or a societal perspective has been taken; and whether effectiveness has been viewed in terms of goal-attainment or as a set of certain desirable characteristics of the organization. Which do we choose?

Each set of views, approaches, models has its own strengths; each has its limitations.

The question arises whether, at all, there can be a universally accepted definition of effectiveness. The case of effectiveness parallels the case of such values as 'good', 'beautiful', 'duty', etc., which despite numerous treatises, have failed to be delineated by universally accepted definitions. Individuals should be good; organizations should be effective. Few will despute this statement, but fewer still will agree with one another on what constitutes 'good' and what constitutes 'effectiveness'. Perhaps the closest we can come to a universal definition, based on the definition of formal organization, is that an effective organization is one which achieves and continues to achieve its purposes. But such a definition does not solve our problem; it only shifts it to another level. We are now faced with another value-laden problem, namely, that of defining 'purpose'.

What should the purpose of an organization be? If we consider organizations to be value adding entities then their effectiveness will be reflected by the extent to which they transform their inputs into higher value outputs. On the other hand we may believe that the role of organizations is to "keep people busy, occasionally entertain them, give them a variety of experiences, keep them off the streets and allow them to socialize. If they do that then they are effective" (Weick 1976: 33). Of course, both the definitions of purpose can be applied to organizations, but each is more applicable to some organizations than to others. Further more, the question remains who decides the purpose of the organization. Is society the arbiter of organizational purpose; is it the managers, the government or the owners? The question does not have any easy answers because each attempted answer is value-laden.

Given the importance that values play in any approach to effectiveness, it is surprising that most theorists do not explicitly state their values. If values are not explicitly stated, then, at times one can fall into the trap of believing that the strongly held values of what ought to be are in fact statements of what actually exists. A strong belief in that organizations ought to strive for effectiveness may lead to an assumption that most organizations do try to be effective. Similarly, one can impute the need for 'growth' and 'improvement' to organizations when one believes that 'growth' and 'improvement' are not only desirable but also essential. There are numerous organizations whose actions seem to reject the above values. Richman and Copen (1973) mention the case of a family owned Indian pharmaceutical company whose owners seem to defy the generally accepted norms of a business organization. They have little interest in growth, in higher profits, etc. They consider the organization to be serving its purpose so long as it continues to provide security of employment and welfare to its employees. What this example illustrates that the purpose of the organization is what those who control it want it to be, based on their own values, and not those of the theorist. Therefore, an approach to 'effectiveness' that is essentially evaluative or prescriptive or both is of little worth unless both the evaluator and prescriptions are accepted by the operative controller of the organization. The poor success of T Groups in transferring their values to organizations testifies to this conclusion.

Is the study of effectiveness necessary? Perhaps the most worthwhile contribution that studies can make is towards the integration of management studies. In the face of increasing differentiation and specialization in the area of organization studies, the study of effectiveness can provide the needed frame around which to integrate organization theory. A further contribution would result if the approaches to effectiveness were to shift from the evaluative and prescriptive to the developmental; from the past-oriented to the future-oriented. Based on a particular set of values of what organizations ought to be, a comprehensive conceptualization of organizations should follow enunciating the purpose of the organization based on those values the various processes that could be used to work towards that purpose, and the development of ways to test the values and the outcomes.

Finally, kin to the various schools in epistemology, such as, rationalism, empiricism, pragmatism, intuitionism, scepticism, mysticism, etc., various schools of effectiveness can be developed with their explicit set of values, processes, and means and evaluations thereby offering the practitioners a choice of comprehensive approaches to organizations. The extent to which each school draws support from society would reveal its inherent strength.

References

Anderson, T.R. and Warkov, S., "Organizational Size and Functional Complexity: A Study of Administration in Hospitals", *Amer. Soc. Rev.*, Vol. 26, 1961, pp. 23-28.

Barnard, C.I., *The Functions of the Executives*, Cambridge, Mass., Hav., Univ. Press, 1938, p. 55.

Bass, Bernard, M., "Ultimate Criteria of Organizational Worth", in Ghorpade (ed.), *Assessment of Organizational Effectiveness*, Pacific Palisades, Calif., Goodyear, 1952.

Bennis, W.G., "Toward a 'Truly' Scientific Management: The Concept of

Organizational Health", *General Systems Yearbook*, Vol. 7, 1962, pp. 269-282.

Blake, R.R. Mouton, J.S., *The Management, Grid*, Gulf Pub. Co., 1964.

Burgess, R.L., "Communication Network and Behavioural Consequences", *Human Relations*, Vol. 22, 1969, pp. 137-160.

Burns, T. Stalker, *The Management of Innovation*, London, Tavistock, 1961.

Campbell, J.P., "Contributions Research Can Make", in Spray, S.L. (ed.) *Organizational Effectiveness*, Kent State Univ., 1976, p. 31.

Caplow, T., *Principles of Organization*, N.Y., Harcourt, Brace and World, 1964.

Carzo, R. Yanonzas, J.N., A.S.Q. 14, 1969.

Chandler, A.D. Jr., *Strategy and Structure*, Cambridge, Mass. M.I.T. Press, 1962.

Child, J., "Organizational Strategy, Environment, Performance: The Role of Strategy Choice", *Soc.*, Vol. 6, 1972, pp. 1-22.

Chung, Kare H., *Motivational Theories and Practices*, Columbus, Ohio, Grid, 1977.

Crozier, Michel, *The Bureaucratic Phenomenon*, London, Tavistock, 1964.

Crozier, Michel, "Cultural Determinants of Organizational Behaviour, in Negandhi (ed.), *Modern Organizational Theory*, Kent State Univ. Press, 1973, pp. 219-228.

Cyert, R.M. March, J.G., A Behavioural Theory of Firm, Englewood Cliffs, N.J. Prentice Hall, 1963.

Davis, R.C., *Industrial Organization and Management*, N.Y., Harper, 1940.

Dill, W.R., "Environment as an influence on Managerial Autonomy", *Adm. Sc. Quat.*, Vol. 24, 1958, pp. 409-443.

Drucker, Peter F., "The Effective Decision", *Hav. Bus. Rev.* (Jan-Feb) 1967, pp. 92-98.

Dubin, Robert, "Organizational Effectiveness: Some Dilemmas of Perspective", in Spray (ed.), *Organizational Effectiveness*, Kent State Univ., 1976.

Duncan, Robert, B., "Multiple Decision-making structures in Adapting to Environmental Uncertainty; the Impact on Organization Performance", *Human Relations*, Vol. 26, 1973, pp. 273-291.

Eitzen, S.D. and Yetman, N.R., "Managerial Change, Longevity and Organizational Effectiveness", *ASQ*, Vol. 17, 1972, pp. 110-117.

Emery F.E. and Trist, E.L., "The Causal Texture of Organizational Environment", *Human Relations*, Vol. 18, 1965, pp. 21-32.

Etzioni, A.W., "Two Approaches to Organizational Management: A Critique and a Suggestion", *Adm. Sc. Quat*, Vol. 5, 1960, pp. 257-278.

Etzioni, A., *Modern Organizations*, Englewood Cliffs, N.J., Prentice Hall, 1964.

Evans, W.M., "Organizational Theory and Effectiveness: A Preliminary Analysis", in Spray (ed.) *Organizational Effectiveness*, Kent State Univer., p. 21.

Feuillette, C., "The Credibility Test for the Firm: A New Rating Grid", European Business (Winter), Vol. 28, pp. 46-52.

Ference, T.P., "Organizational Communication System and the Decision-Process", Mangt. Sc. Vol. 17, 1970, 83-96.

Friedlander, F. and Pickle, H., "Components of Effectiveness in Small Organizations", *ASQ,* Vol. 13, 1968, pp. 289-304.

Georgopoulos, B.S., and Tannenbaum, A.S., "A Study of Organization Effectiveness" in Ghorpade (ed.), *Assessment of Organizational Effectiveness*, Pacific Palisades, Calif., Goodyear, 1957, p. 180.

Ghorpade, J., *Assessment of Organizational Effectiveness*, Pacific Palisades, Calif., Goodyear, 1970.

Georgopoulos, B.S., "An Open System Theory Model for Organizational Research: A Study of Hospitals," in Negandhi (ed.), *Modern Organization Theory*, Kent State Univ., 1973.

Ghorpade, J., "Study of Organizational Effectiveness; Two Prevailing Viewpoints", *The Pacific Soc. Rev.*, Vol. 13, 1971, pp. 31-41.

Gibson, J.L., Ivancevich, John M. and Donnelly, J.H., *Organizations: Structure, Process, Behaviour,* Dallas, BPI, 1973.

Gouldner, A.W., "Organizational Analysis", in Ghorpade (ed.), *Assessment of Organizational Effectiveness*, Pacific Palisades, Calif., Goodyear, 1959.

Graves, D., "Reported Communication Ratios and Informal Status in Managerial Work Groups", *Human Relations*, 25: 159-170, 1972.

Grusky, O., "Managerial Succession and Organizational Effectiveness", *Amer. Jr. of Soc.*, 69: 21-30, 1963.

Gawthrop, Louis, C., "The Environment, Bureaucracy, and Social Change – A Political Progress", in Negandhi (ed.), *Modern Organization Theory*, Kent State Univ., 1973.

Hage, J., Aiken, M., "Routine Technology, Social Strategy, and Organizational Goals", *ASQ,* 14: 366-376, 1969.

Hall, R.H., "Inter-organizational Structural Variation: Application of the Bureaucratic Model", *ASQ*, 7: 295-308, 1962.

Hall, R.H., Hass, J.E. and Jhonson, N., "Organizational Size, Complexity, and Formalization," *Amer: Soc. Rev.* 32: 903-912, 1967.

Hall, R.H., *Organizations: Structure and Process*, Englewood Cliffs, N.J. Prentice Hall, 1972.

Harvey, E., "Technology, and the Structure of Organizations," 33: 247-259, 1968.

Hinnings, C.R. and Lee, G.L., "Dimensions of Organization Structure and their Context: A Replication," *Soc.*, 5: 83-93, 1971.

Hirsch, P.M., "An Organization-Set Analysis of Cultural Industry Systems", in Evan (ed.), *Inter-Organizational Relations*, London, Penguin 1972.

Hirsch, P.M., "Organizational Effectiveness and the Institutional Environment", *ASQ,* 20: 327-344, 1975.

Inkson, J.H.K., Pugh, D.S. and Hickson, D.J., "Organization Context and Structure: An Abbreviated Replication," *ASQ*, 15; 318-329, 1970.

Katz., D. and Kahn, R.L., *The Social Psychology of Organizations*, Wiley, N.Y., 1960, p.149.

Katz, R.L., "Skills of an Effective Administration", *HBR*, Sept-Oct., 90-102, 1974.

Kavic, B., Rus, V. and Tannenbaum, A.S., "Organization Development and Change in Organizational Performance", *ASQ,* 20: 191-206, 1971.

Khandwalla, P.N., "Mass Output Orientation of Operation Technology and Organizational Structure", *ASQ*, 19: 74-97, 1974.

Kimberly, J.R., "Organizational Size and the Structuralist Perspective: A Review, Critique and Proposal", *ASQ*, 21: 571-597, 1976.

Kimberley, J.R., and Nielsen, W.R., "Organization Development and Change in Organizational Performance", *ASQ*, 20: 191-206, 1975.

Kirchoff, B.A., "Organizational Effectiveness Measurement and Policy Research", *Acd. of Mangt. Rev.*, 2(3): 347-355, 1977.

Lawrence, Paul R., and Lorsch, J., *Organization and Environment: Managing Differentiation and Integration*, Boston, Hav. Univ., 1967.

Lefton, M. and Rosengren, W.R., "Organizations and Clients: Lateral and Longitudinal Dimensions", *Amer. Soc., Rev.*, 31: 802-810, 1966.

Leiberson, S., and O'Connor, J., "Leadership and Organizational Performance", *Amer, Soc, Rev.*, 37: 117-130, 1972.

Likert, Rensis, *New Patterns of Management*, N.Y., McGraw Hill, 1961.

Likert, Rensis, *The Human Organization: Its Management and Value*, N.Y, McGraw Hill, 1967.

Maheney, T., "Managerial Models of Organizational Effectiveness", *ASQ*, 14: 357-365.

Maheney, T. and Frost, P., "The Role of Technology in Models of Organizational Effectiveness", *Organ. Beh. and Human Perf.* 11: 127-138, 1974.

Marrow, A.J., Bowers, D.G. and Seashore, S.E., *Management by Participation*, NY, Harper and Row, 1967.

Marsh, Robert M. and Mannari, H., "Employee Performance in Japanese Firms: An Explanation", in Spray (ed). *Organizational Effectiveness*, Kent State Univ., 1976.

Mintzberg, H., "Organizational Power and Goals: A Skeletal Theory", *Policy and Planning* Research Conference, Pittsberg, 1977.

Mott, P.Z., *The Characteristics of Effective Organization*, N.Y., Harper and Row, 1972.

Negandhi, A.R. and Reimann, B.C., "Task Environment Decentralization and Organizational Effectiveness", *Human Relations*, 26: 203-214, 1973.

Q. Reilly 111, C.A. and Roberts, K.H., "Information Filteration in Organizations: Three Experiments", *Orgnl. Beh. and Human Perf.*, 11: 253-265, 1974.

Parsons, T., "Suggestions for a Sociological Approach to the Theory of Organizations: Part 1", *ASQ,*: 63-85, 1956.

Pennings, J.M., "The Relevance of the Structural Contingency Model for Organizational Effectiveness", *ASQ* 20: 393-410, 1975.

Perrow, Charles, "Goals in Complex Organizations", *Amer. Soc. Rev.* 26: 859-866, 1969.

Price, James L., *Organizational Effectiveness: An Inventory Proposition*, Homewood, 111. Irvin, 1968.

Price, J.L., "The Study of Organizational Effectiveness", *Soc. Quat.*, 13: 3-15, 1972.

Pugh, D.S., Hickson, D.J., Hinnings, C.R. and Turner, C., "The Context of Organization Structures", *ASQ*, 14: 91-113, 1969.

Rhenman, E., *Organization Theory for Long-Range Planning*, N.Y. John Wiley, 1973.

Richman, B.M. and Farmer, R.N., *Management and Organizations*, N.Y. Random House, 1975.

Richman, B.M. and Copen, M., "Management Techniques in the Developing Countries", *Columbia Journal of World Business*, 8(2), 49-58, 1973.

Rumelt, R.P., *Strategy, Structure and Economic Performance,* Boston: Harv. Univ., 1974.

Schein, E.H., *Organizational Psychology*, Englewood Cliffs, N.J. Prentice Hall, 1970.

Schoeller, S., Buzzell, R.D.E. and Heany, D.F., "Impact of Strategic Planning on Profit Performance", *Hav. Bus. Rev.*, March-April., 137-145, 1974.

Seashore, S.E. and Yuchtmen, E., "Factorial Analysis of Organizational Performance", *ASQ*, 12: 377-395, 1967.

Spray, S. Lee., *Organizational Effectiveness*: *Theory, Research Utilization*, Kent State Univ., 1976.

Srivastava, Suresh and Salipantte, P., "Autonomy in Work", in Spray (ed.), *Organizational Effectiveness*, Kent State University, 1976.

Steers, R.M., "Problems in the Measurement of Organizational Effectiveness," *ASQ* 20: pp. 546-558, 1975.

Stewart, J.H., "Factors Accounting for Goal Effectiveness: A Longitudinal Study", in Spray (ed.), *Organizational Effectiveness: Theory*-Research – Utilization, Kent State Univ., 1976.

Stodgill, R.M., *Managers, Employees, Organizations*, Columbia, Ohio State Univ. Press, 1965.

Sutton, H. and Porter, L.W., "A Study of the Grapevine in a Governmental Organization", *Personal Psy*. 21: 223-230, 1968.

Webb, R.J., "Organizational Effectiveness and the Voluntary Organization", *Acad. of Mangt. Jr.*, 17: 663-667, 1974.

Weber, M., *The Theory of Social and Economic Organizations*, trans. by A.M. Hendersen, and T. Parsons, Glencose 111., The Free Press, 1947.

Weick, K.E., "On Re-punctuating the Problem of Organizational Effectiveness" (unpublished), 1976.

Woodward, J., *Management and Technology: Problems of Progress, in Industry*. London, HMSO, 1958.

Woodward, J., *Industrial Organization*: Theory and Practice, London, Oxford Univ. Press, 1965.

Yuchtman, E. and Seashore, S.E., "A Systems Resource Approach to Organizational Effectiveness", *Amer*. Soc. Rev. 32: 1967, pp. 891-903.

3

Work Study in Government Organisations

Indrajit Singh and *K.N. Bhutani*

Work Study is an old technique as applied to industry. Its translation to government organizations has been recent. Nevertheless, a considerable amount of literature is available on the manner and method of application of this technique to government organizations in different countries. Work-study has been recently introduced in the Government of India for analysing methods of work and assessing the staffing needs of government organizations. This technique was first employed on an enquiry into the Re-organization of the Income-tax Department; the technique has since been widely used by the Special Re-organization Unit of the Ministry of Finance in the Government of India. The present article deals with the experience of the Special Re-organization Unit and with the problems that generally arise during the course of work study of government organizations. These have been described under the following headings:-

(a) Tools of Analysis
(b) Work Simplification
(c) Work Measurement
(d) Assessment of Staff
(e) Organizational Matters

Tools of Analysis

One of the primary tasks in work study is to analyse the existing procedures of work in detail. We found that if this basic work is done properly and with care, it has considerable impact on the final results. We have therefore selected certain tools of analysis

From *The Indian Journal of Public Administration*, Vol. IV (1), 1958.

which are being used elsewhere and adapted them to our requirements. The basic tools of analysis that were used are mentioned below:-

(i) Organizational Charts: Which display at a glance the disposition of persons constituting the organizational hierarchy, their lines of command and the functions performed by them.

(ii) Duty Lists: Which display in terms of itemised jobs the functions assigned to individuals in the organization under study.

(iii) Job Description Sheets: Which indicate the sequence of steps that occur in the performance of a particular job or piece work and the persons performing each step.

(iv) Job Distributicn Sheets: Which display the load borne by various types of persons in the organization in terms of steps constituting the jobs analysed in the form of Job Description Sheets.

(v) Process Charts: Which are an elaboration of the Job Description Sheets in which various symbols are used to indicate the nature of action performed at various steps in the job.

(vi) Flow Charts: Which display the flow of work in the organization as a whole or in any part in order to locate problem areas from the point of view of work simplification and avoidance of delays, overlaps and waste.

The Job Description and Distribution Sheets are the most important of the tools that we have employed. It will be noticed that they differ in some respect from the standard charts of this character used elsewhere. The basic difference in the Job Description Sheet is that it not only records the steps required to perform a job but also provides for columns which facilitate later the process of work simplification. For example, it enables us to formulate our recommendations relating to standardisation of forms in respect of items of work which are of a repetitive nature. It also assists in designating the strategic steps that should be controlled with a view to more effective supervision.

We have also changed the purpose of the Job Distribution Sheet as used elsewhere. The basic difference is in the fact that the form is employed in standard work study analysis to record the contribution of each participant in a job on the basis of the existing procedures of work. The time content of the various steps constituting the jobs is also indicated simultaneously. We have used the form to indicate the contribution of each participant after the procedures have been simplified. This serves two purposes. In the first place, it gives at a glance the nature of duties of each participant on the basis of which rational duty lists are evolved. Secondly, it enables the contribution to be measured in terms of work units and thus serves as a basis for work measurement studies.

Work Simplification

The information gathered in the Job Description Sheet is analysed with the help of Process and Flow Charts in order to suggest simplifications in the performance of the various jobs constituting the sum-total of the work in the organization. The study for work simplification is always undertaken in collaboration with the persons who are engaged on the performance of the various jobs. Unless we are able to convince them and establish definitely that the revised procedures are not only the simplest but also the less circuitous and the most effective under the circumstances, we do not proceed further with our ideas of simplification. We have however found that it is always possible to arrive at a solution which is acceptable to the actual workers and is also the simplest and the best having regard to the organizational and occupational environments in which the job has to be performed.

It will be interesting to refer here to some of the common types of problems that we have encountered during the course of work simplification:-

(1) Number of stages through which papers have to pass is large.

(2) Number of steps taken to reach decision are large in comparison with the needs of the situation.

(3) More effort is being put into some of the steps constituting the job than is needed for effective performance.

(4) Drafting and typing are being done for processes which are so repetitive that a suitable standard from would meet the requirements.

(5) Statistical reports and statements are capable of being rationalised to give more effective results and reduction in their numbers.

(6) Registration of incoming documents is not analytical enough to enable work to be organized efficiently.

(7) Related jobs are being performed in different work units thus leading to movement of papers which can be avoided.

(8) Methods of exercising control over performance of important procedures need redesigning so as to make exercise of supervisory functions effective as also to enlarge the amplitude of supervision.

(9) Low-cost jobs are being performed by high cost personnel.

It will be noticed that these problems are simple enough but they have raised considerable amount of controversy and a good deal of argumentation and critical references when they are under discussion with the persons actually performing the jobs and their superior officials.

It has been our experience that the process of work simplification not only reduces the number of steps but also throws up valuable material for organizational analysis and work measurement. It is in this process that the germs of the entire solution to the problems that we are investigating are found. It is therefore natural that a good deal of controversy should arise at this stage of the work. The actual workers and the authorities concerned become aware, during the course of work simplification, of the manner in which the mind of the analyst is working and are, therefore, able to anticipate, to some extent, the recommendations that are likely to emerge. We have found considerable enthusiasm in accepting the results of method study. Sometimes even a certain amount of competitive element is introduced in the sense that the organizations anticipate the recommendations of the work study team and begin to formulate their own ideas on the changes that ought to be made having regard to the facts as discovered and analysed by the team. This is in accordance with the objectives of work study and we have several times thought it prudent to let the credit for effecting improvements be passed on to the organizations under study rather than to the work study team.

The attitude however is somewhat different at the stage of work measurement and assessment of staffing needs. Where the recommendations are likely to affect adversely the staffing position of the organization concerned, the actual workers, as well as such of the senior administrative officials who have not full faith in the method of work study, fight their last ditch battle either to delay the completion of the work or to confound the work study analyst. Work simplification has been found by us to be the real test of the success of a work-study analyst.

One could multiply a large number of examples taken from actual case sheets of the Special Re-organization Unit to illustrate the manner in which some of the ideas given above were applied in actual practice. It will, however, make the narrative a little heavy if such examples are introduced at this stage. They have therefore been given as Notes at the end of this article.

Work Measurement

After completion of the Work Simplification programme revised Job Description Sheets are prepared, displaying the redesigned procedures of work. In order to appreciate the contribution of each type of employee, it is necessary to break down the revised Job Descriptions and record them in the Job Distribution Sheet. Ordinarily the constituent elements of a job performed by different employees fall into either of the two categories mentioned below:

(i) Repetitive steps such as diarisation, filing, noting of movement, referencing, indexing, opening of new files, typing, despatch, etc., which are common to almost all the procedures; and

(ii) Non-repetitive steps which are intimately related to the character of the job though some of them may be common to other jobs also. They constitute the real content of the job.

For repetitive steps, agreed 'norms' have been evolved after adjusting past performance in the light of results obtained from the work simplification programme. While the performance of almost all such steps is undoubtedly capable of being time-tested accurately, the stop-watch methods of work measurement have been deliberately avoided because of the reluctance of office workers to such a procedure. It is not as though we have always succeeded in avoiding recourse to the stop watch. In some cases, we were compelled to utilise it as there was no other way of carrying conviction to the organization concerned. However this required considerable education of the organization on the manner in which these studies should be carried out. The following description of an actual instance of this nature brings out some of the difficulties that arise and consequent preparation that has to be made.

We took the following items for time study:-

(i) Perusal of a request for an application form and noting of the applicant's address on wrappers.

(ii) Preparation of folders to contain application forms.

(iii) Entry of a 'receipt' in the Receipt Register.

(iv) Typing of addresses of applicants from wrappers prepared as at (i) above.

(v) Scrutiny of applications for completeness.

For the time-test, the officers in charge of the organization under study offered two persons of 'average' calibre actually engaged in their performance. An interesting innovation in the time-test was the introduction of a 'guinea pig' with the object of importing realism so that the results could be made more acceptable. An inexperienced Clerk drawn from outside the organization under study, who was almost a 'fresher' having had till then experience only of typing work, was the 'guinea pig' employed. The organization itself offered to impart the necessary instruction for the performance of the steps to him for a couple of hours before the actual time test each day. Fairly representative items of work involving the performance of the steps to be time-tested each day were made available by the organization. Before each test, the three persons concerned were clearly told that the time-test was not a 'race' in which performance was to be judged by speed. The results obtained were revealing in sense that the average time taken by each of them was almost the same and this average 'norm' was much less, and for one or two items astonishingly lower than the 'hunches' of many of us, the officers conducting the study as well as officers of the organization itself.

For assessing the work-content of the non-repetitive steps, we have employed the methods of analytical estimation, time synthesis and delay-ratio, which involve extensive case-studies and group discussions. Let us take for example the step involved in the procedure for considering the question of levy of damages against a supplier who has delayed the execution of the contract beyond the stipulated date. Extensive case-studies indicated that the step, namely the consideration of the question, which at first may appear to be a rather intangible process, consists predominantly of the following sub-steps:

1. Perusal of the contract with a view to jotting down:
   (i) The name of the supplier,
   (ii) Particulars of stores,
   (iii) Value of stores, and
   (iv) Stipulated date of delivery etc.
2. Perusal of certificate of completion of delivery.
3. Arithmetical calculation of maximum damages leviable according to prescribed formula.
4. Perusal of supplier's explanation giving reasons for delay.
5. Jotting down of all the above particulars in a standard form.

We would then take a person of "average" calibre actually employed on the job and jot down the time he feels he would take in the light of past experience in the performance of each such sub-step. The advantage of thus estimating the time taken by each sub-step is that it forms a more convincing basis of discussion than an estimation based on the performance of the composite step. The 'norm' so obtained is compared with a similar performance of other 'average' employees and an acceptable 'norm' is evolved. Illustrations of work measurement of such steps could be multiplied but the essence of the scheme is the same: the steps are analysed further into sub-steps, and the time estimation synthesised on the basis of such constituent sub-steps into a standard 'form'.

A synthesis of 'norms' for such steps and repetitive steps in the performance of a particular job or a portion of the job falling to the share of each type of person gives the standard 'norm' for the performance of that job in terms of man-hours of that particular category of employee. For example the standard 'norm' for the performance of a particular job would be X man-hours of a junior clerk, Y man-hours of a senior clerk and Z man-hours of the supervisory staff.

Before we take up the several refinements which had necessarily to be imported into work measurement methods, let us describe briefly the Delay Ratio Method of measurement which was actually applied in evolving standards of performance of some Appellate Officers. The method consists in taking a specified period of past performance and assessing the factors which impeded the more effective performance of the job. For example, such factors, for those Appellate Officers were the frequency of adjournments asked for by the appellants, the delay in receipt of records from lower formations, heterogenity of case fixtures for a particular day etc. etc. Measures were designed to curtail the recurrence of such factors and this way additional productive capacity was generated.

Whichever method is adopted, it does not carry conviction unless a large number of case studies of past performance in respect of identical or similar items of work are made. It is seldom however that case studies indicate the evolution of a simple 'norm' for performance of a particular job. Almost every item of work has been found on case-studies to consist of several categories where even though the work-content differed widely from category to category, it was fairly uniform within each category itself. One of the preliminary steps therefore is to classify the work in such homogenous categories. This enables the norms to be evolved more realistically as fluctuations between the average and extreme types of work are much less pronounced in each category than in the total work.

If the relative frequency of occurrence of each such category is known, or can be predicted to a fair degree of accuracy, a 'weighted' average can be prescribed as the standard 'norm' for the performance of that particular job. We have, however, found it more rational to prescribe different 'norms' for different categories and have future inflow of work registered in Diversified Records. Thus the re-designed Registration Records would display the future complexion of work, not only in terms of items of work requiring differing degree of priority for disposal as explained earlier but also according to degrees of work-content.

In this way, for example, the price finalisation cases in a Purchase Organization were divided into three categories:-

(i) Cases which involved fluctuations in f.o.b. prices.

(ii) Cases which involved fluctuations in the price of raw materials like steel, etc.

(iii) Cases which involved fluctuations in customs duty.

Separate 'norms' were evolved for each one of them since the time required for the performance of the job varied from 5-6 hours for the first category to about half an hour for the last. This scheme of evolution of 'norms' on the basis of actual complexion of the load as against its totality has been found effective in almost every organization studied by us.

A very significant feature of work-measurement studies has been a constant shift from existing 'norms' in terms of incoming documents which are no true index of work-content to 'norms' in terms of distinct items of work, suitably categorised as explained above. Thus standards of performance in purchase units are evolved in terms of indents instead of incoming documents. In price-finalisation units, in terms of various categories of price finalisation cases instead of incoming documents; and in the organization dealing with Government residences, in terms of vacancies instead of total number of residences.

Assessment of Staff

The staffing needs of the organization are worked out by multiplying the standards of performance with total amount of work. The determination of the latter however is not an easy task for the reason that existing records are not maintained to display the work in the same analytical form as indicated by the processes of work simplification and case studies. This difficulty has been overcome by analysing a sample chosen purely at random and projecting its results to cover the whole work provided they square with the judgment of the officers of the organization concerned. This has led sometimes to differences of opinion, but, by persisting with a large enough sample, agreements have been provisionally reached on the volume of total work-counts of different categories. As records will in future be maintained on the basis of the suggestions made, the results obtained from the random sample could be tested after a few months.

In working out the total manpower requirements allowance has always been made for such human factors as fatigue, frictional loss etc. This takes the form of an over-all percentage of the total man-hours worked out on the basis of 'norms' of performance.

Simplification of methods of work inevitably leads to saving in manpower. It is at this stage that the enthusiasm of those that are sceptical of this method begins to decline. The difficulties that arise consume a disproportionate time owing to the unwillingness of the authorities to work, on accepted improved methods, with less staff than was in position at the commencement of the study. This reluctance is understandable as the efficacy of new arrangements cannot be demonstrated except by testing them actually in a part of the organization. Usually this succeeds in converting the authorities or in making the work-study analyst wiser about the factors that he miscalculated. Owing to the short time for which the Special Re-organization Unit has been in existence, we cannot say that full use has been made of installing methods to prove their efficacy. We propose to make greater use of this in future as it is a vital part of the system of work study.

Organizational Matters

The work studies, made by us so far, have revealed some interesting problems in organizational planning. The important issue that arose was whether the methods study, work simplification programme, etc., should precede an analysis of the organization at the top, or should it succeed it? Having regard to the circumstances of administrative set-up in the country, it has been found more profitable to make an analysis of the organizational structure only after the methods of work have been carefully planned out and simplified. This is specially true in the organizational set-up of the secretariat of the government. The higher structure is meant partly for some high-grade original work and partly for span of control. Since the latter is more than half the part of the ingredients of supervision, it is necessary that the analysis of the superstructure of the organization should follow the evolution of the design of the basic primary unit, the quality of work and the volume of load that it has to carry.

In this respect we have departed from the normal practice of work analysis adopted elsewhere of segregating organizational studies from methods studies and pursuing both of them more or less as independent assignments to be linked up later. We have considered them as a continuing part of the same assignment and reversed the normal pattern of priorities assigned to it in view of the circumstances in which we have to function.

The study of organizational structure is somewhat limited in that certain patterns of a rigid character already exist. The work analyst has therefore to proceed on certain pre-determined systems but the scope for fresh thinking is considerable in spite of the restrictive nature of the atmosphere in which we have to work.

We indicate below some of the organizational problems that emerged from our work-studies:

(i) Grading of Personnel: An assessment of the intrinsic worth of the non-routine steps involved in the performance of jobs entrusted to a work unit indicates the gradation of the person required for the effective performance of that job. Thus, we have found quite often that high cost personnel were being used for intrinsically low cost jobs either because of a strict adherence to the prescribed structure of the primary unit of work or because of high cost and low cost functions being mixed in a work unit. Thus, to a substantial extent, it was the nature of the steps required to be performed that determined the structure of the primary unit of work itself.

(ii) Assessment of need for functional specialists: Detailed work analysis and extensive case-study of the non-routine steps have actually indicated in several studies the need for functional specialists not only in the line but in the lower echelons of organizations entrusted with policy-making so that work gets expedited with the availability of experts at the earliest stage in policy formulation. Such a need was felt in work-units dealing with price finalisation work, Sales-tax work, etc.

(iii) Supervisory functions: Work-studies have indicated the need and extent of supervision necessary for the proper performance of jobs. Methods designed to provide the control mechanism determine the span of control of supervisory staff, their means of communication etc. and therefore determine the structural arrangements necessary for effective supervision.

(iv) Need for segregation of policy and executive functions: A heterogeneous assignment of functions, involving the exercise of policy as well as executive functions, gets revealed by work studies which involve analysis of procedures emanating from the exercise of those functions. Apart from the organizational merit of segregation of such functions, amalgamation of executive functions with policy functions automatically results in high cost personnel being brought to engage their attention on low cost jobs because of set high-cost patterns of staffing for policy-making organizations.

(v) Need for functional distribution of work: Analysis of procedures of work have indicated often the need for functional distribution of work. It was a study of the existing methods of work for dealing with procurement of stores which indicated the separable nature of planning of procurement, process of procurement, and finalisation work and led to functionalisation of

purchase work into a Planning Wing, Purchase Wing and Finalisation Wing.

(vi) Need for avoiding over-functionalisation: Conversely analysis of existing procedures of work indicated the existence of a swing of the pendulum to the other extreme. Over-functionalisation of work into a Medical Section and Personnel Section in a particular organization lengthened the process of disposal of some items of work and enhanced their work-content.

(vii) Multiplicity of consideration of important issues: Analysis of work and case-studies of the non-routine steps in many organizations have indicated, that while for resolution of important issues or formulation of policy, there has to be a multiplicity of 'consideration' at various levels in the organizational hierarchy, the need for papers to move through each level in the hierarchy between the level of first handling and the level of final decision needs to be re-assessed.

(viii) Structure of the primary unit of work: By far the most important results brought out by work studies has been the importance of the structure of the primary unit of work. Under existing arrangements, there was almost a uniform pattern of staffing of the primary work-unit, viz. a Section Officer in charge of the section with a fixed number of persons 'dealing' with work flowing into the section, assisted by a fixed number of junior clerks for routine work like typing etc. Work studies indicated that with rapidly expanding activities of Government, the complexion of functions now performed is so different that the setting up of the primary unit of work into pre-designed inflexible structures requires reconsideration.

Training Work Study Personnel

Lastly, we would like to refer to some of our difficulties. One of them is the lack of trained personnel for work study. We have heard the argument that almost anybody could be inducted into this business. We have found from experience that it is just the wrong way of organising work of this character. New personnel put on this work has brought more troubles and difficulties with the organization under study than we had bargained for. Trained personnel, on the other hand, has considerably assisted the Unit to remove misunderstandings about the nature of work that is being done by us. The personal qualities required of those undertaking work study have been described in many text-books and we can testify that much of what is written about their intelligence, tact, perseverance, resourcefulness etc., is fully justified. A work-study analyst need not be super-human but he has certainly got to be fully trained in the art of analysis and has to have patience and persuasiveness which should be somewhat extra-ordinary. Such men cannot obviously be found any where but have to be fashioned out of good material that is available in the various organizations with which a work-study analyst has to deal. We have therefore adopted a number of methods by which the art of work study is not confined to a small unit in the government organization but is broad-based. In several cases we have given a demonstration of the manner in which the work should be done in a couple of primary units and left the rest of the analysis to be made by a person trained from the organization itself but under the general guidance of the Special Re-organization Unit. Secondly, we have undertaken a work study course of persons drawn from different organizations so that they can go back and apply the methods that they have learnt from the Special Re-organization Unit. The first batch has already completed its training. We are also receiving requests from State Governments for either material on the manner in which work study is being carried out or for training their men for that purpose. One of the objectives of work study is that each one of the persons should be able to analyse his work in order to economise on time and increase his efficiency. This is being amply fulfilled by the manner in which we are trying to decentralise this work so that it continues to be done where it is most needed.

Notes

Actual Examples of Improvements Resulting from the Application of 'Work Study' Techniques

(i) Problems of Registration : There is almost a dogmatic adherence to chronological registration of incoming documents in most of the government organizations. We have been exploring the possibility, where opportunities exist, of registering documents on the basis of certain identifiable categories, to which varying priorities could be attached for disposal and control. In a Purchase organization, we came across about four categories of incoming documents which accounted for 60-70% of the total work-load. We indicated that at a certain stage the registration of these documents should be changed from a chronological to a diversified character. This not only serves the purpose of easy identification of important items of work which must be controlled if efficiency and economy were desired, but also offered a ready means of supervision on the bulk of the important work of the unit by senior officials.

(ii) Organizational Issues : We have generally found that much

of the confusion in organizational matters arises from the fact that duties are allotted on a composite basis making it possible for the officials at the level of the primary unit of work to concentrate on one type of work at the expense of another. As far as practicable we have tried to form basic units of work on the consideration that they should carry out predominantly unified types of duties so that they could not disregard one if there was greater pressure to dispose off the other. This reform was specially introduced in one of the supply organizations for finalisation of contracts. It was observed that by combining purchase and finalisation work the official in charge of the primary unit gave greater attention to the purchase work as it was of an immediate consequence. The lack of proper attention to the finalisation work resulted in a large amount of final payments to suppliers being held up which ultimately reacted on the prices offered for stores in response to tenders. The creation of a separate Finalisation Wing with its own primary units of work is likely to result in improvement in the payment of final bills.

(iii) Bulking of Indents : A purchase organization normally bulks in indents with a view to getting most favourable prices for the largest possible quantities that it undertakes to purchase. It is however necessary that this intention should be followed by carefully laying out the procedure by which bulking becomes an automatic process. It was observed in a supply organization the bulking was being left to the initiative of the lowest official. A procedure was designed, which involved registration of indents in a diversified form, designing of cards for bulking and suggestions for drawing up a time-schedule for receipt of various types of stores, progressive standardisation of indenting vocabulary etc. etc.

(iv) Applications for Allotment of Residential Accommodation : It is one of the interesting features of work in offices that sometimes information is called for which is not directly required or necessary for the purpose of the objective with which the organization is charged. We found that in one of the organizations dealing with allotment of government residence, the existing procedure stipulated that every government employee, even if he were already in occupation of government accommodation, should submit an annual application giving all the relevant particulars. This is no doubt necessary when the application is submitted for the first time, but the important purpose of getting this information annually was to enable the organization concerned to revise the rent owing to changes that might occur in the interval in the emoluments of

the tenant. It was suggested that it would be enough if information was obtained for changes in respect of emoluments as they affected the recoverable rent. Under the existing procedure the changes called for in annual applications were categorised, classified and put into many registers and this process was repeated every year though no substantial change had occurred in the particulars of many tenants. In place of existing registers the system of card indices has been suggested which would eliminate the necessity of the annual re-writing of registers and also accelerate the process of allotment.

(v) Sometimes the existing Rules and Regulations governing the conduct of business, result in uneconomic procedures of work because the circumstances under which the Rules were originally framed have completely altered. An instance of this was found in the organization which dealt with allotment of Government residences. This was the provision for allowing the tenant of a Government residence an option to ask for a change of residence. This led to a considerable amount of infructuous work without commensurate benefit to the tenants, since extensive case-studies showed that in about 75% of the cases, changes in residence offered in accordance with the preferences exercised by the tenants themselves, were not being accepted by them. This was because the existing Rules permitted the tenant to repeat his request for a change even if he had earlier refused the offer made in response to his own request. The only penalty he incurred was that he could not repeat the request for a period of six months. This provision in the Rules actually accentuated the tendency to apply for change of residence irrespective of the genuine needs of the tenants and incidentally added considerably to the cost both in terms of volume of work involved and the loss of rent as a result of quarters remaining vacant in the process of accommodating the variety of requests for change.

An acceptable suggestion made was that the option for change should be restricted to cases based on economic or other compelling grounds, e.g., distance, lack of educational and other facilities, health grounds, etc. Accordingly, it was suggested that Government residential accommodation be clearly demarcated into various territorial zones within which facilities of the type referred to above would not be materially different. After this the option of 'change' could be restricted to change from one zone to another only. Secondly, to ensure elimination of capricious requests for 'change' it was agreed that failure to accept the change offered in response to the tenant's request should result in his forfeiting his right to a 'change'.

(vi) No Objection Certificate : Another interesting example of work simplification is the procedure for dealing with requests from employees for a No Objection Certificate. Before payment of Pension or Provident Fund is sanctioned, the employee is required to produce a certificate that no rent dues are outstanding against him in respect of any of the Government residence he may have occupied in the past. To be able to furnish this certificate the organization concerned had to search through a large number of rent cards, collect all the rent cards in respect of houses occupied by the employee concerned at any time in the past, scrutinise them, effect outstanding recovery if any and then issue the certificate. Since 'rent cards' had necessarily to be maintained 'house wise' and their number is very large, a search for all the rent cards relating to houses occupied by a particular person, was a very laborious process which resulted in considerable delay in the issue of 'No Objection Certificate'. An evident solution which readily suggested itself was the maintenance of occupant-wise cards (or personal ledger accounts) in addition to the house-wise rent cards, which for valid accounting reasons could not be dispensed with. But the maintenance of such cards in addition to the rent cards was likely to result in an almost doubling of the effort necessitating the additional employment of about hundred persons. This was considered incommensurate with the percentage of defaulters which constituted hardly 5% of the total number of tenants. An acceptable solution was found in this, that every time a new rent card was opened for a person who had shifted from an earlier Government residence the distinctive number of the old rent card was jotted down on the new rent card to facilitate back reference if and when necessary. To eliminate the need for back reference, a suitable table was suggested to be superscribed on the rent cards themselves so that any arrears of rent relating to the earlier house could be carried forward to the new rent card.

(vii) Utilisation of Personnel : An illustration of high cost personnel being utilised on low cost jobs because of defective procedures of work was found in an organization dealing with grant of scholarships. Under the existing method, applications on first receipt were made into convenient bundles and passed round the various Sections. Each Section Officer in his turn scrutinised all the applications in a bundle to pick out those dealt with in his Section and passed the rest on to other Section Officers. This procedure of sorting was entrusted to senior supervisory staff. An acceptable solution to speedier and less expensive sorting was found in prominently superscribing on the prescribed form of

application, a check table in which the applicant could indicate the necessary particulars such as the State of Domicile etc. which formed the basis of work distribution in the organization. In this way sorting could be effected at the very stage of receipt by low cost 'sorters'.

(viii) Work content of Jobs : An interesting illustration of methods analysis leading to reduction of work-content of jobs was found in a unit of work charged with accounting work ancilliary to the grant of scholarships. One of the items of work in this unit was the compilation of a list of students awarded scholarship arranged State-wise/caste-wise/institution-wise. Under the existing procedure, this was compiled from a Register in which relevant entries were being ledgerised. The basic record from which this posting was made was a copy of the Bills sent to this Unit by the Units dealing with the award of scholarships. This annual posting involved a lot of effort. As a result of study of a large number of copies of the bills which formed the basis of posting it was suggested that if the object of maintenance of the Register was only to prepare a classified compendium of awards, it would be much more easily and effectively done if the copies of the bills themselves could be sorted out and classified instead of being posted into Ledgers. This was actually tried out in one working season and found to result in a speedier disposal of work with much less effort.

4

Speed and Efficiency in Development Administration

Tarlok Singh

This paper outlines suggestions for measures to be taken in the immediate future for speeding implementation, raising administrative efficiency and standards, securing better management in public enterprises and simplifying procedures relating to planning. It is common ground that the volume of administrative work and its complexity have increased to such an extent in recent years that the present machinery is severely strained. At many vital points there is inadequate follow-up. There is insufficient emphasis on individual responsibility and on the observance of time schedules. Delays in the disposal of the day-to-day business of government also occur frequently. Public enterprises, especially those engaged in industrial activities, present a growing number of difficult managerial problems. With increase in the tempo of development and in the range of Government's responsibilities, these problems have assumed greater urgency and demand far-reaching changes in procedures and approaoch. It is being increasingly urged that as far as possible each Department should have "self-contained powers" and that the need for constant reference to other Departments should be minimized. This observation has relevance as much to the Planning Commission's own work as to other fields. Suggestions in this paper, which are based on a considerable volume of discussion, may be conveniently set out under the following heads:

(i) Machinery within the Government for improving administrative efficiency and standards;

From *The Indian Journal of Public Administration*, Vol. VII, July-Sept. 1961.

(ii) Measures for speeding implementation;
(iii) Problems of public enterprises;
(iv) Other administrative problems; and
(v) Reduction of references to the Planning Commission.

(i) Machinery within the Government for Improving Administrative Efficiency and Standards

Important questions of policy and approach in administration require the directions of the Government from time to time. Within the administration there is need for machinery which will be charged with the duty of locating key administrative problems, arranging for their investigation by special study groups, advising on policy decisions and, generally, suggesting measures for raising administrative efficiency and standards. In an administrative structure based on parliamentary institutions, the higher ranks of the public services have both the obligation and the opportunity of assisting the Cabinet in providing direction and guidance on these lines. Accordingly, it is proposed that at the Centre there should be a Committee on Administration consisting of the Cabinet Secretary and a few other senior officials who, as a body, are given a continuing responsibility for the tasks mentioned above and report to the Cabinet periodically on action taken by Ministries and authorities subordinate to them. In the States also, it is proposed that there should be similar committees on administration, including the Chief Secretary and a group of senior officials, who report to the Chief Minister and the State Cabinet.

(ii) Measures for Speeding Implementation

Avoidance of delays within any organization depends largely on the quality of the personnel at different levels, the extent to which they have been trained for the work entrusted to them, arrangements for supervision, distribution of work and delegation of responsibilities. Improvement of work along these lines has to be necessarily a process which goes forward purposefully all the time, and the responsibility for ensuring this devolves at the Centre on the Organization and Methods Division of the Cabinet Secretariat and in the States on the appropriate units which have now been set up in most State. Suggestions offered here may be broadly grouped as follows:

(i) Need to fix individual responsibility and to reduce 'consultation' with other authorities;
(ii) Procedures relating to financial control;

(iii) Administration of secretariat services; and

(iv) References to the Union Public Service Commission.

Two other problems to which attention is frequently drawn are not dealt with in this paper. These are delays in the execution of civil works due to the concentration of responsibility in the Central Public Works Department and delays in procuring stores for which responsibility has been placed on the Directorate General of Supplies and Disposals in the Ministry of Works, Housing and Supply.

Need to fix individual responsibility and reduce 'consultation' with other authorities: It has been frequently pointed out that in the present administrative practice, there is insufficient stress on individual responsibility and that the requirements for consultation with or seeking of concurrences from other authorities are excessive. Both speedy disposal of business and effective delegation of powers on the part of Ministries to their subordinate authorities are consequently impeded. It is essential that in each field responsibility for producing results should be cast more definitely both on the Department or agency concerned and, within it, on the individuals entrusted with particular tasks, and that consultation with other authorities should be confined to broader matters. These processes are closely connected and are indispensable if delays are to be reduced and implementation speeded up.

The propositions stated above apply equally as between Ministries and as between a Ministry and the executive Departments subordinate to it. It should be pointed out that in recent years Ministries at the Centre and Secretariat Departments in the States have tended to assume responsibility for an increasing amount of original work, thus reducing the initiative of the executive departments and offices and their ability to function without frequent reference to and consultation with the Ministries. Both in the First and in the Second Plan it was stressed that the primary concern of Ministries and Secretariat Departments should be with matters of policy, general supervision and enforcement of standards and that executive tasks should be left to be carried out by Departments and authorities specially designated for the purpose. As there is general agreement in principle on this approach, there is need for a Government directive that Ministries should review their existing delegations of powers to the executive Departments subordinate to them and provide for larger delegations of authority to them. Action taken should be followed up by the Organization and Methods Division of the Cabinet Secretariat, which should also review the scheme of delegations within individual Departments, as this is an essential aspect of the same process.

Procedures relating to financial control: A scheme of delegation of financial powers to Ministries and Departments was introduced in August 1958. This envisaged that the major scrutiny of the Finance Ministry would be exercised before the framing of the budget and once this had been done administrative Ministries would be free to spend sums provided in their budgets up to Rs. 50 lakhs in each case in consultation with their 'internal' financial advisers. Towards the end of 1959, some further delegations of financial powers were agreed to. It has been suggested that the scheme of delegations has not had a chance to work as intended mainly because Ministries have not found it possible as a rule to furnish adequate details of their schemes before the framing of the budget. On the other hand, it has been urged that the new procedure has not materially reduced the need for consultation with the Finance Ministry especially in establishment matters, and that there is need for a much larger measure of delegation of powers to individual Ministries in the use of funds provided in their budgets.

Control of expenditure presents different sets of problems in respect of (a) projects and schemes and (b) staff and salaries. As regards (a), the estimates prepared by Ministries are frequently incomplete and defective mainly because enough time and personnel are not assigned for the planning phase. The most important requirements here are, firstly, to ensure that the Ministries are adequately equipped in personnel for thorough planning of projects and schemes and, secondly, that the Ministry of Finance are also equipped for similar study of cost estimates. Provided there is careful planning and close association from the beginning between financial and technical experts, after funds have been budgeted, references to the Finance Ministry should be required only where substantial variations take place in the scope or in the costs of a project.

As regards staff and salaries, note has to be taken of the criticism that civil expenditure has risen considerably and that the cost of administration must be kept in check. At the same time, it is important that while adhering to agreed financial limits and to standards based on approved practice or, where necessary, on systematic work studies, Departments should have much greater discretion in determining their staff structure and requirements. In this connection, the general policy of Government regarding the levels of salaries of highly paid employees and the need to avoid competitive bidding by Government Departments for personnel in categories in which there is shortage should be kept in view. Further delegations in favour of Ministries and project authorities in matters affecting staff and salaries should now be worked out.

Administration of Secretariat services: Secretariat services are controlled by the Ministry of Home Affairs with the help of a Board which also includes officials from some other Ministries. The total strength of the Secretariat services now runs to more than 20,000. It has been felt that with larger control over their Secretariat personnel it should be possible to secure greater efficiency and better human relations within various administrative organizations. The principle of transfer of control over specified categories of Secretariat personnel is acceptable to the Home Ministry. There is general agreement that selection of officers of the rank of Under Secretary and above should be on a common basis for the Government as a whole. The practical issue for consideration is whether the transfer of control to individual Ministries should extend to the level of Section Officers or to that of Assistants. On a balance of considerations, it is considered that up to the level of Section Officer, administrative control should be entrusted to individual Ministries, but certain safeguards regarding standards, promotion, reporting, etc. should be provided.

References to the Union Public Service Commission: Suggestions have been made that the Union Public Service Commission might limit itself to recruitment to the higher grades of the public service and, in respect of promotion and confirmation, it might leave decisions to Ministries to a greater extent than at present. Matters of common interest to Government and the Union Public Service Commission are kept under constant review and there does not appear to be need for any fundamental change in the scope of consultation with the UPSC. It is open to Government to determine the posts for which recruitment should be undertaken through the UPSC. In disciplinary cases, consultation with the UPSC provides protection which is helpful to the morale of the public services. It should be considered whether references regarding promotion or confirmation within the same grade or class could be reduced. Two questions which deserve to be examined are: (1) whether the present arrangements for recruitment to technical and scientific posts need to be strengthened further, and (2) whether delays which occur at present in the disposal of references regarding vigilance cases could be further reduced.

Action-orientation in administration: The changes in organization and procedures suggested above will go some distance to remove causes of delay. They have to be supported, of course, by greater attention to the training of personnel, to supervision and to reporting and evaluation. All these measures, however, will be of little avail without a major effort to make the administration much more action-oriented than it is at present. With growth in the volume and range of work in the Central Government, despite considerable increase in staffs, the situation is far from satisfactory. Dr. Appleby's observations are still true:

"A general fault of the Indian Administrative process exists in the practice of seeking agreement on everything by everybody before anything is done. Worse, the practice requires that these agreements cover not only general objectives, general allocations of funds, general personnel arrangements, and the fixing of general lines of responsibility, but also over specific applications of these general determinations in a continuing and heavy flow. The criticism in rather crude terms is that there is much too much sharing of responsibility for action before the fact, and too little review in appropriate terms focusing on accomplishment after the fact."

There is no single remedy for this situation but, along with other measures, the four essential conditions which need to be stressed are:

(1) Policy directives: Although policy and administration are closely connected, there is a clear distinction between them which is often overlooked. Administration is necessarily concerned with detail; what gives meaning and focus to it is policy. In every important field, the quality of execution can be greatly improved if the Government's policy directives, while being based on a proper study of facts, are set out in bold and specific terms, so that they provide a definite perspective for positive and sustained implementation.

(2) Responsibility for execution: Although they have their place in the scheme of administration, there is at present far too much resort to committees, groups, boards, etc. for carrying out the policies of Government. What is important is that for the execution of any programme or project, specific responsibility should be placed on the agency concerned and, within it, on particular individuals. Within defined limits, each individual should be given full responsibility and, with it, the necessary measure of support and trust. If he fails in the discharge of his responsibility, he should

be replaced. But so long as he holds an office, he should accept all its obligations and equally he should be placed in a position effectively to discharge them. With responsibility thus specified, it should be open to him to seek such advice and consultation as he may require, but these should not become the necessary ingredients of the executive process itself.

(3) Test of performance: Success or failure must be judged rigorously by the test of results. This is possible only if in the planning stage the aims to be achieved, the tasks to be undertaken, the means to be employed, the obligations of the various agencies or individuals concerned, and the time-sequence in which different operations must flow and dovetail into one another are clearly stated in advance, and are subjected to systematic review from stage to stage. In these aspects there are marked deficiencies in the existing procedures, which have to be removed urgently.

(4) Personnel policies: The importance of appropriate personnel policies in securing results can scarcely be exaggerated. Perhaps the most crucial consideration is that for all vital jobs, not only should the responsible officials be selected with the utmost care and suitably trained, but they should remain long enough to grow to the full measure of their responsibility and produce the results expected of the assignment. In any major enterprise a period of less than five to ten years is rarely sufficient for producing large results. Frequently, in service transfers, the factors which are taken into consideration are not of the first importance in terms of public interest or the success of the undertaking. Such transfers tend to injure both continuity of operations and the morale of organizations whose tasks are nearly always of a difficult and pioneering character.

It is unfortunately true that there is a great deal of slowness, even retardation, built into the existing administrative structure, and there is urgent need for procedures which will make for radical reorientation in attitudes both at the level of policy and of execution. This central porblem must now be attacked from many sides and continuously if the implementation of plans is to be speeded up in any marked degree.

(iii) Problems of Public Enterprises

The critical role of public enterprises in the planned development of the country is being rightly stressed. The future rate of growth will be determined to an overwhelming degree by the efficiency of the public sector and by the contribution which public enterprises make to domestic savings. Problems relating to the organization and management of public enterprises have been reviewed extensively in reports by the Estimates Committee, studies by high-level experts, a special report on Parliamentary Supervision over State Undertakings, and an international seminar on management of public industrial enterprises organized jointly by the Government of India and the United Nations in December 1959. There is also considerable experience within the country which can be drawn upon and which it would now be desirable to collate and consolidate.

It has been recently agreed that there should be a separate Committee of Parliament for State Undertakings which, in respect of State undertakings brought within its purview, would replace the Public Accounts Committee and the Estimates Committee. In working out the functions and powers of the proposed committee, the principle has been laid down that State undertakings should have more autonomy and greater freedom from detailed control. The powers of Boards of State undertakings are to be enlarged and there is to be provision for further delegations to chairmen and general managers. These problems as well as problems connected with the financing and internal administration of public enterprises fall outside the purview of this paper. Here it is proposed to refer only to those aspects of the subject which have a bearing at the governmental level on the speed and efficiency of implementation in respect of public enterprises.

One of the main difficulties which has been observed is that frequently when the Government has to approve a project, say, for inclusion in a Five Year Plan, it has not been worked out fully, nor is it presented in any adequate form. For irrigation and power projects, there has been in existence for several years within the Planning Commission an Advisory Committee which is assisted in its technical work by the Central Water and Power Commission. All projects costing more than Rs. one crore are considered by it before their execution is taken in hand. The items in respect of which project information should be supplied by State Governments have been indicated in details and every effort is made to secure the necessary reports in time. Industrial and mineral development projects present more varied and complex problems. A checklist of items included in the cost estimates of projects was circulated to the Central Ministries concerned early in March 1960, but Ministries found it difficult to provide the minimum data required. The consequence is that for a large proportion of projects included in the Third Five Year Plan, the information available is still far from satisfactory. This deficiency arises in part from lack of the requisite technical personnel, but equally it is due to the absence of arrangements, for preparation of projects well in advance of the time for their consideration and approval by Government. It is suggested that while the preparation of projects included in the Third Plan must go forward with the utmost speed, the Ministries concerned with industrial projects should take in hand forthwith project studies relating to the Fourth Five Year Plan, so as to complete these as far as possible in the course of the next three years. The question is essentially one of technical and administrative preparation on the part of these Ministries, there should be no great difficulty in making available the funds needed.

The Ministries concerned with industrial and mineral development projects should have strong technical planning cells. These should be maintained as permanent nuclei to be supplemented by additional ad hoc personnel according to requirements. It is not, of course, necessary that the preparation of every new project should be taken up by a technical cell located in a Ministry, for, progressively, existing enterprises should be in a position to undertake this task successfully within their own fields. It is, therefore, suggested that steps should be taken to strengthen and, where necessary, to set up suitable design and research units within major State undertakings. This is already being done to an extent, but there is need for greater emphasis as well as effort on a larger scale. If the preparation of projects becomes a primary responsibility, wherever feasible, of existing enterprises, the planning cells within the Ministries can devote themselves to the broader technical and economic aspects of the project, defining the stages of execution and ensuring that the various related steps for which other authorities are responsible are also precisely co-ordinated.

A weakness which still persists is the inadequacy of existing arrangements within the Ministry of Finance for the examination of cost estimates. The Ministry of Finance have already a 'projects co-ordination cell'. This cell needs to be strengthened. Its responsibility should extend, not only to a scrutiny of cost estimates and the broader economic aspects of projects but also to the presentation of a report each year on the financial and economic aspects of State industrial undertakings as a whole. The absence of such a review at present leaves an important lacuna which needs to be filled.

Apart from technical personnel employed in State industrial undertakings and within Ministries, the Ministries also need to draw upon the advice and assistance of engineers, technologists, economists and financial experts outside the service of Government. It would be helpful for Ministries to arrange for technical advisers for different groups of industries, so that the technical knowledge and experience within the country, which are, of course, growing rapidly, can be readily utilized by Government in developing public sector. The example of the Advisory Committee for Irrigation and Power projects suggests that such association with leading technical and other experts will yield good results and at small cost.

In the Draft Outline of the Third Plan, it was suggested that in major projects or groups of allied projects under the same overall management, there should be special units assisting the management in keeping down costs, raising productivity, setting norms and checking performance, so that the physical assets created are commensurate with the original estimates and designs, time-schedules are maintained, and the responsible authorities are in a position to enforce efficiency, economy and integrity. Speaking on the Third Plan in the Lok Sabha in August 1960, the Prime Minister also stressed the need for evaluation of performance in major projects. It is suggested that the Ministries concerned with large industrial and other projects should review the existing arrangements in these projects and should provide for suitable units for evaluation and review of progress, which will function independently of day-to-day operations, but under the control of the top management authorities. In giving effect to this proposal, the personnel should be chosen with care and the sense of responsibility of those in the direct line of supervision should not be interfered with.

In view of the strategic importance of public enterprises the Planning Commission has to keep in much closer touch with their working and problems than in the past and be in a position to offer its independent advice on large issues whenever necessary.

(iv) Other Administrative Problems

Administration in the States: Efficiency of administration on the part of the Central Government is closely bound up with efficiency in the States and vice versa. Problems of administrative efficiency, standards and morale have, therefore, to be approached from now on as a matter of common concern between the Centre and the States. A large part of the implementation of the Plan rests with the States. In the execution of the Central Government's projects also, State administrations are involved at many points. Both the Centre and the States should keep themselves informed regarding measures taken to strengthen administration and make effective arrangements for exchange of information and experience in matters like personnel, training methods, raising standards, etc.

At the instance of the Planning Commission two aspects of administration in the States are at present being studied with a view to making proposals for the Third Plan. The first relates to administrative personnel at different levels in the States and involves a review of requirements for the Third Plan and of the existing arrangements for training and supervision and other aspects on which the quality of administrative personnel depends to a large extent. The second aspect concerns district administration where a series of new and difficult problems are now cropping up as a result of the introduction of democratic institutions at district and block levels. The National Development Council has agreed that steps should be taken along these lines, but it is important that the effective implementation of the Plan and satisfactory standards of administration should be ensured at each point within the district structure and, in particular, the agricultural production programmes should be carried out successfully.

Relations with the public: One of the main aims in administration must be to ensure right public relations, co-operation from and with the public, and a sense of confidence on the part of citizens generally that where the administration comes into contact with them, it can be relied upon to function with efficiency and integrity and without fear or favour. In this respect, it is true that an atmosphere of complaint and criticism exists, often vague perhaps, but real enough to demand serious attention jointly on the part of the Central as well as the State Governments. Many of the major fields of administrative activity which involve public relations lie in the province of State and local administration. Because of the complexity of the subject and the difficulty of proposing precise remedies, there has not been enough practical effort to bring about a marked change in public opinion in relation to the administration.

If delays could be reduced, accurate information regarding policies and procedures made available and due courtesy shown to citizens by officials at all levels (including promptitude in correspondence), there would doubtless be a change for the better. It would also be worthwhile to make a systematic effort to analyze public attitudes with a view to identifying and removing some of the causes of discontent and adverse public feeling. It is suggested that this task might be entrusted to the Indian Institute of Public Administration and its regional branches and that through this project they should be assisted in undertaking a series of limited but specific studies in collaboration with the local authorities, the object in each case being to analyze problems with a view to finding practical solutions for them and then watching how these work. It is possible that in respect of a number of complaints, which are frequently made by the public, through such a scientific approach to the study of public opinion, measures and procedures capable of producing a favorable response could be evolved. If the general public sensed positive improvement even in a few significant directions and in a few selected areas, this might help turn public thinking into constructive channels and thus suggest ways of bringing about improvements in other directions as well. In a democracy the problems which agitate the public mind can only be solved through co-operation between official agencies, local authorities and citizens based on a sense of common purpose and responsibility for the welfare of the community as a whole.

(v) Reduction of References to the Planning Commission

References to the Planning Commission relate broadly to-

(a) inclusion of new schemes in the Five Year Plan,

(b) revision of cost estimates and outlays for schemes included in the Plan,

(c) provision of funds and the formulation of annual plans,

(d) central assistance included in the Plans of States and for Centrally sponsored schemes,

(e) progress reports, and

(f) general questions of policy and procedure.

Inclusion of new schemes: Schemes to be included in a Five Year Plan fall broadly into two groups, those concerning the Central Ministries alone, and those undertaken in the States. The inclusion of the schemes of the Central Ministries in the Plan requires agreement between the administrative Ministry, the Ministry of Finance and the Planning Commission. Under the present procedure the Planning Commission's concurrence is required, firstly in principle and, secondly, for securing an appropriate allocation within the Plan. The acceptance of a scheme and determination of the outlay required are connected processes in the case of projects which involve considerable expenditure. The Planning Commission has indicated to the Ministries that in the case of new projects it will be guided by the examination of cost estimates undertaken by the Ministry of Finance. In respect of

Central schemes, there has to be greater emphasis than in the past on thorough examination of estimates of cost by the Ministry of Finance for the larger projects accompanied by an enlargement of discretion on the part of the administrative Ministries in formulating detailed schemes within broadly agreed heads and financial allocations.

Schemes undertaken by the states fall into two groups – those whose entire cost is shown in the plans of States and those which are "sponsored" by the Central Ministries for which the provision for assistance is made within their budgets, while the plans of States indicate only their contributions. The acceptance of new schemes in either category takes place, in the main, at the time of the formulation of the Five Year Plan, in which process State representatives, the Ministries and the Planning Commission jointly participate.

The question of technical examination of projects to be undertaken in the States arises where large expenditures are involved, notably in the fields of irrigation and power and for large-scale industries. Industrial projects from the States are yet few in number. In respect of irrigation and power projects, it has been agreed that detailed examination by the Central Water and Power Commission and the Advisory Committee for Irrigation and Power should not be undertaken in respect of schemes costing Rs. one crore or less. For such schemes it is sufficient if a prescribed proforma is completed by the States with a view to providing the essential information. Once a scheme costing up to Rs. one crore has been included, the State Government can proceed with the execution according to its Plan except where inter-State considerations may be involved. The principle that schemes costing Rs. one crore or less prepared by State Governments should not be subject to technical examination by the Central Ministries is also being extended to housing programmes.

Revision of cost estimates and outlays: It is desirable that cases of substantial revision in cost estimates of projects entailing large expenditures or where the scope of a project is altered should be considered by the Planning Commission on the advice of the Ministry of Finance before changes are accepted in the Plan. In the past, large variations in estimates have taken place to the detriment of the Plan. There should, however, be no objection to variation in cost estimates upto 10 per cent or Rs. one crore, whichever is less, being approved by the Ministries without reference to the Planning Commission. The same procedure could be adopted by the States in respect of irrigation and power projects which are now referred to the Advisory Committee on Irrigation and Power projects.

Provision of funds and formulation of annual plans: The annual plans of Ministries are drawn up largely as a by-product of the preparation of the capital budget for which the Ministry of Finance are responsible. In the case of States, the annual plans are formulated jointly by the representatives of the States and the Ministries working in collaboration with the Planning Commission. The Planning Commission indicates overall outlays and Central assistance for States in consultation with the Ministry of Finance. The existing procedures involve the visit to Delhi of fairly large numbers of officials from States. The preparation of the annual plans for 1961-62 was integrated with the discussions on proposals for the Third Plan and no separate meetings were arranged. It is proposed that in future discussions regarding annual plans should be confined to the more important projects and programmes, and before State Governments draw up their proposals, a fair indication of the likely outlays and Central assistance should be given to them in terms of the magnitudes agreed under the Five Year Plan. In fields not covered by specific discussions, the States could report the decisions taken by them. Where they consider necessary, the Ministries could confer informally with individual States well in advance of the time for drawing up annual plans.

Central assistance: Considerable simplification of procedure for Central assistance was undertaken in May 1958. This was followed by further liberalization in May 1959. For the Third Plan, a number of improvements are being undertaken in co-operation with the Ministry of Finance and the administrative Ministries, the guiding principles being the following:

(a) The list of Centrally sponsored schemes is being drastically reduced. Only selected schemes will be accepted as "Centrally sponsored" as-

   (i) relate to demonstrations, pilot projects, surveys and research,

   (ii) have a regional or inter-State character,

   (iii) require lump sum provisions to be made until these can be broken down territorially, or

   (iv) are placed in this group for reasons of overall significance from an all-India angle.

(b) A large variety of Central assistance patterns have grown up in recent years. It is proposed to retain patterns of assistance for a limited number of schemes only. For the rest, Central assistance by way of loans and grants will be intimated under different heads of development. The total amount of assistance due to a State each year is worked out with reference to the plan to be carried out and the assessment of resources which the State can provide. The distribution of schemes within each head into 'groups' which has been in force since 1958 is being discontinued. This will enable State Governments, over a large field, to make such adjustments as they consider necessary within a head of development. However, in the interest of implementation, adjustments between heads of development and diversions of funds provided for important projects should not take place without further consultation.

(c) The All-India Boards present some special problems. It was agreed in May 1958 that only new schemes should be referred to them by States for technical scrutiny. Recent instructions have rendered this unnecessary in respect of most of the All-India Boards. The programmes of the Khadi and Village Industries Commission, though undertaken in the States through State Boards, are at present shown as Central schemes. The Khadi and Village Industries Commission, however, constitutes a somewhat distinct category.

Progress Reports: It is proposed that progress reports on projects and programmes undertaken in the States should be received at a single point within the Government of India, namely, the Ministry concerned, and copies should be made available for the use of the Planning Commission. To the extent additional information is required by the Planning Commission, this will be provided for in forms drawn up by the Ministries in co-operation with the Commission.

General issues of policy and procedure: These arise from time to time and in the interest of planning and co-ordination, it is considered that there is advantage in the Planning Commission having an opportunity to offer its comments and suggestions before decisions are reached. Frequently consideration by the Planning Commission is only a preliminary stage leading to consideration by the Cabinet.

5

Concept of Efficiency in Administration: From Curzon Onward

S.K. Pachauri

Tracing roots of concern for efficiency in Indian administration, the author starts off with contributions made by Lord Curzon 100 years ago and his successors under the British rule. He then highlights the features introduced in Indian administrative system to safeguard efficiency following independence. He follows up the discussion with contributions made by few individual scholars, findings of reform bodies like ARC and Sarkaria Commission. Among most significant recent developments in this area, he discusses 73rd Constitutional Amendment, pressure of liberalization, adoption of concept of efficiency audit in U.K., recommendations of Fifth Pay Commission, availing of information technology benefits in government along with certain other proposed measures which may help promote the cause of efficiency.

Introduction

In the 50th year of Independence, Indian Administration is facing a crisis with a very deep concern for how the country can march forward and live up to the ideals and expectations of the makers of our Constitution. B.R. Ambedkar summed up the debates in the Constituent Assembly when he said that all of us were interested in seeing that the administration was maintained at a high level not only in efficiency but also in purity. Almost exactly

From *The Indian Journal of Public Administration*, Vol. XLIII, Oct.-Dec. 1997.

a hundred year ago, Lord Curzon was faced with a similar problem. His concern was maintenance of the British Government in India and prevention of its impending collapse if the administration did not perform well and efficiently. When Curzon became Viceroy, the country had passed through one of its worst famines in 1897. There was stagnation in the administration and virtually no economic reforms, as India did not reap the benefits of Industrial Revolution of the West in a significant way.

Curzon was influenced by thinkers like Bentham of the 19th Century England, who emphasized on the utilitarian aspects of life and stressed on the greatest happiness of the greatest number. "Efficiency", as he read and declared "has been our gospel, the key-note of our administration". His justification for it was expressed in the following way, "Efficiency of administration is, in my view, a synonym for the contentment of the governed. It is the one means of affecting the people in their homes and of adding only one atom, it may be, but still an atom, to the happiness of the people." Like many other Victorians, he held that national prosperity lay in their material well-being.

Curzon's main effort was in the direction of providing a credible structure of government which would survive for many years after his Viceroyalty and would form the foundation of modern Government in India. Curzon was also consumed by his over-powering zeal and passion for 'efficiency' which was the watchword dictating all his actions as an administrator. He accomplished the task by firstly cutting down the red-tapism, which included discouraging long notings on files and inter-departmental rivalries. As a result, a new set of Secretariat Instructions were formulated and these were complied with by all the Provincial Governments of the day. Curzon had a very clear vision about the role of the Indian administrative system and the personnel manning administrative positions in India. He expected the people, who came from England to serve in India, to have a love for the country and give their very best in terms of time, efforts and efficiency to the Indian people. He feared if this were not the case, the British Empire in India will collapse one day. This is reflected in his letter of May 21, 1902 to Lord Hamilton, then Secretary of State for India, stating:

I wish I had the time to deal at some length with....the future of the English Civilian and indeed of British Rule generally in this country....Lord Beacons Field uttered what was thought to be a very wise and remarkable epigram when he said that the keys of India were not at Herat but in England, in London, and in the possession of the British people. I do not regard this aphorism as true...it seems to me only a half-truth....The Empire here may suffer perhaps from their ignorance but will not in the last resort be lost by their neglect. No, the cause of India are concerned neither in England nor in the House of Commons. They are in the office desk of every young civilian in this country. He, by his character and conduct, is insensibly but materially contributing to the future maintenance or collapse of the British dominion in India. If he is...keen about his work, has the high sense of duty and is interested in and likes the people then the British dominion will be secured for a century to come. If he is indifferent or incompetent or slack, if he dislikes the country and his people and has no taste for his work, then the great structure of which we are all so proud will one day breakdown.

Curzon's Contributions

To evolve the system, Curzon took following steps:

1. He set about reforming the Civil services and bureaucracy.
2. He removed all old established procedures of correspondence and substituted these with more effective methods of functioning in terms of simplification of office procedure. He brought about uniformity of approach and encouraged individual initiative for those who were dedicated and devoted to duty. This particularly applied in the case of civilians serving in the country.
3. He established new norms of administration and set up a large number of Commissions and implemented their recommendations. He also systematized administration and set up new departments where activities were dormant. He introduced scientific principles in the management of Government.

The distinguishing features of Curzon Administration were the innovations brought about by him, namely, establishing a Department of Industries and Commerce, tackling the problem of agricultural indebtedness by introducing the concept of cooperative credit, and adding muscle to agriculture by founding the Indian Council of Agricultural Research. He also carried out reforms in higher education and established the University Grants Commission. He even had remarkable foresight about the use of Hindi in the coming times. His greatest contribution perhaps lay in the preservation of art and culture by establishing the Archaeological Survey of India. Pandit Nehru once told the Earl of Swinton, who was Secretary of State for Commonwealth Relations during 1952-55, as follows: "After every other Viceroy has been forgotten, Curzon will be remembered because he restored all that was beautiful in India"

Post-Curzon Developments

After Curzon's departure, the British Government in India got involved with checking the rise of the National Movement. In tackling the rising demands of nationalism, several constitutional experiments were made by the British Government. Initially there were the Morely-Minto Reforms of 1909, which proved to be a non-starter. Then came the disastrous Montague-Chelmsford Reforms and establishment of diarchy. In all these endeavours, an attempt was made to involve Indians in the decision-making process and governing the country. Moreover, because of the World Wars I and II, and the inter-War years, conditions were, by and large, unsettled. This paved the way for independence and the enactment of the Indian Constitution.

Features Contributing to Efficiency since Independence

Creation of All India Services

It was Sardar Patel's idea to constitute the All India Services and make the Indian Administrative Service (IAS) as a successor to the Indian Civil Service. An efficient and responsive civil service would go a long way in implementing the dreams and hopes of independent India. Sardar Patel reposed a great deal of trust and confidence in the Indian administrative system and was responsible for integrating the country into one Union. Accession of the Indian Princely States to the Indian Union was, by and large, brought about by Sardar Patel, and it was Sardar Patel's leadership and efficient manner of execution which resulted in the final successful outcome. Sardar Patel was all in favour of preserving the Indian cultural traditions and, therefore, did not tamper much with the system inherited from the British. "The key to efficient administration," Patel said, "is the sense of security in the service at the top and non-interference by Congressmen or with the people connected either with the Congressmen or with the Ministers in the administration. The Ministers should not give orders to any subordinate officers and they must deal with them through their superiors."

Emphasis on Hard Work

Pandit Jawaharlal Nehru's concern for hard work and efficiency is epitomized in his slogan "Aaram Haram Hai". He had rightly proclaimed, "This generation is condemned to hard labour". In fact, Pandit Nehru did his utmost to establish democracy in India and nurtured the institution of Parliament very lovingly and devotedly. His fortnightly and monthly letters to the Chief Ministers can be considered as sine qua non of democratic functioning and efficient leadership in the newly born nation of India.

Indira Gandhi imparted a great fillip to Indian Administration by emphasizing the importance of the Twenty-Point Programme, which became an integral part of the Indian planning process.

Demarcation of Tasks and Powers under the Federal System

Another new feature of the Indian Constitution was the establishment of a federal system where the subject of executive powers and its administration was divided into three lists. Subjects included in the First List were exclusively under the purview of the Centre; in the Second List were State subjects; and the Third List incorporated concurrent subjects. The State subjects were exclusively under the purview of the State Government. In order to increase the efficiency of the government expenditure, planned development and economic development of the country's Five Year Plans were launched. Another significant feature was introduction of community development programmes and setting up of Panchayati Raj bodies with its three-tier system for bringing the administration closer to the people.

Findings of Research Studies and Recommendations of Reform Commission

Studies on Indian bureaucracy carried out by two eminent scholars – The Government and Politics of India by W.H. Morris Jones (1964), and Political Order in Changing Societies by Samuel P. Huntington (1968) – which cover the first two decades after independence, provide some insights into the working of the All India Services. They concluded that Indian bureaucracy, which during the British rule had remained almost unchecked by any political or other countervailing forces, adapted itself well to Parliamentary democracy. This, according to them, happened mainly because the members of the All-India Services displayed a quick understanding of the new political system and the art of handling it, combined with a zeal for development work. The stable, effective and democratic government in India during this period rested to a large extent on this institutional inheritance.

In the search for efficiency and economy in public administration, the administration has to become result-oriented and productive and observe norms of properly handling scarce resources. While dealing with the problem of efficiency, questions of morality and ethics also creep in. The common good and welfare of society at large is the objective of good governance and government spending. It is against this background that the administration has to subserve itself to the ideals laid down by the Constitution makers wherein equality of opportunity and achieving social justice has to be delivered efficiently.

Administration comprises civil servants who have to assist the elected government in policy formulation and implementation. There has to be close rapport and mutual trust between the Ministers and Civil Servants. Ministers have to defend in the legislature the bonafide decisions and actions of civil servants. The latter are expected to implement faithfully the policies of the government in power, whatever its political complexion and policies, and to remain faceless and nameless in the legislature.

Reports of Administrative Reforms Commission

In the report on Personnel Administration, the Administrative Reforms Commission (1967) (ARC) observed that the intention behind All-India Services was mainly to ensure uniformly high standards of administration in all States in key activities, to provide for interchange of experience between State Administration and the Centre at the decision-making levels. As common areas of administration in the States are expanding, it would be in the public interest to establish more All-India Services.

In regard to the IAS, the ARC recommended that a functional field should be carved out for it. This field could consist of land revenue administration, exercise of magisterial functions and regulatory work in the States in fields other than those looked after by other functional services. The ARC went on to recommend a functional classification of posts in the field, the field headquarters and the secretariat to be manned by members of the corresponding functional services.

The Union Government, however, did not accept the above mentioned recommendations on the ground that limiting the role of the IAS to a narrow area of district administration would defeat the very purpose for which the service was constituted as an All-India Service, viz., the forging of a link between the Centre and the States. The Union Government decided that the existing role and functions of the IAS should continue.

Report of Sarkaria Commission

The Sarkaria Commission, in its report on Centre-State Relations in 1988, had recommended that there should be more decentralization of power to State Governments and their officers and authorities. Although the Constitution has distributed executive power between Union and States, yet executive power defies a precise definition. Ordinarily, it connotes "the residue of Governmental functions that remain after legislative and judicial functions are taken away". The exercise of the executive function "comprises both the determination of the policy as well as carrying it into executive the maintenance of order, the promotion of social and economic welfare...., in fact, the carrying on or supervision of the general administration of the State" (Ram Jawaya Vs. State of Punjab, 1955, 2 SCR 255).

The Sarkaria Commission recommended that the All-India Services should be further strengthened and greater emphasis given on the role expected to be played by them. This can be achieved through well-planned improvements in selection, training, deployment, development, and promotion policies and methods. The present accent on generalism should yield place to greater specialization in one or more areas of public administration. Training and career development policies should be geared to this objective. Disciplinary control should aim at nurturing the best service traditions and relentless weeding out of those who fail to make the grade. Finally, there should be greater coordination and periodical dialogue between the authorities in the Union and the State Governments, who are responsible for management of these services. It recommended that State Governments, with the assistance of the Union Government, may evolve modern and more enlightened system of incentives for the officers of the All-India Service cadres. The political authorities in each State should strive to create an atmosphere of mutual trust and cooperation vis-à-vis the civil servant by ensuring fair and just treatment to them and encouraging promotion of positive qualities of honesty, fearlessness, independence of judgment, and dedication to duty. An efficient, disciplined and contented service, assured of its prospects as a result of diligent and honest work is a sine qua non of sound administration under a democratic regime.

Recent Significant Developments

Power to Local Bodies

The devolution of power to local bodies was given a stamp of approval by the 73rd Constitutional Amendment Act 1992 on Panchayats. The three-tier system was incorporated in Article 243 B as follows: "There shall be constituted in every State, panchayats at the village, intermediate and district levels in accordance with the provisions of this article."

The objective of devolution of power to Panchayats was, namely, preparation of plans for economic development and securing social justice as may be entrusted to them, including those in relation to the matters listed in the Eleventh Schedule. It may be seen that the long cherished dream of the founding fathers and the Father of the Nation to have Panchayati Raj all over the country was, thus, given a practical shape by amending the Constitution. Simultaneously, the recommendations of the Sarkaria Commission on devolution of more powers were implemented. By making Panchayati Raj an integral part of the country's political system would ensure a sound and efficient administration with people at grassroot level as the real watch-dogs.

Compulsions of Liberalization

More recently, with a wave of economic liberalization sweeping away the old system of permit and license raj, administration is now required to attain new heights of efficiency and quick disposal of business. This has resulted in restructuring and streamlining of the administration paving the way for the new ethos in administration. In this regard, we have a lot to learn from the practices more recently adopted in the UK. When Margaret Thatcher became the Prime Minister, a new strategy of management was evolved, termed as the Efficiency Strategy, which aimed mainly at showing increasing cost consciousness and selecting management tools and techniques to economize on resources and promoting greater efficiency in their use. Another way of describing it would be to cut down the size of Government and "rolling back the frontiers of the State". Initially, an Efficiency Unit was set up within the Prime Minister's office. A series of scrutinizes were conducted within individual departments which aimed at identifying and eliminating areas of waste, inefficiency, duplication and overlap. The second part of the strategy was designed to consolidate and integrate the evidence emerging from scrutinies and building a case for reform that would be credible and lead to better managed and more efficient civil service in the future. The long-term goal was lasting reforms of structures, systems, personnel policies and deeply ingrained attitudes and beliefs.

Concept of Efficiency Audit

The Report from the Efficiency Unit, entitled "Improving Management in Government: the Next Step", had recommended following three main priorities to be pursued with vigour in service delivery, in the departments and in the Central departments of Whitehall, the Treasury and the Cabinet Office:

1. The work of each department must be organized in a way which focuses on the job to be done; the systems and

structures must enhance the effective delivery of policies and services.

2. The management of each department must ensure that their staff have the relevant experience and skills needed to do the tasks that are essential for effective government.
3. There must be a real and sustained pressure on and within each department for continuous improvement in the value for money obtained in the delivery of policies and services.

This report was accepted by the UK Government

Recommendations of Fifth Pay Commission

In February 1997, the Fifth Pay Commission submitted its report, which perhaps drew lot of inspiration from the work methods, adopted in UK. It aimed at reducing the role of Central Government to the core functions; shift some items on Concurrent List, like Education to the state; bringing down the number of schemes listed as Centrally sponsored schemes to 10, and State Government to have a large share of revenue receipts. It recommended abolition of certain ministries; amalgamation of certain departments in ministries and reduction in the size of ministries. The most radical changes recommended were with regard to restructuring of Government in order to tone up the efficiency of Government and to obtain quicker and better results in administration. These recommendations are as follows:

1. The number of Secretaries to the Government should be drastically reduced. For example, since Health is a State subject, more administrative powers should rest with States. And, therefore, the three Secretaries in the Ministry of Health should be replaced by one; the same should apply to the Ministry of Industry.
2. The Department of Programme Implementation be abolished and the Prime Minister's Office should have a less visible role.
3. Twenty four ministries and departments should be merged in the existing eleven Ministries.
4. The Government should abolish all 3.5 lakh vacant posts in one stroke. This will straightway reduce flab. Put a freeze on recruitment of auxiliary and supporting staff.
5. Work out a 10-year manpower reduction exercise. Plan for a 30 per cent cut across the board within a time-frame of 10 years. Launch campaigns for retirements of a compulsory nature is departments where redundancies are noticed.

Suggestions for Transfer of Centrally-Sponsored Schemes and Holding Mid-Career Exams for Civil Servants

It is also learnt that the Government is planning to transfer most of the Centrally-sponsored schemes to the States, along with the funds for speedier and efficient implementation. The Planning Commission, after a detailed exercise, had identified 179 Centrally sponsored schemes administered by various Ministries and Departments. Of these, 115 schemes are proposed to be transferred to the States. The move stems from the Government's concern over the tardy progress of various Central projects, which has retarded the desired pace of development in the country. After identifying these 179 schemes, whose total outlay was estimated at about Rs. 16,000 crore in 1996-97, the Planning Commission said that 64 schemes, with an outlay of about Rs. 4,000 crore, should continue to be operated as Centrally sponsored. Out of the remaining 115 schemes, 89 schemes with an outlay of Rs. 9,000 crore, are proposed to be transferred after earmarking of funds for the schemes, while nine schemes with an outlay of Rs. 1,129 crore were identified to be transferred in a phased manner.

Very recently, a Parliamentary Committee has recommended that in order to increase the efficiency and output of the services, a middle level or mid-career examination system should be introduced within the civil services, in order to give a fillip to efficiency and to improve performance and ability. This system of examination will weed out those who are incompetent and unable to cope with the realities of the new administration.

Introduction of Information Technology

With the introduction of information technology in administration, a new vista has been opened on the Indian administration scenario. It has given a tremendous boost to efficiency and quickened the pace of decision-making process. Information technology has come to stay in India, which now forms an integral part of Indian Administration from the grassroots to the uppermost echelons of Government. In the decades to come, it will become a vital part of our administrative machinery.

Need to Take Closer Look at Policies of Transfers and Postings

One factor which has eroded performance and efficiency is transfer policies adopted by various Government. It has been noticed that transfers are resorted to generally on the eve of elections to post pliant officers in sensitive areas. Frequent changes in Government also result in numerous transfers. The most glaring example of such transfers is evidenced in some State Governments in the recent past. Usually, whenever there is a change in Government, amongst the first to fall victim of the transfers is the Chief Secretary, the Director General of Police and other top-ranking officers. It has been seen that if a civil servant does not obey or tow the line prescribed by those in power or the most influential persons in a Government then transfer follows. Such transfers do not inspire confidence nor does it lead to building confidence among the officials and the public. By carrying out a spate of transfers, it is ultimately the people who suffer because these cause delay in implementation of welfare schemes. In many cases, officers, even before they get a grip on the issues requiring solutions, are transferred on political and extraneous considerations resulting in wastage of skills and insights acquired by such incumbents during their tenure. Hence, it has been suggested in the letter written by Margret Alva as Union Minister of State for Personnel, to the Orissa Chief Minister that "frequent transfers and postings of IAS Officers, especially on grounds other than administrative imperatives have a demoralizing effect on the officers and ultimately on the quality of administration". But how many Chief Ministers adhere to these instructions?

It has been suggested at various fora time and again that posting to an assignment should be for a fixed tenure. The Centre has a mechanism for posting and transferring officers, which is managed by a Committee of Secretaries chaired by the Cabinet Secretary. But no such system exists in the States.

In 1902, Lord Curzon had addressed the Secretary of State about the establishment of a Police Commission, which he regarded as his most important reform.

He stated as follows:

...I myself rate the efficiency of our Police System more highly than any other subject of intenal reform in as much as its ramifications effect all classes of the community and leave no single individual untouched. We cannot, of course, hope to reform the native character or by a stroke of his pen or by a grant of a few lakhs or even crores to make the police forces honest instead of corrupt, but we can at least find out where it is that we are going wrong and communicate an impulse to have that improved in time....*

Summing Up

It is necessary to emphasize that administration must be viewed in a holistic manner by which it is suggested that both regulatory and developmental functions have to be fused and looked upon as dependent on each other. It is not merely enough to have 'growth with justice' but also 'growth with stability', and this is where the strength and efficiency of the administration has to reveal its real character. No doubt, India has made significant strides and has achieved a growth rate of six to seven per cent, but since the quantification of the growth rate is based merely on measuring indicators like GNP and GDP, the exercise is incomplete. We have to take Indian polity as a whole into consideration. The indicators of human development have to be integrated to those of economic development so that the holistic pattern is obtained and presented. From the times of Curzon to the present day, a great metamorphosis has taken place in the polity of India. A colonial State has been replaced by a self-governing secular, socialist, sovereign, democratic republic. It will be no exaggeration to say that the administrative apparatus has stood the test of times and faced all the ravages and fury over the years. It has accomplished the tasks set before it. India is now on the threshold of emerging as a major industrial power in the world and thanks to the silent efficiency of the administration, it has become possible.

However, the current mood is reflected by stating that the Government needs to trim the fat of its bloated bureaucracy, slim down administrative overheads in the shape of reduced inputs and provide a strict regime. Efficiency has acquired a new meaning, that is having a leaner and fitter bureaucracy. Saving will stimulate and improve efficiency and effectiveness. It can be said that reducing inputs of money and manpower reduces cost directly and stimulates productivity, and forces officials to cut out waste and irrelevant expenditure, resulting in greater harmony, more disciplined performance, and increase in efficiency.

Select Readings

Earl of Ronaldshy, The Life of Lord Curzon, Volume II, London, Earnes Benn, 1928.

S. Gopal, British Policy in India, 1858-1905, New Delhi, Orient Longman in association with Cambridge University, 2nd Edition, 1984.

Lovat Fraser, India Under Curzon and After, London, William Heinemann, 1911.

David Dilks, Curzon in India, Vols. I & II, London, Rupert Hard Davis, 1970.

Kenneth Rose, Curzon – A Most Superior Person, London, Macmillan, 1983.

Rani Dhavan Shankardass, Vallabhbhai Patel: Power and Organization in Indian Politics, New Delhi, Orient Longman.

Les Metcalfe and Sue Richards, Improving Public Management, London, European Institute of Public Administration and Sage Publications, 1990, (second edition).

India, Report of the Commission on Centre-State Relations, Nasik, Government of India Press, 1988.

Mohit Bhattacharya, Public Administration – Structure, Process and Behaviour, Calcutta, The World Press 1987.

Bhabani Sen Gupta, India – Problems of Governance, New Delhi, Konark Publishers, 1996.

Ajit M. Banerjee and K.A. Chandrasekaran, Renewing Governance – Issues and Options, New Delhi, Tata Mc Graw-Hill, 1996.

Note

* Curzon Papers Microfilm, Lord Curzon's letter to the Right Hon'ble Lord G. Hamilton, Secretary of State, dated March 13, 1902. p. 74. No. 86, National Archieves of India.

6

Understanding Organisations Through Perceptions of Organisational Goals

Raj Nandy

Perhaps 'Organisational Goals' is one of those terms which cannot be easily fenced in by a narrow meaning. A number of social scientists and organizational theorists, since the turn of the present century, have either just referred to this concept in their writings or made rigorous attempts to define and/or clarify it. For example, Michels[1] in his study (1911) mentioned it when he tried to show how organizational processes turned political parties/unions into centralized bureaucracies and, subsequently, modified their radical goals into modest reform programmes. Max Weber[2] (1922) did not directly address himself to the concept but merely referred to it when he conceived of a bureaucratic organization as a rational instrument for accomplishing certain goals. How actual practices (informal organizations) did not follow the formal goals of an organisation was brought out by the now-famous Hawthorne Experiments (1939).[3] Merton's[4] central thesis (1940) was 'displacement of goals', i.e., how formal procedures – the 'means' – were pursued as 'ends' in themselves. Selznick[5] (1949) showed how a government agency, in its bid to adjust to a hostile local environment, accepted fundamental changes in its official goals by co-opting some opposition elements.

A least known fact that needs emphasis here is that while the subject of 'formal organisations' claimed a great deal of theoretical attention and research work during these few decades, yet a basic issue, namely, "what is the definition of organizational goal" appears to have gone by unnoticed. Gross notes this omission in the following words: "It seems to be taken for granted in most studies,

From *The Indian Journal of Public Administration*, Vol. XXVI, 1980.

and yet what the goal or goals of particular organizations are is an empirical matter and needs to be discovered."[6]

Thus, it is only for the past 15-20 years that a whole body of literature has emerged which is aimed at both clarifying as well as defining the very concept of organizational goal. Thompson and McEwen[7] and Parsons[8] seem to have set the ball rolling when they tried to define the term as a kind of output the organisation produces and offers to its environment. However, it is Etzioni who is known to have made the first major attempt in this direction when he criticized the use of traditional 'goal model' as an evaluative criterion for measuring organizational effectiveness, i.e., the tendency to assess effectiveness of an organisation (a real state) against its primary goal/mission (an ideal state). His argument, which he later carried forward to his book Modern Organisations, was: "One who expects a light bulb to turn most of its electrical power into light would not be very interested in the differences between a bulb that utilizes 4.5 per cent of the power as compared with one that utilizes 5.5 per cent. Both are extremely ineffective. A more realistic observer would compare the two bulbs with each other and find one of them relatively good. The same holds for organizational studies that compare actual states of organizations to each other, as when the organizational output is measured at different points in time."[9] Hence, rather than comparing existing organizations to their ideals, we may assess their performance, relative to one another, he pleaded.

Thus, rejecting the 'goal model' as an unrealistic tool, he suggested, as an alternative, the adoption of what he called the 'system model'. The use of this model, he said, would enable us to "see a basic distortion in the analysis of organizations that is not visible or explicable from the perspective of goal model evaluation".[10] In other words, if one goes by the goal model, effectiveness of an organisation shall be expected to increase with the assignment of more means to the organisation's goals. As a contrast to this, the 'system model', he argued, would suggest that "just as there may be too little allocation of resources to meet the goals of the organisation, so there may also be an over-allocation of the resources".[11] His 'system model' also recognized that the organisation solves certain problems other than those directly involved in the achievement of goal, and that excessive concern with the latter may result in insufficient attention to other necessary organizational activities. In support, he cited the example of a bank which "may pay all its attention to making money and completely ignore the morale of its employees. This lack of attention to non-goal activities may result in staff dissatisfaction which may express itself in poor work by the clerks which, in turn, results in decreased efficiency or even in a wave of embezzlements which ultimately reduces the bank's effectiveness"[12].

Etzioni's system model is made up of two parts: (1) the survival model an 'optimum' or 'balanced' allocation of resources, and (2) the 'effectiveness' model – a pattern of interrelations among the elements of the system which would make it most effective in the service of a given goal.[13] Here, Mohr, finds a weakness in Etzioni's two-part model. According to him, while the 'survival model' offers no criteria for determining an optimal balance of resources, in his second part (the 'effectiveness' model) Etzioni returns explicitly to goal attainment as the criterion of effectiveness, though with a difference, i.e., the central concept is no longer simple assumed to be the primary goal/mission, and he defined an organisation goal as a desired state of affairs which the organisation attempts to realize and as that future state of affairs which the organisation as a collectivity is trying to bring about.[14] But, questions Gross: "...of whose state of affairs it is that is desired?" For, "Theoretically, there could be as many desired states for the organization as there are persons in it, if not more. What appear to be goals from the point of view of the top administrators may not be goals at all from the point of view of those further down",[15] he adds.

Simon brought in a new perspective when he challenged the very utility of the concept of organizational goal by contending that in actual organizations the goal of an action is seldom unitary and generally consists of a whole set of constraints the action must satisfy.[16] Indeed, in the words of Mohr for Simon, no goal is the goal – that in order to understand why people do the things they do in organizations, one must take into consideration a whole host of goals.[17]

The literature that has emerged in recent times also attempts to grapple with the issue of classification of organizational goals. Perrow, for instance, distinguished six categories of goals. Of these, he said, three have 'external' referents, i.e., society, the public in contact with the organization, and the investors – and labeled them as societal goals – output goals and investor goals, respectively. The other three have 'internal' referents, i.e., to the organization and its members and named them as system goals, product goals, and derived goals.[18] Although his new classification scheme which he advanced later recognized five types of goals, i.e., societal goals, output goals, system goals, product goals and derived goals, yet "the scheme", he thought, "was not as neat as one might like".[19] Gross's way of inducting some order in the area of classification was different: he suggested only two categories – (1) 'Output goals" which the organization produces or distributes to persons or systems outside of itself, and (2) 'Non-output or support goals" which refer to conditions or activities necessary for the maintenance of the organization itself.[20] Mohr, however, deals with this problem by viewing organizations as having two types of goals, namely, 'Transitive goals' and 'Reflexive goals' – though he adds the proviso that his classification "in no way precludes or questions the utility of various sub-classification schemes, such as those used by Perrow or Gross".[21]

And so the controversy limps along, with quite a few other writers joining into give the subject their own theoretical treatments. But a significant aspect of this controversy is that it is not just restricted to 'what should be labeled a goal, or how to categorize the goals'; indeed, it deepens further when closely-related issues, such as, 'where it comes from', how it changes' and 'what impact it has'[22] also jump into the fray.

Purpose

The purpose of this study was to understand an organization through the goals it pursues because, as Perrow suggests, the goals "provide the best single clue to the distinctive character of an organisation".[23] Perhaps a better understanding of the goals an organization pursues – whether states or not – can be obtained if one also tries to understand the 'perceptions' of these goals, as seen by the members of that organization. An underlying assumption here is that understanding of the employees' perceptions of their organization's goals provide a very valuable entry point for a researcher to monitor some aspects of the general functioning or the health of the organization. After all, as it has been said, the "place of perception in the attitude-formation and behaviour is significant" and if, "behaviours occur as a result of perceptions,"[24] then it follows that precision in perception of organizational goals can lead to precision in the goal-directed behaviour of the employees. Conversely, the absence of such a condition can be detrimental, if not disastrous, for organizational effectiveness.

Putting in operational terms, the intent of this research effort was : (a) to lay bare the perceptions of a group of senior and middle-level officers with respect to the goals of their organization, and, then, (b) to examine how far their perceptions were in harmony with or at variance with each other's.

Methodology

The organization selected for this research exercise was the traffic police department in a metropolitan city. No written goals were given to it when it came into existence several years ago, nor did they exist at the time of this research exercise. As many as 18 (including the present incumbent) chiefs have presided over this department since it was established.

Those chosen to provide information on 'perceptions' of the organization's goals were a group of officers of that department, such as assistant commissioners, inspectors and sub-inspectors. These officers, as is evident from their official titles, bear the principal responsibility for carrying out the departmental policies and decisions. Besides, these are the men supposed to not only control the behaviour of their subordinates, such as, head constables and constables, but also lead and motivate them and, finally, direct them towards goal-accomplishment.

The exercise consisted of a 6-item questionnaire, administered to five assistant commissioners, eight inspectors, and nine sub-inspectors, representing 100, 50 and 15 per cent of the total strengths of these three management levels in the city's traffic police hierarchy.

Questions included inquiries about their perceptions of the organization's goals, resources provided to attain the goals, the degree of commitment of their superiors and subordinates to the goals or organization, etc. The officers were asked to mention only their 'ranks' and not their 'names.'

The data in the study was fairly controlled in the sense that the officers had assembled for a lecture-discussion on 'Organizational Goals – A System's View' and were handed the questionnaire and asked to fill it out on the spot, thereby eliminating the possibility of influences resulting from mutual consultations or social relationships. All forms (22 in number) were returned then and there.

Analysis

Perceptions

Question 1: Like individuals, all organizations, pursue some goals or the other, and then try to conduct their operations in a manner so as to achieve those goals....Traffic police, as an organization, also has its own goals. Could you please list below these goals?

Analysis of the answers to question 1 disclosed a wide range of perceptions on the part of these officers. These are coded below:

1. to save people and vehicles from accidents;
2. to regulate traffic smoothly;
3. to enforce traffic laws;
4. to minimize deaths on road;
5. to educate public in road safety;
6. to reduce accidents to the minimum;
7. to educate younger generation;
8. to check atmospheric and noise pollution;
9. to keep TSR/taxi drivers under discipline;
10. to plan for future;
11. to be smartly dressed;
12. to be very courteous but firm in action;
13. to improve behaviour of traffic police toward public;
14. to build our country by giving better services;
15. to make our subordinates more effective;
16. to make good use of our time and resources;
17. to train staff in road-safety;
18. to remove obstructions on roads; and
19. to study the causes of accidents.

As can be seen, the above mentioned 19 items were perceived as 'goals' of the traffic police department by the respondents, thereby clearly demonstrating that there is considerable variation amongst them on how they perceived the goals of their organization.

However, if the number of respondents mentioning a particular 'perception' can be interpreted as indicative of the importance attached to that by most of them, then 'to educate public in road-safety', 'to regulate traffic smoothly', and 'to enforce traffic laws' clearly emerge as supreme goals of the traffic police department, for these were named by as many as 17 in the case of first two (i.e. 77 percent) and 14 in the case of the third (i.e. 64, per cent).

'To reduce accidents to the minimum' and 'to save people and vehicles from accidents' seem to dominate the thinking of 10 (45 per cent) and 7 (32 per cent) respectively of the officers surveyed. Three of them (14 per cent) named ' to improve police behaviour toward public'.

The perceptions mentioned by two (9 per cent) in each case are: 'to plan for future', 'to remove obstructions on roads', 'to study causes of accidents'. The remaining ones found only one supporter (i.e., 5 per cent).

The data when stratified by participants' status produced almost the same outlook, i.e. 'to regulate traffic smoothly', 'to educate public in road safety' and 'to enforce traffic laws' were found to be the most commonly-cited perceptions by the three management levels.

A point that arises here is: Are all the perceptions that, in the view of the respondents, seem to pass for 'goals' of their organizations, actually the 'goals'? Indeed, a closer inspection of these perceptions reveal that of the 19 items perceived by them as 'goals', most cannot be considered as goal.[25] They are, as a matter of fact, either individual activities/tasks or broad strategies/ programmes undertaken by the employees of the organization, as a whole, towards goal attainment. A few examples are: 'to keep the TSR/-Taxi drivers under discipline', 'to be smartly dressed', 'to be very courteous but firm in action', 'to educate the public in road-safety', 'to plan for future', etc.

Priorities

Question 2: Now, list the goals (as you have described them above) in order of your priority.

The results of this question are best summed up in Table 1.

Table 1

	Perceptions of Goals Priorities	*1st*	*2nd*	*3rd*	*4th*	*5th*	*6th*
1.	Save people and vehicles from accidents	4	1	1	1	-	-
2.	Regulate traffic smoothly	7	6	3	1	-	-
3.	Enforce traffic laws	1	-	3	5	-	1
4.	Minimize deaths on road	1	-	-	-	-	-
5.	Educate public in road-safety	4	2	2	5	3	1
6.	Reduce the number of accidents	1	7	2	-	-	-

Contd...

7.	Educate younger generation in road-safety	1	-	-	-	-	-
8.	Check atmospheric and noise pollution	-	-	-	-	1	-
9.	Keep TSR/taxi drivers under discipline	-	-	1	-	-	-
10.	Plan for future	-	-	-	-	2	-
11.	Be smartly dressed	1	-	-	-	-	-
12.	Be very courteous but firm in action	-	1	-	-	-	-
13.	Improve behaviour of police towards public	-	2	1	-	-	-
14.	Build our country by giving better service	1	-	-	-	-	-
15.	Make our subordinates more effective	-	1	-	-	-	-
16.	Make good use of our time and resources	-	-	1	-	-	-
17.	Train staff in road-safety	-	-	1	-	-	-
18.	Remove obstructions on roads	-	1	1	-	-	-
19.	Study the causes of accidents	-	1	1	-	-	-

It is interesting to note that when it came to according their own priorities to the 'goals' described by them, the participants showed differences in their preferences.

For example, while 'to educate public in road safety' and 'to regulate traffic smoothly' shared the top position as the most popular perceptions/goals of the organization, but the former slipped to second position (18 per cent) in terms of Ist priority, the latter claiming the top rating (32 per cent).

Another interesting highlight here is that 'to save people and vehicles from accidents' which occupied the fourth position earlier moved up to share the second (18 per cent) with 'to educate public in road-safety', and 'to enforce traffic laws' earlier mentioned by 60 per cent, was given first priority only by 5 per cent.

The 'perceptions/goals' that merited second priority are in this order: 'to reduce the number of accidents', 'to regulate traffic smoothly'.

Precedence in third priority was received by: 'to regulate traffic smoothly' and 'to enforce traffic laws'.

Satisfaction with Given Resources

Question 3: How satisfied are you with the resources placed at your disposal to achieve your organization's goals?

This is how the respondents showed their satisfactions/ dissatisfactions so far as the adequacy of organizational resources is concerned (Table 2).

Table 2

Very satis-fied	*Fairly-well satisfied*	*Neither satisfied nor dissatisfied*	*Fairly dissatis-fied*	*Very dissat-isfied*
1	8	5	6	2

As is apparent, at least 36 per cent are either 'fairly dissatisfied' or 'very dissatisfied'. But they are out-numbered by those who seem to be happy with the sufficiency of the organizational resources to attain goals (41 per cent). Five of them said they were 'neither satisfied nor dissatisfied'.

But, how did the actual 'men in the field' – inspectors and sub-inspectors (17 in all) – feel about the resources? Taking them as one category, it was found that 35 per cent of them were 'neither satisfied nor dissatisfied'. Those who were 'fairly dissatisfied' or 'very dissatisfied' (30 per cent) were once again found to be out-numbered by those who were either 'very satisfied' or 'fairly well satisfied' (35 per cent).

Factors, other than Resources, Hindering Achievement of Organisational Goals

A related question to the one concerning internal resources was:

Question 4: Apart from resources, what other factors, do you think, generally stand in the way of your achieving organizational goals?

The factors indicated by the respondents were:

Indisciplined and ill-behaved public; non-cooperation from bodies, such as, the municipal corporation, the electricity undertaking, and the public works department; political/official influences/pressures; lack of coordination within the organization; bad roads; unhelpful attitude of judiciary; weaknesses in laws; inordinate delays in disposal of traffic offences by courts; non-availability of modern equipment to staff; soft punishments for serious traffic offences and accidents; absence of promotional opportunities for staff; corruption resulting from frustration and work-attitudes, such as, 'make hay while the sun shines'; too much obsession with statistics at the expense of genuine work; lack of proper perspective; poor training and imperfect briefing at different levels; incomprehension of actual problems at lower levels; practice of issuing driving licenses without vigorous testing; frequent postings of senior officers; lack of clarity about their respective roles both at junior and senor levels; inter-personal problems amongst the staff; and, suppression of ideas in the rank-wise system.

Amongst these goal-thwarting factors, 'indisciplined and ill-behaved public', and 'non-cooperation from bodies, such as, the municipal corporation, the electricity undertaking, and the public works department' were decidedly the severest obstructions, as experienced by the officers (57 per cent and 35 per cent respectively).

Political/official influences/pressures was mentioned by 18 per cent and three other factors, namely, 'lack of coordination within organization', 'weaknesses in laws' and 'non-availability of modern equipment to staff' found support from 14 per cent in each case. Two each (9 per cent) named: 'unhelpful attitude of judiciary', and 'poor training and imperfect briefing at different levels'.

All the other factors were reported by a distant percentage: 4 per cent in each case.

Commitment to Organizational Goals

Question 5: How would you rate the commitment of your subordinates in the attainment of organizational goals?

Question 6: How would you rate the commitment of your superiors in the attainment of organizational goals?

Two kinds of data were generated by the two questions, i.e., how did the participants feel the pulse of their subordinates as well as those of their superiors to gauge the degree of their commitment to organizational goals?

The group, as a whole, visualized the commitment of their subordinates as follows (Table 3):

Table 3

Excellent	*Good*	*Average*	*Fair*	*Poor*
1	8	9	3	1

And of their superiors as follows (Table 4):

Table 4

Excellent	*Good*	*Average*	*Fair*	*Poor*
7	13	-	2	-

When the same data were looked at separately from the different angles of the three management levels, represented in the group, the following picture emerged:

Assistant Commissioners: Four of them gave a rather gloomy view of the commitment of their subordinates, i.e, either 'average' (3) or 'poor' (1). Only one of them thought it was 'good'.

Their evaluation of the superiors' commitment was either 'excellent' (4) or 'good' (1).

Inspectors: They spoke highly of their subordinates' commitment and rated them as 'excellent' (1), 'good' (5). Only two said: 'average'.

As for the superiors' commitment, no one gave a bad chit. Three said 'excellent' and five 'good'.

Sub-Inspectors: Most of them (7) saw the commitment of their subordinates as 'average' or 'fair' (1) Two found it 'good'.

On the superiors' commitment, they tended to regard it either as 'good' (7) or 'fair' (2).

Two conclusions stand out: one, when it came to rating the commitment of the superiors, each lower level gave a favourable judgemnt on the higher levels, and, two, of the three levels, only the inspectors (6 out of 8) gave a good chit to their subordinates. The other two ranks, namely, the assistant commissioners (4 out of 5) and sub-inspectors (7 out of 9) gave either 'average' or 'fair' rating to their subordinates commitment to organizational goals.

Implications and Recommendations

In view of the findings above, a few implications and recommendations seem to be in order.

One is that a fairly large percentage of officers are not clear about the goals of their organization and seem to be mistaking their day-to-day functions or activities as 'goals' of the organization. It is apparent that when organizational members (especially those at the supervisory levels) perceive the organizational goals wrongly, confusion follows because there is always the likelihood of a whole chain of erroneous activities and behaviours on the part of members, such as, faulty or disproportionate allocation of organizational resources by the superiors. Take, for instance, 'to improve beahaviour of traffic police toward public,' perceived as a 'high priority goal' by a section of officers in all the three levels. It is evident that such a perception might induce an assistant commissioner of police, an inspector or a sub-inspector to commit a larger chunk of organizational resources at his disposal (including 'time' as a resource) to an improvement in human relations between the public and the members of his group, as compared to other organizational goals, say, 'safety of human lives on roads', or 'law-enforcement' which, incidentally, in their perceptions, stand as 'low priority goals'. The resultant behaviours of these men would mean greater emphasis on cultivating a pleasant, friendly manner towards road users and less emphasis on prevention of accidents and law enforcement, meaning that more people could get injured or killed on roads which, in turn, is sure to worsen the already bad image of the traffic police in the eyes of the public.

For, when the local press carries reports about increasing injuries and deaths on roads, these are certain to stimulate greater public discussion of police apathy and inefficiency in homes, streets or in angry letters to the editor. Thus, if any effort to improve police-public relationship is to fructify, it must be recognized that the 'route' to the achievement of the (lower) goals lies through the achievement of other (higher) goals, such as, 'safety of human lives on roads', etc. In other words, first things must come first and that calls for an orderly arrangement of the multiple organizational goals of the traffic police department and, then, understanding of that 'order' by every member of the organization.

Consider yet another 'perception', namely, 'to be smartly dressed', mentioned by a sub-inspector and, on top of it, rallied by him as a 'high priority goal' for the traffic police. It would not be surprising if a host of communication problems, conscious or not, arise between him and his immediate superiors at the circle/ division levels who tend to regard 'to educate public in road-safety' as a 'high priority goal', opposed to that of being 'smartly dressed'. Thus, two members of the same organizational team, caged by and confined to different perception, are likely to trigger messages about expected or desired behaviours/activities at each other, yet oblivious of the reasons as to why they are not being 'received' or are being misunderstood at the other end. In extreme cases, such a situation could even result in friction amongst team members, and possibly lead even to an adverse effect on the morale and performance of the individual members as well as that of the group.

Since the purpose of this research was purely descriptive and was not aimed at determining the causes behind the discrepancies in the perceptions (research would be needed to understand this process), suffice to say that a question that should be the focus of the higher-ups who manage and direct the traffic police department is: Whether those at the implementation level of the system perceive the goals of their organization as they are intended to. If they are not, then urgent attention needs to be paid to the indoctrination of traffic police personnel at all levels regarding the goals of their organization and their importance with respect to the community as a whole.

Second, there is clear evidence of the helplessness expressed by the officers in meeting the goals of the organization because of 'indisciplined and ill-behaved public' and 'non-cooperation from bodies, such as Municipal Corporation, electricity undertaking, and the public works department'. If these men have to be more effective, a determined and organized attack on these two fronts has to be mounted; that is, the process of safety education has to be accelerated by strengthening the road-safety education wing of the department, and some of the energies of the department concentrated on removing (or, at least reducing) some of the restraining external factors posed by the civil bodies, etc.

Third, the analysis suggests another dark area, namely, lack of commitment on the part of the personnel to the organizational goals. It is too well known to be repeated that commitment to goals cannot be forced or bought out. It can only arise out of the interaction of the employee with the quality of environment surrounding his work situation. Hence, the right conditions for winning over the commitment of the men have to be created and responsibility for this squarely rests with the management.

To sum up, once goals are clarified, arranged in order, and then understood and internalized, it should be possible to bring about considerable change in the organizational behaviour of the officers to facilitate the attainment of organizational goals whether it is the traffic department of the police or any other.

References

1. Robert Michels (1911), 1915, Political Parties: A Sociological Study of the Oligarchical Tendencies of Modern Democracy, translated by Eden and Cedar Paul, The Free Press, Glencoe, III.
2. Max Weber (1922), 1964, "Bureaucracy" in Max Weber, From Max Weber: Essays in Sociology, pp. 196-244 translated and edited by H.H. Gerth and C. Wright Mills, Routledge & Kegan Paul Ltd., London.
3. Fritz J. Roethlisberger and William J. Dickson, Management and the Worker: An Account of a Research Programme, conducted by the Western Electric Company, Hawthorne Works, 1939, Chicago, Cambridge, Mass., Harward University Press.
4. Robert K Merton (1949), "Bureaucratic Structure and Personality" in Robert K. Merton, Social Theory and Social Structure, Glencoe, III., The Free Press, pp. 195-206.
5. Phillip Selznick, TVA and the Grass Roots: A Study in the Sociology of Formal Organizations, 1949, Berkley, University of California Press.
6. Edward Gross, "The Definition of Organizational Goals", British Journal of Sociology, Vol. XX, September 1969, p. 278.
7. James D. Thompson and W.J: McEwen, "Organization Goals and Environment", American Sociological Review, Vol. 23, 1958, pp. 23-58.
8. Talcot Parsons, "A Sociological Approach to the Theory of Formal Organizations", in Talcot Parsons, Structure and Process in Modern Societies, New York, The Free Press, Glencoe, III.
9. Amitai Etzioni, "Two Approaches to Organizational Analysis: A Critique and a Suggestion," Administrative Science Quarterly, September 1960, pp. 259-269.
10. Amitai Etzioni, Modern Organizations, 1965, New Delhi, Prentice-Hall of India (Private) Ltd., p. 17.
11. Amitai Etzioni, Modern Organizations, *op. cit.*
12. *Ibid.*, p. 17.
13. *Ibid.*, p. 19.
14. *Ibid.*, p. 6.
15. Edward Gross, The Definition of Organizational Goals, p. 278.
16. Herbert A. Simon, "On the Concept of Organizational Goal", Administrative Science Quarterly, June 1964, pp. 1-22.
17. Lawrence B. Mohr, "The Concept of Organizational Goal", The American Political Science Review, Vol. LXVII, June 1973, p. 472.

18. Charles Perrow, in "International Encyclopedia of the Social Sciences", ed. Sills L. David, The Macmillan Co. & The Free Press, New York, 1969, Vol. 11, pp. 306-309.

19. Charles Perrow, Organizational Analysis: A Sociological Review, Belmont, Calif., Wadsworth, 1970, pp. 135-136.

20. Edward Gross, *op. cit.*, pp. 285-294.

21. Lawrence, B. Mohr, The Concept of Organizational Goal, p. 476.

22. Charles Perrow, International Encyclopedia of the Social Sciences, ed. Sills, L. David, p. 309.

23. Charles Perrow, Organizational Analysis: A Sociological Review, p. 180.

24. Theodore, T. Herbert, Dimensions of Organizational Behavior, Macmillan, New York, 1976, p. 201.

25. A goal or an objective is a 'condition'; an 'activity' represents some effort of programme-personnel to bring that condition about. See Lawrence, B. Mohr, The Concept of Organizational Goal, p. 474, and also see Edward, Gross, The Definition of Organization Goal, p. 284.

7

Improving State Administration–Search for Directions

A.P. Saxena

A variety of reasons in the recent past have converged to focus attention on improving State administration. The scenario of State administration today reflects sharp changes in scope as well as content and function. It is commonly agreed that the extent of Government purposes has radically altered in the decades following Independence. Along with enlargement in scope, there has been a resultant complexity as well in all directions of State level administration. It will, therefore, be useful to note that the profile of State administration in the country has a radically different stance today. In the context of the emerging objectives in the new national ethos, it is thus appropriate that the subject of the improvement of State administration should be considered as one of contemporary relevance and poriority.[1]

A quick survey of the functional coverage in the areas of state administration is worth a close look. There has been extensive proliferation of activities and it is not uncommon for a State administration to evolve a policy and administer it as well, be it the production and supply of text books or the development of electronic complexes.[2] Frequently, State administrations had to take over under their control extensive industrial organizations in the form of sick mills. It is important to realize that the taking over of giant industrially sick units and their administration involve an entirely different set of activities as compared to the industrial administration of viable enterprises with assured profitability and future prospects. Yet, as a logical part of the pursuit of public policies, State administrations in the country

From *The Indian Journal of Public Administration*, Vol. XXII, 1976.

have been called upon to shoulder these onerous responsibilities within the framework of public accountability. The extent of the strain involved in this element of administration needs to be fully recognized, since a realistic assessment can alone establish reliable and responsive guidelines for improvement.

There can be scores of directions for improving State administration and any discussion group on the subject can generate a long agenda for action and priorities, subject to particular profiles. In such exercises a speculative analysis may supersede mere factual interpretations of current challenges. Against the pressing urge of the present-day action programmes, State administrations can no longer simply regulate and react but must take on themselves the responsibility for directing vastly new social and economic changes. "Government's functions have increased as people's assertiveness and requirements have increased."[3] The concept of public interest, general welfare and net benefit to the society as a whole emerge as the obvious determinants of public action by State administrations. Obviously the new role of state administration in the context of these dominating forces will not only increase the size and complexity of administration, but will necessitate new approaches and techniques to achieve improvement and secure assurances for the timely completion of policy goals and public tasks. It is this contextual consideration which would help the search for directions in improving state administration.

Agricultural Administration

As an illustration, the subject of agriculture may be examined as part of State administration. In the recent past, with increasing emphasis and commitment, agriculture has assumed a new concern for performance and productivity. Thus, it can be argued that the subject of agriculture as an element of State administration has radically changed as compared to, say, a decade or so back. Agricultural administration does not begin or end with the traditional tasks of State level organization created for administering it; instead, it has assumed entirely new directions with technology as the dominating theme, and has created emphasis on the judicious availability of inputs to the farmers. A string of State, regional and national research institutes and agricultural universities continuously pour out new findings and developments which must be expeditiously translated into action for providing the eventual fruits to the tillers of the land.[4] It cannot be conceived that any State administrative apparatus will delay and thereby deny the conversion of technology into a field reality. The subject of availability of inputs is by itself an enormous area of administration and it is no wonder that a wide pattern of departments and organizations has been created at various levels with the common objective of assuring inputs availability. State administration in this subject has not stopped at this stage and extensive studies are being made to categorize the farmer and the land which he tills.[5] This has been done on an inescapable logic that neither all farmers nor all the land is alike and, therefore, separate treatment must be found to meet and match their requirements.[6] The objective and content of administration involved in, say, the Small Farmers Development Agencies and Command Area Development Project[7] will be substantially different – a difference which will be accentuated further by the time horizon of the problem, which each is seeking to resolve. Since agriculture as a subject is emerging more and more important as part of the larger area of State administration, it is being increasingly realized that there is need as well as scope for improvement and what should now be discussed is in effect 'management of agriculture'*. If this proposition is accepted, this is surely a fruitful direction towards improving State administration.

In pursuing the subject of management of agriculture as part of improving State administration, a set of postulates are to be noted. The range of inputs needed to secure optimal agricultural production is, today, far and wide, and several of these have continuously to be juxtaposed to meet the requirements of the farmer.[8] New developments pushed by agricultural scientists and swift changes in the technology involved, make it imperative that the apparatus of State administration should take the leadership role in ensuring the quality, quantity and timely availability of the inputs. These features need to be noted especially as an area of administration – because several of the inputs have mutually conflicting inter-dependencies and the non-availability of one may provoke a chain reaction and upset the beneficial results of other inputs.[9] Also, the range of manipulation needed to achieve an optimum pattern of input availability is limited, both in terms of resources and inherent implementation difficulties. For example, in several situations apart from the matter of physical resources, attitudinal blocks emanating from long standing social and cultural stances, will need to be tackled before the inputs can led to the desired results.[10] It is possible to add a set of similar issues, which at each stage can thwart the quest for productivity and development of agriculture.

Several studies in the recent past have also highlighted the interplay of administrative procedure and organization setting as an important variable in this task. The large number of organizations available for these tasks do not always ensure appropriate and timely coordination, with the result that there is avoidable duplication, waste and delay. If this organizational aspect is a problem, the inputs could be managed, thereby implying a sharp shift in the traditional stance of administration. To enlarge the analogy, it can be visualized that the management of agriculture ought to be the style of administration of this sector and State administrations should come forward and react with adaptability to accept this proposition and thus provide a framework and impetus for improving State administration in this critical sector.

Technology and Organisational Change

As an elaboration, mention may be made here of the interrelated area of the introduction of technology and the corresponding organizational change with particular reference to agriculture. The experience of the developed countries suggests that the acceptance and introduction of technology are a prime reason for ensuring the requisite organizational change – the logical assumption being that organizations must change before they will accept and practice a new technology**. This has led to a set of situations where it has been possible to prepare organizations for the change implicit in the introduction of new technology. There is evidence to suggest that organizational resistance to the change, implicit in the introduction of new technology, can seriously disrupt production gains and even lead to dysfunctional situations. At the level of State administration it is a moot question to what extent the introduction of technology has been attempted with a clear, prior understanding and concern for organizational change. A cautious view can be taken that even if there was awareness of this correlation, there are not discernible decisions to suggest that new organizational designs and structures were conceived as part of the process of the organizational change flowing out of the introduction of new technology. In fact, evidence to the contrary asserts that either organizational structures were replicated or allowed to continue unchanged, irrespective of the introduction of technology. These issues become more dominant in the State administration of a subject such as agriculture where the impact of technology is assuming a more and more dominant role and in fact has emerged as the key determinant of higher producticvity.[11] Therefore, a deep study of this correlation could well form a key area for improving State administration.

The problem of organizational change and the introduction of new technology is equally relevant to a more basic question, namely, the pattern of organization as a vehicle of State administration. Without going into the historical perspective and evolution of State administration before Independence, it can be noted that organizations in State administration normally portray characteristics which are peculiar to 'formal' organizations.[12] Contemporary research in this area indicates a series of related in-built advantages and disadvantages in the broad category of formal and informal organizations. The burden of the findings stipulate that in complex and fast emerging developmental administration, formal organizations may be inherently constrained in achieving their goals. At the level of individuals, forming part of the formal organization, the extent of the strain is fairly well-recognized. Individuals report experiencing frustration because their self-expression is blocked. They also experience failure because they are not permitted to define their goals or the paths to these goals in relation to central needs. They experience short-term perspectives and even conflict, because of a feeling that change of job situations may not result in a different task configuration. Because of the implied degree of dependence and subordination, the directive element in administration also increases along with controls. In extreme situations there is even individual withdrawal, lack of involvement and alienation as a form of defence mechanism against the formal organization. Conversely, a similar pattern of lack of fulfillment is in evidence in higher administrative levels also, who may feel curbed by limited authority, under-utilization of abilities, hierarchical controls and a relatively non-participative administration style. Evidently, these will lead to inter-personal difficulties and distort organizational behaviour and goal achievement.

Some recent research studies state that a set of points for intervention can be established to secure the desired change at the organization level and prepare it to meet the new pressures of change, with adaptation. It has been noted that organizational change as a deliberate activity requires a theory to guide the selection of points of intervention. Attempts to change organizations by changing individuals alone have been heavily criticized, and currently the practitioners are stressing the importance of developing approaches that are focussed upon the whole organization as a functioning entity. In this background, planned organizational change will proceed by identifying and manipulating variables, which are most readily controlled. As an illustration, the suggested intervention points[13] are:

(a) Tasks which refer to the objective of the organization.

(b) Technology which is the requirement for the organization at a point of time and will go beyond equipment, plant, and buildings because changes in technology might arise indirectly from changes in tasks or directly through improved methods of production. The existence of one form of technology will, therefore, be bound to determine the range of tasks.

(c) Structure, referring to systems of authority, workflow, information systems, coordination and communication. Areas of centralized decision-making and established methods of problem-solving would be relevant.

(d) People who constitute the organization including their attitude and expectations, their extent of involvement and their appreciation of the extent of change implied as an adjustment to changes in task, technology or structure.

It must be stressed that these intervention points are highly inter-dependent, so a change in one may almost certainly force a change in the other leading to a situation of associated change of strategy.

The merit of stipulating these intervention points is manifold. They suggest the possibilities for multiple points of entry to secure organization change. They also pin-point that whatever may be the limitation in isolating these points, they do open a positive direction for improving administration. This becomes particularly relevant when one is attempting to analyze the vast complex field of State administration and the directions for improvement. A score of guidelines and milestones will be needed and as an initial intervention strategy, the points mentioned above may provide the start for improving administration at an aggregate level – the State level.

It will be necessary to take note of the dissatisfaction with traditional bureaucratic styles of administration in coping with the problems of development and change, which today face State administration. Students of public policy and political science suggest that administration is prone to be easily permeated with the evils of bureaucracy, implying thereby that if the administrators behave as bureaucrats they reflect all the dysfunctional features of bureaucracy***.

A writer on bureaucracy has even suggested that "nobody can be at the same time a correct bureaucrat and an innovator. Progress is precisely that which the rules and regulations do not foresee. It is necessarily outside the field of bureaucratic activities."[14]

There is even talk of debureaucratising administration, but we do not precisely know how administrative systems move from a conventional model towards a more adaptive organizational system. In the case of State administration, the relevance of the political and legal nature of decision-making can pose a problem for this transformation and since it is a reality, it cannot be wished away. If administration is 'a basic social technique' and implies the guidance, leadership and control of the efforts of a group of individuals towards some common goal, then, clearly, good administration will be one which enables the group to achieve its objectives with minimum expenditure of resources and effort and the least interference with other worthwhile activities.[15] In this exercise, the combined pressure of achieving better results while dealing with more complex situations places a high premium on improvements in administrative ability. It is this conclusion which reinforces the need for introducing management techniques in order to improve State administration.

Use of Management Techniques

The need for examining the application of modern management approaches and techniques for improving State administration can now be argued against the above background. According to many management theorists, the choice is not between using or not using the important resource of management in administration.[16] Their use is imperative, if Government has to play a meaningful role directed towards economic and social change. The real issue is, to what extent will administration pro-act to promote the use of management in a judicious, systematic and dynamic way or continue to operate in outdated styles. The relevance for using management approaches and techniques in State administration can be further pressed on a number of reasons, e.g.,

(1) Science and technology cannot be harnessed to the pursuit of all-round national development without the support of sophisticated organization and effectively planned management systems.

(2) Development planning which is today accepted as a major element of State administration cannot be attempted without a number of conceptual, analytical and other tools and techniques.

(3) Design and installation of selected planning and control systems and techniques is essential for efficient management or regulation of a wide range of state enterprises –social commercial or industrial, and

(4) Social welfare programmes for sizable weaker sections of society can only be administered and successfully monitored with the help of management systems.

To take an overall look, any State administration may find it difficult to effectively accomplish the above areas without appropriate management systems and the supporting range of analytical skills.

A planned acceptance and introduction of management techniques in administration will have a number of related benefits also. In the vast field of State administration, management approaches can generate emphasis on creativity, innovation and acceptance of change. While much progress has been made, there is also evidence of increasing concern with both the rate and degree of developmental change. From the standpoint of management, it is possible to highlight the reality of obsolescence of individuals, their thinking styles and the organizations they represent. In a positive sense, the techniques and approaches can enthuse State administration systems to learn to live and cope with complexity. It must be realized that organizations and individuals in any part of administration, if overwhelmed by change or complexity are unlikely to make their contribution to the current requirements of economic and social development.

Role of Training

In the context of these tasks eventually designed to improve State administration the role of planned training as an input can hardly be over-emphasized. It is increasingly accepted that training can provide effective intervention for upgrading levels of performance of individuals and thereby of organizations. This premise can be effectively extended to the larger objective of improving State administration. The Government's interest and commitment to training of its public personnel is today well known.[17] The five year plans have stressed training as a desirable ingredient for accelerating the process of national development.[18] At the State level, a series of administrative reforms commissions, instituted in the last two decades have unequivocally stressed the need for training of State personnel for improving State administration.[19] Against this emerging acceptance of training there is also an increasing awareness on the part of the public personnel that they need training for improving performance, since they have necessarily to operate and survive in an environment which is dominated by an explosion of new knowledge and new skills.[20] Public personnel at various levels in administration today accept that training – formal as well as informal – alone can help them face the threat of obsolescence which can take place before their official superannuating. A number of State Governments have set up extensive training institutions, which are doing a commendable task of providing training to a wide range of State personnel. Some of these institutions have done exceptional work and have to their credit standard publications and journals which periodically communicate the quality and quantity of their efforts.[21] The Department of Personnel and Administrative Reforms in the Central Government has provided an equally valuable leadership role and strengthened the process of training of public personnel.

However, at the level of State administration, there is need to take a fresh look and develop a two prong short term strategy for training. Firstly, there is need for a planned exercise of identification of training needs. It is well known that public personnel in the State administration display an unusual diversity of background, experience and skills. In large States, they are also geographically distributed in wide areas and that reduces professional interaction. Opportunities for formal training needed for large numbers of public personnel are equally limited and the supporting component of on-the-job training is not infrequently up to the desired level needed for individual and institutional development. There is, therefore, need for a careful exercise of identification of needs to cover, as extensively as possible, State organizations and development functions. In the absence of an individual based analysis of needs, a group based approach can be followed with advantage.[22] Several departments in the State Governments are adopting this approach and there is no reason why it should not become an important plank of the identification exercise.

Secondly, it is important that need-based plans for the training of public personnel are prepared for State administration. A training plan is visualized here as a statement of training requirements, which will reflect both short and long range training objectives designed to solve the immediate or anticipated problems of State administration. A good need-based plan would rank training needs in priority and include an estimate of resources required to meet the predicted needs. It will be seen that a plan which states needs and resources can indeed be a useful tool for improving the State administration. Besides, the availability of a need-based plan will have a number of other advantages as well. It will kill ad hocism, which is in evidence in the performance of training functions. It will generate a useful input for career development planning and can be eventually linked to overall manpower planning. It can also be evaluated. If the plan is prepared in the background of an earlier identification need exercise, it will also help public personnel to improve their present performance; it will assist them reach their full potential and prepare them to meet the challenges of technology and change. Above all, it will provide the personnel with an adequate input of knowledge and skills necessary to perform certain functions which are relatively unique to the emerging profile of State administration. A need-based training plan will thus assist in fulfilling predetermined needs and in achieving the objectives of training. It will equip the State institutions to design and forecast available training programmes in the context of the new challenges before the State administration.

The Search

It must be acknowledged that the pattern of State administration has reflected equally positive changes indicating genuine concern for efficiency and improvement. There is also evidence of confidence to cope with unforeseen challenges which keep on recurring. Almost continuously, procedural and structural adjustments are also being suggested to upgrade the capability of State administration to face the current urge for all round development. These are undoubtedly encouraging signs, but yet they point to a continuing question, whether administrative improvement is to be achieved through short-term, ad-hoc arrangements or by more deep-rooted solutions. Some time back, the Prime Minister suggested: "What we need, therefore, is revolution in the administrative system without which no enduring change can be brought about in any field." Today more than ever before, when all-out attempts are being made to push closer the streams of development to the weakest sections of the community, the administrative system must aspire to "reflect the individual's contribution to human welfare and economic gain". It will be a challenging task for state administration to ensure that it is able to cope objectively, responsively and in time with the impulses of development processes which will dominate the content of administration in the next decade or even beyond and require high visibility in improvements at all levels in State administration. But while the issues are being analyzed, it will be appropriate if there is a search for directions to secure, if possible, a congruence in the manifested goals of State administration. Let it be noted that there may not be a approach for improvement, instead there may be a range. It may, thus, be necessary to concurrently operate over a range to secure the validity of directions for improving State administration.

Notes

*The Indian Institute of Public Administration in collaboration with United Nations Economic and Social Commission for Asia and the Pacific and United Nations Asian Centre for Development Administration recently conducted a Regional Programme on Management of Agriculture (6-24 Sept. 1976). The programme was designed to stimulate creative thinking on the role of managers in agricultural development. The programme objectives included identification of key management issues involved in implementing national agriculture policy and consideration of appropriate managerial interventions.

**For discussion of this theme in the Indian context see Edward A. Kieloch, "Innovation in Administration and Economic Development", *Indian Journal of Public Administration*, Vol. XII, No. 3, July-Sept. 1966.

***Bureaucracy has been recognized as a misused concept; for a workable basis there are different approaches to be examined but Hall's formulation appears worthy of note. See R. Hall, "The Concept of Bureaucracy: Its Empirical Assessment", *American Journal of Sociology*, Vol. 69, No. 1, July 1963.

References

1. Inaugural address by Prime Minister at the Conference of Chief Secretaries on Administrative Improvement and Personnel Management, New Delhi, May 7, 1976.
2. For details of State enterprises and departmental undertakings – See 'Commerce Year Book of Public Sector 1974-75', Commerce, Bombay, 1975.
3. "Address by Shrimati Indira Gandhi", *The Indian Journal of Public Administration*, Vol. XVII, Oct-Dec. 1971, No. 4.
4. M.S. Swaminathan, Our Agricultural Future – Sardar Patel Memorial Lectures 1973, All India Radio, New Delhi.
5. Khan, Waheeduddin and R.N. Tripathy, Intensive Agriculture and Modern Inputs – Prospects of Small Farmers: A Study in West Godavari District, Hyderabad, National Institute of Community Development, 1972.
6. Gopalakrishnan, V.S. "Organisation for Command Area Administration in India", *Indian Journal of Public Administration*, Vol. XIX, No. 2 (April-June 1973), pp. 177-86.

   Sudan, M.L., "SFDA and MFALA Ambala: Some observations", *Journal of LBS National Academy of Administration*, 20:4 Winter 1975, 1269-80.
7. See Seshadri, K., Agricultural Administration in Andhra Pradesh: A Study of the Process of Implementation of Intensive Agricultural

Development Programme, Bombay, Popular Prakashan, 1974.

8. Swaminathan, M.S. "Perspectives in Agriculture", Seminar (Jan.1973), pp. 63-6.
9. J.C. Finn, "The Simulation of Crop-Irrigation Systems" in J.B. Dent and J.R. Anderson (ed), Systems Analysis in Agricultural Management, John Wiley, 1971.

   Also see, Luz Mario Bassoco and Roger D. Norton, "A Quantitative Approach to Agricultural Policy Planning: Annals of Economic and Social Measurement", 4 (October-November, 1975).
10. For a detailed treatment see: Hunter, Guy, "The Administration of agricultural development: Lessons from India", London, Oxford University Press, 1970.
11. Ch. Hanumantha Rao, Technological Change in Distribution of Gains in Indian Agriculture, New Delhi, Macmillan of India, 1975.
12. See for discussion, Richman, Barry M. And Farmer, Richard N., Management and Organizations, New York, Random House, 1975.
13. Leavitt, H.J., in Cooper, *et al.*, New Perspectives in Organizational Research, New York, Wiley, 1964.
14. Ludwig Von Mise, Bureaucracy, New Haven, Yale University Press, 1944, p. 67.
15. William Newman, The Administration Action, Prentice-Hall, 1965.
16. "Inter-regional Seminar on the Use of Modern Management Techniques in the Public Administration of Developing Countries", Oct-Nov., 1970, Vol. II: Technical Papers, United Nations, 1971.
17. See for example, the Prime Minister's Address at the Annual Meeting of the Indian Institute of Public Administration, New Delhi, Oct. 22, 1971.
18. Training Division, Ministry of Home Affairs, Government of India, "Five Year Plans Training", Training Monograph No. 1, 1969.
19. Ibid., "State Administrative Reforms Commission on Training", Training Monograph No. 7, 1970.
20. A.P. Saxena, "Training and Development in Government", The Indian Institute of Public Administration, New Delhi, 1974.

   T.N. Chaturvedi, Public Service and Modern Challenges: Need for Continuing Education, Training Abstracts 10, Training Division, Government of India, 1970 (mimeo).
21. See for example, The bi-annual journal, Development Policy and Administration Review, published by the State Institute of Public Administration, Jaipur.
22. A.P. Saxena, "Identification of Training Needs: A Group Approach", *Indian Journal of Public Administration*, Vol. XX No. 1, Jan-March, 1974.

8

Reforms in the System of Filing, Noting and Inter-Departmental References

We are reproducing below a minute recorded by Lord Curzon as Governor General of India on May 24, 1899, on the system of filing, noting and inter-departmental references in the Government of India. The minute is not merely of historical interest; many of the maladies which Lord Curzon mentioned are still there.-Ed.

I desire in this Note to invite the attention of my Colleagues and of the Secretaries of Departments to the manner in which business is conducted in the various Offices of the Government of India, to the excessive noting and writing which are the characteristics of that system, to the delays involved in inter-departmental communication, with its complicated chain of reference and annotation, to the method in which the record of our proceedings is printed and kept, and to the effect which these features of the Indian practice are demonstrably exercising upon the dispatch of business and the efficiency of Government.

It is in no academic spirit that I initiate this discussion but with the definite and practical object of suggesting alterations and improvements which shall bring the Indian system more into harmony with the results of administrative experience elsewhere, and with the exigencies of Government in India itself. Not even the most confirmed adherents of the existing system, who have been brought up under its influence, affect to deny the exaggeration by which some of its best features have been defeated.

From *The Indian Journal of Public Administration*, Vol. XII, 1966.

It is, however, so powerful, and has established so masterful a hold over the faculties of its victims that all previous attempts at reform have failed or have been abandoned; while the whole of the Civil Service of India, trained up in a method to which they know of no alternative, and which is repeated, with very slight modifications, in every Presidential or Provincial Government throughout the country, is thus engaged in stereotyping the worst anomalies of an anomalous system. If for these reasons the stimulus outside criticism, and of experience acquired in different schools of Government, may be useful, as tending to apply an independent test to the Indian practice, the advocates of the latter will at the same time be enabled, by the procedure which I am about to suggest, to enter any defence that there may be of a procedure which has presumably not been founded on caprice, but has grown up, however unscientifically, in response to definite requirements, and for which it is conceivable that pleas are capable of being urged, that would not at once suggest themselves to a critic from the outside world. It has been with the view of ascertaining some of these pleas and of escaping the dangers of a premature judgment, that I have refrained from raising this question until I have seen the machine at work for five months. I dare not wait any longer; lest like previous would be reformers, my senses become dulled by the routine of everyday contact, and I end by being merely an additional cog in the machine itself.

I have alluded to previous but abortive efforts at reform. The last of these was made in 1894-95. The question was raised by a Note in the Home Department in August 1894, and after being referred by the Viceroy (Lord Elgin) to the Departments, meandered peacefully through them in the normal fashion for several months, eventually emerging in September 1895. A Committee of Secretaries then met in order to arrive at a common agreement upon the desirable points of reform and to formulate orders thereupon. These orders were finally issued in November and December 1895.

I have carefully studied the whole of these proceedings; and without my disrespect to the labours of the Committee, or to the opinions placed on record in the Notes that preceded it, I have formed the conclusions (1) that the enquiries made and views expressed barely touched the fringe of the subject; (2) that the recommendations agreed upon did no more than tinker instead of reforming the system; (3) that no serious attempt has been made to carry out the most important of these suggestions, or to obey the orders that were framed for their enforcement. For instance, strict regulations were issued as to the number of Office Notes, as to the character of précis, and as to the elimination from the final record in print of all purely routine references. The fact that these orders have been, and are every day being complacently infringed, has sharpened my anxiety to reopen a case which I should anyhow have taken up on its own merits.

The procedure which I now have in view, and in which I solicit the cooperation of my Colleagues is as follows. In this Note I propose to detail the anomalies of the existing system, as they have presented themselves to me from the experience of the past five months; and to make certain tentative suggestions as to their modification or removal. I do not propose that this Note should then itself inaugurate that perambulatory process through the Departments of whose length and delays I am complaining; but that the Member and the Secretary of each Department either independently, or if they prefer to do so in collaboration, should favour me with their views upon the question at issue, both in its general aspect, and with special reference to the experience of their own Department. After collating these views, I will either submit a scheme of proposed regulations applicable to all the Departments to my Colleagues, or, if it seems preferable, will convene a meeting of all those whose opinions have been given, at which we can discuss, and, I hope, decide upon a plan of common reform. Should we be of opinion that our plan is capable of a wider application than in the offices of the Government of India, I would then propose to send it round to all the Local Governments with a request to them to embody it, so far as practicable, in their own official and departmental procedure.

Before advancing further I should like to say that I am conscious of one great and ineradicable difference between the Indian system, and the practice of those English or foreign departments with the working of which two of my Colleagues as well as myself are familiar. In Great Britain the offices of Government are manned from top to bottom by clerks or Secretaries, all of whom have passed a severe and often a special competitive examination, whose life-service will be devoted to the department, and who acquire early and carry with them through their careers the traditions and a great deal of the unwritten knowledge of the office. Here the case is widely different. The lower grades of the Departments are filled with non-gazetted officials of a class and attainments not comparable with those of the corresponding ranks in the English offices. These clerks in India carry on with great fidelity the ministerial work of the department, but without sharing, or ever hoping to share, any of its larger responsibilities. The responsible officers at the upper end of the scale are few in number – what is far more serious – are constantly changing. This system has a double consequence. In the first place, it throws upon the administrative officers a labour of which they cannot expect to be relieved by their subordinates to the same extent as in English departments. Secondly, owing to the fluctuating nature of the gazetted establishment, there is much greater need for a permanent record of what may be styled the inner history of cases than there is in England. There such a record is to a large extent preserved in the inherited memory of the department. Here it requires to be perpetually put into print for the use of novices at a later stage.

There is also another difference inseparable from our Indian system of Government (though as I think absurdly exaggerated in practice) which must be borne in mind. I allude to the necessity for inter-departmental reference, so much greater in the case of an administration which undertakes many functions not ordinarily associated with Government, e.g. the building and management of railways, than it is in the case of a Government organized like that in England. These references and counter references cannot be dispensed with here, although I think it can be shown that they are at present pursued with needless prolixity and delays. Nevertheless they are a feature inseparable from the Indian system, for which due allowance must be made.

I will notice only one more difference, which is not without its effect in adding to the circumlocation of the existing system; viz. the somewhat indefinite subdivision of responsibility in the Government of India between the Member of Council, who represents a Department, and the Secretary of the Department itself. In England a Department speaks only with one voice, and that the voice of the Secretary of State who is its Parliamentary Chief. In India the loyalty of the service, and the traditions of administration, have as a rule prevented anything like schism. But in theory there are two voices – that of the Secretary and that of the Member – in the case of any disagreement between whom the Viceroy is called upon to decide (a condition of affairs that has no parallel in England). Whether position be ideally right or the reverse, it is one that does not tend to the contraction of official noting upon cases, but rather to the reverse.

Of similar effect is another feature of the Indian system, unknown at home, and, in my judgement, susceptible of reform here, viz. the practice by which Members of Council, largely owing to conditions of accommodation, etc., for which they are not responsible, frequently do their business and write their Minutes at a distance from the Office of which they are the responsible heads. This means in nine cases out of ten a Note from the Secretary and a subsequent Note from the Member, a certain amount of time being consumed while the file is being conveyed from the one to the other, and while the two Notes are being written. In England where a Secretary of State is daily in his office, this stage is constantly dispensed with by a few minutes conversation between the two parties. I should like, as is known, to see a further development of this most sensible practice in India.

There is one alleged difference between Indian and English standards which I only note in passing, in order to dispute the value of the pretensions which are based upon it. It is said that Secretaries, Deputy Secretaries, Under-Secretaries, and Assistant Secretaries, in India must write in order to prove their mettle; that only by so doing can they vindicate their abilities to the Secretary of the Department and in the last resort to the Viceroy; and that if they did not thus exercise their faculties, the faculties themselves would remain untrained, and their owners would not qualify for the higher positions which they may hope at a later stage to fill. There is some plausibility in this plea. But I decline to accept it on more grounds than one. Firstly, official noting is designed as a help to the authority finally called upon to decide, not as a drill ground for raw recruits. Secondly, the promotion of the latter, in due ratio to their abilities and deserts, will not, in any properly organized system, depend upon the facility or even the acumen with which they may have written, but upon the opinion formed and recorded of them by their official superior, the Secretary of the Department. Thirdly, the Secretary will, under the system which I shall presently explain and recommend, give as full an opening as is required by the circumstances of the case to the young lions of his department. Fourthly, writing is not the main or final test by which we promote our young men in England; nor is there any reason why it should be or have become so here. A young man is far more likely to learn the formation and the expression of sound judgements by studying the performances of his seniors than by prematurely experimentalsing himself.

With these remarks on the differences between the English and Indian systems, which must not be forgotten in any attempt to deduce conclusions from the experience of the one for the advantage of the other, I pass to an examination of the Indian system as it has so far come under my notice.

(i) Method of keeping and circulating papers

The Government of India has only arrived at its present system after trying and discarding several others. The history, as traced from the practice of the Foreign Department, has been as follows:

(1) Originally all papers were kept in MS. and were folded in four, and docketed on the outside back. During this period there seems to have been very little noting. What there was appears to have been appended is separate covers or little books.

I may mention that this system of folding is still adopted in the Foreign Office in London. The MS. dispatch, invariably written upon a light blue foolscap sheet, is upon arrival folded into four, docketed, noted upon on the back of the sheet by a clerk or Under-Secretary (unless a note of unusual length requires to be written in which case minute paper of corresponding shape and size is employed, and the note is appended), and is then submitted to the Secretary of State, who initials the Note if he approves, or writes his own instructions if he does not.

Each paper or dispatch therefore carries upon its own back the orders passed upon it. The dispatch itself is subsequently printed on a single sheet, as one of a series, and these are bound up yearly, or more often, into volumes. None of the Notes or orders issued upon the dispatch are ever printed. Should reference to them be necessary, to illustrate or to explain the history of a case, the particular folded dispatches are picked out from the file, placed together in an elastic band, and submitted for perusal. Whereas in India we preserve the humblest effort of a clerk: the orders of a Secretary of State and even of a Prime Minister in England are not recorded in print.

I do not propose to advocate the re-introduction of this system of folding in India, nor the introduction of this system of quasi-marginal and unprinted noting; the former, because paper perishes more quickly in the Indian climate, and a folded document soon becomes frayed along the folds; the latter, for the reason already mentioned, namely, that, owing to the personnel of our departments, printed records are more necessary here than in England. I may, however, say that both for the expeditious discharge of business and for ease of reference, it seems to me the best system that I have so far seen.

(2) The next stage in the evolution of our papers was from 1863 to 1869. During this period they were for the first time printed, but still folded in four.

(3) From 1870 to 1882 folding in two (the papers being folded longitudinally down the center) was the practice. During this period the notes (called, at least in the Foreign Department, K-W or Keep-with) were separately printed; and the sheets containing them were, as now, prefixed to the Official Proceedings when the latter were bound together. During this simple and Saturnian age, however (for it is only since then that corruption on a large scale has set in), there were four particulars in which the system differed materially from that which now prevails, greatly to the discredit of the latter. (a) No one noted, or at least the Note of no one was finally printed, except a Secretary of Department, a Member of Council, or the Viceroy. The new criterion of Government, according to which men can only qualify for promotion by writing, had not then been discovered. (b) These Notes were of the briefest and most business-like dimensions. (c) What are now treated as demi-official communications, and separately collected, were included in the K.W. with the Office Notes. (d) Office numbers, figures, hieroglyphics, precis, paraphrases, dockets, were unknown. In one section of the print were the Proceedings duly numbered. In the other or K.W. were the Printed Notes with corresponding numbers. The Notes had no connecting link with the Proceedings beyond the numbers. This was slight but sufficient.

(4) From 1882 onwards that Flat File system was adopted, under which the papers were laid, unfolded, upon each other, both as originally received in MS., and as ultimately bound up in print. This was a salutary change, and one, which is not now likely to be departed from. Unfortunately, at the same time or soon after, were sown the first seeds of that fatal malady that has ever since increased and tightened its hold upon its victim.

The Flat File system is that adopted in the India Office and Colonial Office (and I believe in the majority of the Offices) in London. But there is this difference. The Notes upon each paper are in the London Offices written in the first place, and subsequently either typed or printed, upon sheets corresponding in size to the paper received, and are affixed to it by a tag. Each paper therefore carried its own Notes or instructions not actually upon its back, as in the case of the Foreign Office papers, but attached to it. This I believe to be the best system where an office is independent and self-sufficing. I understand that the main drawback to its adoption here is that we send home from time to time our Official Proceedings to the India Office, and that there is convenience therefore in keeping them, both in MS. and in print, separate from the Notes or K.W. There is also perhaps some convenience in our system, for the rapid tracing of the departmental history of any case that has extended, as do most Indian cases, over a long period of time.

As regards the method of folding and preserving papers here, I do not recommend any departure, in main principles, from the existing system. But I think that it would be to the convenience of the departments, and certainly of Members of Council, if in circulating the files attention were paid to the following points, individually insignificant but collectively providing a perceptible relief:

(i) All files should have a board at the bottom (as generally supplied).

(ii) The tapes attached to these boards should not be of the flimsy and breakable type in use in most of the Departments, but the stouter sort, in use in the Public Works Department.

(iii) When a file attains any size or weight a strap should be employed to hold it together for submission. This strap should be of better make, less stiff and coarse, and with shorter and sharper prongs to the buckle, than that in common use here. A sample, as employed in the India Office, London, will be sent round to each Office.

(iv) A dispatch sheet or card with the title of Department concerned printed at the top, and the subject-matter written legibly across the sheet, must be placed upon the top of every file, immediately inside the tape or strap, so that the Viceroy may see at a glance, without undoing the tape or strap, what are the Department and the subject concerned. Copies of those in use in Foreign Department can be procured.

(v) Blank sheets for noting by the Viceroy should invariably be attached to the MS. Notes or K.W. Cases are constantly occurring, in which owing to departmental carelessness, no such sheets are attached. The Department, after expanding itself over pages of MS. only leaves the Viceroy to give dumb witness by his initials to their lucubrations.

(vi) The system of Linked Files is (though in rare occasions necessary) a cumbrous system, and has been greatly abused. I am constantly having enormous Linked Files submitted to me which, having perhaps started from different points, have gradually converged, until both contain the same papers, and discuss the same problem. This is perhaps inevitable, e.g., in a case where the Military and the Foreign Departments are engaged in discussing a case which may have a military as well as a political aspect. But in the majority of cases the separation and linked presentation of the files are only a nuisance which a little forethought might avoid. An intelligent selection of the papers required from both files by the Deputy Secretary, and their submission with an explanatory Note, would probably save the Viceroy many a quarter of an hour of valuable time.

(vii) Similarly, with reference not only to Linked Files but to any file, there is no necessity to submit to the Viceroy, or I should imagine to any Member of Council, prodigious files which start almost from the commencement of time. Such a system would bring the work of the Foreign Office in England to a standstill in 24 hours. When I was Under-Secretary there, I frequently had in the course of a single day to read from 50 to 100 despatches or papers relating to different subjects. These came round to me in boxes, with a few previous papers, required for the understanding of each, attached to them by elastic bands. Had each paper carried on it back, like a snail, its entire official history and tenement, a regiment of porters would have been required to carry to and fro, between the "Foreign Office and the House of Commons, the pre-posterous burden. Why cannot a similar intelligence, in selection and in reduction of burden, be exhibited here? Why cannot the vast mass of the file be left in the Department, and the necessary papers alone be sent? Of course, the Secretary would be held responsible; and if he omitted essential papers, the blame would fall upon him, or upon the particular subordinate to whom had been delegated the selection. But such a responsibility is after all only a feature of any and every departmental system. I remember a case here in which there was circulated to Members of Council, prior to its being mentioned there, an Inland Steam Vessels Act. The papers constituted a file nearly a foot high, with which chaprassis struggled about Calcutta for a week.

(II) Noting on Cases in the Departments

Here I come to the main abuse and scandal of the present system. I have already pointed the contrast between the practice now in vogue, under which everybody from a clerk to a Member of Council paraphrases, initials, notes, or recommends and is handed down to posterity in print – and the sensible system that prevailed in the days of Lord Mayo and Lord Northbrook. The present system has the following obvious drawback. Firstly, people write who have no business to write. Secondly, a case is delayed for days and sometimes for weeks in a department (and a fortiori still longer in cases of inter-departmental reference), while it is passing through this dismal ordeal of irresponsible loquacity. Thirdly, in the wilderness of diverse opinions, its original proportions and point are eventually lost to view, until no one is able to say what is the issue, or at what stage it has arrived. I have myself had to pick out unsolved cases, which have been literally buried under the superincumbent mass of writing and would, unless disturbed, have lain mumified in the departmental tomb, until one day accidentally unearthed by a later generation. Fourthly, all these opinions, disquisitions, trivial departmental stages and even initials of clerks, preserved as they are in print, swell the volume of our official records to point at which the Notes far exceed the Officials Proceedings in bulk and length; and must, in the long run, require a library like that of the British Museum to contain them. I will give, before passing on, an illustration of the prolixity of the existing system. A dispatch from the Secretary of State arrived in one of the Departments of the Government of India in my predecessor's time. It covered 3 ½ pages of print. After being somewhat gingerly touched by a few clerks it was taken in hand by an Under-Secretary who paraphrased it (with glosses and readings of his own) in 1¾ pages of print, and then added a Note recording his own opinions in 4½ additional pages of print. This brave example was eagerly followed by his colleagues in an ascending scale; and by the time the Viceroy and Members of Council had noted upon it the recorded Notes amounted to 28 pages of small print, as compared with the 3½ pages of large print from the Secretary of State which had provoked this lamentable effusion. I need hardly add that no final decision was arrived at; and that the case was one of many left over to me for settlement. I am glad to think that we settled it with less than half a dozen more pages of print, followed by an hour's discussion in Council.

I now turn to the remedies. They are based upon the old practice of the Indian Government, upon the practice of the London Departments, and upon what I should imagine to be the practice of every sensible Government in the world. This practice rests upon the simple principle that the Head of the Department (here styled Secretary, in England Permanent Under-Secretary) is officially responsible for the presentation to his Chief (in India a Member of Council and ultimately the Viceroy, in England a Secretary of State or other Minister, and ultimately the Prime Minister) of the case upon which the latter is required to decide. In the preparation of the case, he may employ at his own discretion the industry or abilities of his own subordinates, be they clerks or Under-Secretaries; he may even delegate his responsibility to one or other of them, signifying his own assent by appending his initials. But this discretion must have obvious limitations. There must be a limit to the number of subordinates who are permitted to note, the selection being determined not by their grade in the official scale, but by their aptitude to deal with the particular question under notice. Secondly, the reference to the ultimate authority must not consist of a jumble of heterogeneous and discordant opinions, out of which he is called upon to pick one for himself. The manner in which I would apply this principle to our Indian practice is as follows:

(i) When the question of noting was discussed in 1895, a great deal turned upon the question as to the side of the page upon which clerks or gazetted officers should sign their initials, and as to whether the higher officials should sign their initials or their names. The principle that I would desire now to establish is this; that from the Office there should come up to the administrative ranks but one Note. Let the Superintendent select which clerk he pleases to write it. If he approves of the note, let him pass it on with his initials. If he disapproves, let him have it revised or modified, or let him substitute for it a Note by himself. When the paper has passed to the gazetted officials, as a general rule not more than two of them (including the Secretary) should note upon it before passing it on to the Hon'ble Member. The Secretary will doubtless select whichever of his subordinates he pleases to write the preliminary Note, or the selection will be made automatically by the sub-division of labour in the Department. I have said 'as a general rule', and I think that it should be of almost universal acceptance, but I would not exclude the possibility in exceptional cases of three Notes, though I hope that such a contingency may very rarely occur.

(ii) Precis and paraphrases should only be adopted on a very limited scale. If the letter or dispatch under examination is one of a character and importance that are certain to require its perusal by the higher officials and ultimately by the Viceroy, it will, in nine cases out of ten, be unnecessary to précis or paraphrase it at all. The subject-heading will indicate the general character of its contents. Only in the event of the document being one of great length or complexity, may a précis of its proposals or contents, for sake of convenience, be required. Occasions will also occur from time to time when a précis, either of the facts or of the previous history of a case may be useful in order to avoid much reference to old files, and to create, so to speak, a fresh starting point. Similarly, with regard to paraphrases, no higher official requires a paraphrase, much less a sequence of paraphrases, by subordinate, of a letter, which he is bound to read himself. Still less does he want to know (though he is often now invited to read) what his subordinates think was, or may have been, in the mind of the original writer. He requires references to precedents, former papers and so on, and suggestions for action. Another vice of the present system is the habit of reproducing verbatim in the Notes entire extracts from the letter or despatch under discussion. This is entirely unnecessary and should be discontinued.

(iii) The rule should be of universal acceptance, that when at any stage an official agrees with the preceding Note or recommendation, he should append his initials (and date) and nothing more.

(iv) Cases are constantly occurring in which, even without superfluity or delay in noting, a paper will take several days in passing through a department, simply owing to a want of elasticity in the interpretation of the existing system. An official who is seated in one room, will keep a file lying on his desk one or two days, and then initial it, and pass it on by a chaprassi to another official seated next door, who will treat it in similar fashion. I was asked the other day by a Local Government when I would sanction the journey of a native Prince to Europe. The application reached the Department on May 12th. The Chief proposed to sail on the 20th. The file, after leisurely and uneventful procession through the office chambers, reached me on the night of 18th, too late to make permission of value, or refusal possible. If the officials of the departments would only remember that they live in the same building, and would in cases demanding early decision (and I may add in many others) substitute a few words of conversation with each other for the pedestrian procession of the files, they would greatly expedite the despatch of business.

Inter-Departmental Reference

(i) The last remark applies with even greater force to the references that, under our complex system, are inevitable from one department to another. In the event of any difference of opinion between the two each is disposed to act as if it were the inhabitant of a separate planet, firing off its missive to another world; whereas the offices, from which this interchange of formal compliments proceeds, are usually within a few yards of each other, which might be traversed in a few moments by the rival correspondents, who might in a few minutes settle a matter that otherwise drags its weary course along for months, I will give an illustration that has occurred in my time. There was a question as to whether a Colonel W was or was not deserving of promotion, and whether the unfavourable comments of the Provincial Government upon his capacities should or should not be communicated to him. It entered the Departments in December 1897. It came up to me for decision in February 1899. In the interval the departmental Note had amounted to 53 pages of print.

The same sort of official pedantry appears to prevent a settlement, by meeting and conversation, of any question upon which an acute controversy has arisen between two Departments, or between their officials heads. I have more than once, in commenting upon these displays, employed the simile of Lawn Tennis or Badminton, and I repeat it here. When once the departments have, so to speak, got their flannels on and the game has begun, they appear to lose sight of all other considerations but that of keeping up the ball or the shuttle cock (and as a rule, the latter is the fairer parallel) over the net, while the faithful official marker calls out the strokes and records them (in print) for the admiration of later ages. I had a case the other day, in which the Secretary of State had, in June 1897, invited the Government of India to express an opinion as to a change in the marking of their confidential maps. From that date until May 1899, the rally was heroically sustained, and might, but for an accident, have gone on, till the crack of doom. Can we not in our departments abandon this system? In England if the Foreign Office disagrees with the Colonial Office, the Permanent Under-Secretary of the one puts on his hat and walks across the quadrangle to discuss the matter with the corresponding official of the other. If they fail to come to terms, the two Secretaries of State meet and talk it over. They do not pursue for months and exchange of vocal amenities from the rival house-tops.

(ii) The rules that I have already suggested for the conduct of any one Department, in respect of noting, will of course equally apply, but with increased economy of time and space, in cases where more than one Department is involved. I had a case before me concerning the supply of winter great coats to the Khyber Rifles. After the usual departmental formulas had been gone through I referred it back for some additional information to the three Departments who were affected. It was returned to me with 14 separate and distinct opinions! There is a further abuse in the same connection which is capable of easy correction. Where a case is being bandied to and fro between different departments, after the officials of the first had had their say, and the officials of the second have commented upon the opinions of the first, the papers frequently go back to the latter, who then begin in the same old order commenting again upon the comments of the second; until presently the chain of argument and repetition reminds one of the nursery rhyme about the "House that Jack built". I suggest that in such cases the Secretary of the original department alone should note upon the papers after they have been returned to his office.

Arrangement and Printing of Proceedings and Notes

(i) The papers of the Government of India (I believe in every Department) consist of two sections; the Official Proceedings, and the Office Notes. These are under our system, kept distinct from each other, both in MS. and in print. I would not propose to interfere with this distinction. Some officers print the Notes and the Proceedings afterwards, others vice versa. I think that a uniform system should be adopted; and, unless any good reason can be shown to the contrary, I would propose that the Notes should be printed first, since they are in the majority of cases a prelude to rather than a sequel of, the official decisions recorded in the other section.

(ii) The Notes, when printed, are in many departments called Keep-Withs, and are designated as K-W. This is part of the barbarous jargon that has grown up pari passu with a barbarous system. I see no reasons why in the Government of India we should call ordinary things by any other than their ordinary names. I would therefore propose in future to designate K.W. simply as Notes. In the Foreign Department I have further found the Index or Table of Contents of the separate volumes of papers, when bound up, variously designated as "Brief Subject", "List of Papers", and "Precis-Docket". As I see no reason for calling it by any other than its proper name, I have ordered this Index-age in future to be headed "Table of Contents".

(iii) As each press letter, despatch or telegram, comes into the office, and is added to the MS. file, the heading or docket under which it is entered in the MS. Notes, prior to noting, is in the

Foreign Department written in red ink. I daresay this is done in other offices. If not, I recommend it as a useful system of distinguishing the various stages of a case, as well as each stage in turn, from the MS. Notes upon it.

(iv) I now come to a peculiarly malignant abuse of the present system, which is itself the outcome of a further, and equally culpable abuse, viz. the extent to which official correspondence (I speak particularly of the Foreign Department), has become supplemented, and almost in many cases superseded, by private or demi-official communications. The privilege of private correspondence between officials in the department and officers or persons outside is a valuable one, inasmuch as it places the former in possession of information which may be essential to the due comprehension of a case, but which it may be impossible, for various reasons, to include in the official letters or telegrams. But it is a privilege which is capable of being, and has been, greatly abused; and hence has arisen the question of how to deal with this sort of communication in the records of a Department. It has been solved by constituting a separate branch or sub-head of the K-W's for demi-official papers. This branch requires again a separate index of its own. Accordingly, it has happened to be in studying a case, in a printed volume of our Proceedings, that in order to preserve the chronological sequence of discussion and decision, I had had to keep my fingers in three or four different places in the same volume, and to dart backwards and forwards, from one to the other, at what a cost of time and temper I need hardly say.

I lay down the proposition, therefore, which cannot, I think, be disputed, that a demi-official, personal, or private letter, differs only from an office note in the fact that it is written by an official outside the department and often at a distance, instead of by an official inside the Department at his desk. It must as a consequence be similarly treated, i.e. it must, if printed at all, be places not in a category a part, but in the Notes in the order of its arrival. The decision whether it should be printed, and if so how much of it should be printed, must rest with the officer concerned, subject of course to the decision of the Secretary. By this method there will be in every printed collection of papers in every department, three sections only – (a) Table of Contents, with references to former and later cases; (b) Notes; (c) Proceedings. There must be no extras of any description.

(v) In printing both the Notes and Proceedings, it is possible to avoid a good many sources of subsequent confusion by always using the same type for the same thing, i.e., one type for Notes, another for Proceedings, and again in each class, one type for headings, another for contents, and so on. At present all kinds of type are used promiscuously, according to what may be handy in the printing press at the moment. Similarly, in printing both the Notes and the Proceedings, all numbers, alphabetical letters and purely departmental hieroglyphics, except such as may be essential for subsequent reference, should also be omitted. Too often a printed volume of our records is more a puzzle than it is of a guide.

(vi) I come to the main cause of plethora of print, as distinct from writing from which our records suffer in so marked a degree. This is the preservation in print of any and every Note, mark, sign, date, or even initial – in a word of the inevitable but worthless ministerial routine of the Department.

In the conduct of all business there must be an immense amount of such surplus ages. Under the Indian system, it is swollen at every point by the abuses, which I have been describing. But its main and differentiating feature is this, that here alone, as I conceive, of all Governments in the world is it accorded the honour of print. The Notes of our official volumes are augmented to three or four times their needful dimensions by long columns – I have often seen entire pages – of initials and dates, by the record of the passage of the case from department to department, by the questions asked by officials of their subordinates (which ought to be sent round on a slip of paper instead of officially recorded upon the Notes) and by banalities of many and various types.

The reduction of this abuse was one of the questions that was only perfunctorily dealt with by the Committee of Secretaries in 1895. They recommended a strict enforcement of Rule XIV in the Rules of Business, which ran as follows:

"References of no permanent importance, such as requests for former papers, should be made on separate slips, which should not be filed, but destroyed when done with."

In the revised Secretariat instructions which were issued in August 1898, this rule re-appeared as No. 5(3) in the following form:

"References of no permanent importance such as requests for former papers, calls for proofs or drafts, orders to print, etc. shall be written on separate slips and destroyed without being filed."

But it is obvious that this went neither far enough nor in the right direction. For what is wanted is not merely the destruction of routine slips such as those alluded to, but orders to prevent the printing of matter, which must appear upon the files, but which is not worthy of being printed. All that is wanted is that in every department, some officer, responsible to the Secretary, shall, before the MS. file goes to the printer, run a blue or red pencil through the stuff that does not require reproduction in print. In this way we shall find that the bulk of our printed Notes will speedily be diminished by more than one-half. I circulate for inspection an ordinary Foreign Department file, prepared under the existing system; and a revised proof of the Notes or K.W. of the same as amended under the process that I am about to introduce. The length is thereby reduced from 11 printed pages to 4.

Other aids to dispatch

I should like to invite the aid of my Colleagues and of the Secretaries in respect of any suggestions that they may dare to make under the above heading, in addition to, or in corroboration of, the remarks which I am about to submit. Some check appears to me to be wanted in order to prevent the interminable delays that now occur, and the complete oblivion that is apt to overtake departments as to the whereabouts, or fate or future, of cases in the course of their departmental career. These delays and this carelessness occur:

(1) in the cases of answers to communications from the Secretary of State-concerning which I am continually receiving telegrams, couched in the following terms: "When may I expect an answer to my telegram or despatch of such and such a date?";

(2) in the case of questions that are pursuing their weary pilgrimage through the departments;

(3) in the case of questions that have been referred to a Local Government but have not returned therefrom. Let me give an illustration of the latter. I was called upon not long ago to give a decision affecting certain canal rates in one of the provinces. The question had originally been referred to the Government of India in October 1892. It had then been sent to the Local Government with whom it had remained, without reminder, or rebuke, for 3 ½ years. After returning from this long holiday, it had then wandered like an uneasy spirit through the departments of the Government of India for another 3 years, until at length in April 1899 it came up to me to be exercised and laid.

Now in all these cases, there ought to be some practical, and not merely illusory, check. I know that in each department some sort of statement is drawn up quarterly, or perhaps at other intervals, of the cases in the department, of the orders that have been issued upon them, and of the present stage of their wandering. But clearly this check must at present be what I call an illusory check, since it does not prevent cases like that which I have just mentioned, and which is only one among many that have come under my own notice. My impression is that these quarterly statements, which are drawn up by clerks and are, I believe, divided into classes for submission to the Secretary and Deputy Assistant, and Under-Secretary, severally are only glanced at or are completely ignored by them, a convenient initial being substituted for a bona fide scrutiny. I cannot dogmatize upon such a question as this; but having indicated what I believe to be the evil, I shall be grateful to the Secretaries if they will submit to me what their experience suggests to them as the remedy.

I have now completed what I have to say upon this branch of the question. At a later date I shall submit another memorandum to my Colleagues upon an abuse, equal in intensity and even more pernicious in its results than over-writing inside the Secretariats, upon which I have here been commenting viz. over-writing, not of Notes but of reports, in every branch of the Local and Imperial Governments. But for the moment I confine myself to the departments of the Supreme Government with which we are here officially connected. This is a long Note; but a long Note has been required to deal with an abuse of such long standing; nor if one long Note from a single Viceroy has the effect of saving many scores and hundreds of long Notes from hard worked subordinate officials in the future, will its length have been wasted. The reforms that I have indicated, I can undertake to carry out – in fact most of them are already in successful operation – in my own, i.e. the Foreign Department. While I could impose them by a ukase, it is obvious that it would be out of my power to supervise their enactment, still less to ensure their ready acceptance, in the other departments of the Government of India, without the cordial cooperation both of my Colleagues and of the present and future Secretaries of those Offices. I invite this cooperation, in the interests, not merely of Members of Council whose work may be somewhat lightened by more reasonable and businesslike methods; nor merely of the departments themselves, though I believe that when a better regime has once been fairly started, it will prove to be of incalculable relief to them; but for the sake of the efficiency of British administration in India, in which from the Viceroy to the humblest clerk, we are all engaged, and which is being seriously and detrimentally affected by a continuance of the existing indefensible system.

May 24th, 1899. CURZON OF KEDLESTON

9

The Reform of Administrative Procedures

Arthur J. Naftalin

The success of a government depends considerably upon the quality of the persons engaged in its administration. Personnel, however, is by no means the only factor in successful management. Effective procedures and an efficient organizational structure are also essential. Even the best personnel system cannot overcome basic procedural or structural deficiencies that disturb or obstruct the flow of administration. There is obviously a close relationship between personnel management and administrative procedures, just as there is between both of these areas and the problems of organizational reform. In fact, all these three ingredients of an effective system of administration – personnel, procedures and organization – are closely interrelated and each of them cannot, in my view, be effectively studied in isolation from the others.

In considering the problems of procedural improvement – the second factor, it is proposed to deal here primarily with trends and experience in American public administration. Administration everywhere shares many common qualities and it can safely be assumed that the experience of administrators in one country has meaning for others who are engaged in essentially the same activity. Much is to be gained by the exchange of ideas and experiences across national boundaries.

Some Questions and Criteria

In the area of procedures, some of the main problems the administrator faces today are:

From *The Indian Journal of Public Administration*, Vol. IV, 1958.

(1) How does a government achieve internal and external security and stability and still avoid bureaucratic excesses?

(2) How can a government ensure equal and fair administration in accordance with fixed routines and, at the same time, remain flexible and responsive in meeting individual situations?

(3) How can a government keep its operations continuously alive and moving, avoiding inertia and indecision that result from procedures and methods that are too rigid?

(4) How can the tendency to "bottleneck" decision-making at the top levels of administration be resisted and greater delegation of authority achieved?

(5) How can a government develop an effective division of labour among its employees and, at the same time, successfully coordinate all operations?

(6) How can a government ensure continuous four-way communication, from the top down and from the bottom up within the administrative organization and outward and inward with the public that it serves?

(7) And, finally, how can all of these elements be efficiently coordinated into an effective functioning unity?

These are, of course, difficult questions to which there are no easy answers. They are examined here only in general terms, because there are a great variety of approaches and each administrator, in seeking meaningful solutions, must fashion answers that fit particular needs and special circumstances. There are, however, certain common criteria that define the essential requirements of any effective administrative system.

The first of these is simplicity and clarity. In the United States, as elsewhere, administrators are engaged in a continuous struggle to keep rules and regulations and methods and procedures in their simplest possible form. It is often easier, in meeting a new need, to add a new operation than to eliminate or modify an old one. As the years pass an administration may find itself encumbered with procedures and regulations that no longer serve the purpose for which they were originally intended. The need for the sixth copy of a form may have ended years ago (if, in fact, it was ever needed) but the requirement remains unchanged. A particular certification may no longer serve any purpose, yet it will still be required. Such practices clutter up the administrative process, slowing down the flow of activity and consuming valuable time and materials.

If administration in the United States is a fair example, all governments could benefit greatly from continuous revision of its procedures. In the Minnesota Self-Survey project*, hundreds of instances came to notice where state law or traditional practice had imposed expensive and complicated administrative routine that were serving little or no purpose. It was found that many administrative forms were unnecessarily complicated and confusing; many operations involved a variety of certifications and approvals that far exceeded the requirements of a sound system of internal audit or control; thousands of valuable man-hours were being consumed in the gathering of statistical and other data that had been serving no purpose for many years; and hundreds of rules and regulations were in force which might once have served a purpose but which were no longer of any value. In the field of financé, there existed more than 200 separate funds for accounting purposes when 10 or 12 would have been sufficient. The State was paying its employees on 118 separate payrolls, and, with further study, it became clear that the number could be reduced to five and, eventually, to one single, comprehensive system. As the result of this Self-Survey and the reform activity that grew out of it, substantial progress was made in clarifying and simplifying procedures.

The indignant and complaining taxpayer is a familiar figure the world over. In the United States it is something like a national pastime to complain about the cost of government and to criticize the bureaucracy for its tendency to move at its own slow pace in providing service. We all know that the taxpayer at times can be very unreasonable. Yet, when we reflect upon how unnecessarily cumbersome and confusing many governmental procedures have become in the United States, we wonder if the citizens we serve are not too passive and too uncomplaining. The prod of the complaining citizen is a wholesome influence on administration, and one sometimes feels that governments would be better served if more citizens were to demand full explanations for the continuance of procedures that have no apparent justification.

Administration must be constantly re-examined to be effective and such re-examination requires a strong act of will on the part of administrators. It is far easier to repeat the routines that were in operation yesterday, letting rules and regulations, and forms and methods grow and multiply in response to immediate and pressing needs, than it is to re-examine and re-evaluate one's operations, asking oneself simple, honest, and basic questions such as: "Is this procedure really necessary?" "Is this certification necessary?" "Is there a quicker way to accomplish this task?" "Why do we need so many copies of this form?" "Do we need to maintain this particular file?" The questions are infinite. It is, of course, this more difficult course of continuous re-examination that must be pursued if administration is to be fully successful.

Administration is basically nothing more nor less than common-sense, and common-sense begins with simplicity and clarity. These must be the cornerstone of any effective procedural system.

A second criterion for effective procedures is flexibility. Administration must not only be clear and simple, it must also be responsive to needed changes. Again, judging by our experience in the United States, bureaucracy's major evils are its unwillingness to shed outworn regulations and procedures and its inability to adjust to new situations or to allow for necessary deviations from fixed requirements. The successful system adapts to new needs and new circumstances and meets special situations rationally and efficiently. The unsuccessful system is one in which the procedures are so rigid that they limit and obstruct the administrative flow. Some governmental agencies have procedures that are so inflexible and so precise that administration has become as ceremonial as a religious observance. When this happens, the procedures have become the ends of administration rather than the means, and the entire process becomes stultified.

Achieving flexibility, adaptability and adjustment is a never ending struggle. It requires constant re-evaluation of all administrative operations and a continuous restatement of the aims and purposes sought by the government so that all procedures can be sensibly related to their proper objectives.

A third criterion of sound procedures is definiteness and uniformity. Similar operations in different agencies should be directed and controlled in similar fashion. The public that is served comes to know government's procedures, and, if they are definite and uniform from one agency to another, the flow of administrative activity will be expedited. The abuse of this principle reaches absurd limits in some governments. Different administrative agencies in the same government, for example, will sometimes maintain different hourly schedules. Sometimes employees in different agencies have different rights and privileges. Often agencies performing similar operations will use different forms that seek the same information.

There is apparently some contradiction between, on the one hand, the need for uniformity and definiteness in administration, and, on the other hand, the need for flexibility that permits the exercise of individual discretion. But the two must be reconciled for effective administration. This is another point at which the art and the science of administration must be joined. A successful system strikes a balance between basic formality, in which all procedures are set forth with simplicity, clarity and definiteness, and with internal freedom and flexibility that allow for individual judgment, discretion and originality.

Procedural improvement in administration, as noted earlier, is aimed at achieving internal and external stability, at ensuring flexibility and responsiveness, at overcoming inertia, at smashing bottlenecks, at developing an appropriate division of labour and an effective coordination, and at achieving continuous communication in all directions. To realize these objectives requires endless and intensive planning, analysis and programming. The more complex administration becomes, the greater the need for these internal administrative functions. Thus, modern government is turning more and more to systematic and continuous administrative planning.

In the United States today there is increasing emphasis on the function of management research and analysis. There is a growing awareness that the internal problems of administration require the expert attention of persons specially trained for this function. As a result, there has emerged in the United States a new group of professional and technical experts who devote their time to the problems of administrative management. Not only are there general experts trained in the larger problems of organization and methods, there are specialists among the specialists, some specifically trained in the application of machine methods, others in forms control and records management, others in physical plant utilization, others in work measurement. Many governmental jurisdictions in the United States now have well-defined units devoted to the analysis and study of the administrative operation itself. Such units have a variety of names, such as "planning and research," "systems and procedures," or "organization and methods" (O & M). While they perform a variety of analytical or planning functions, they share in common the pursuit of improved administrative operations.

The recognition of the importance of administrative planning has not come about without a struggle of its own. Legislators and even top executives often must be persuaded that special funds should be made available for this purpose. In paring operating budgets it is always tempting to remove items labeled "research": or "planning" or "analysis" on the grounds that they are of long-term concern and can be postponed until the presumably more pressing short-term demands are met. The foolhardiness of this policy has been demonstrated again and again. For lack of a carefully devised administrative plan that could have been developed with a small appropriation, inefficient operations are continued month after month and year after year at a cost many times the amount that would have been needed for proper planning.

The new almost overwhelming, emphasis on the study of systems and procedures and on research into organization and methods is due in large measure to the almost fantastic progress that is being made in the manufacture and use of high-speed business machines. The new machines can perform in seconds hundreds of operations that previously required minutes and even hours. As a result they have opened up extraordinary new opportunities for efficiency and economy. This has compelled administrators to re-examine their entire operations not only particular procedures but their complete organizational frame work. They are finding it necessary, if the machines are to be used efficiently, to re-educate and retrain large numbers of employees who can programme the work for the machines and who can operate and service them.

The interest in high-speed equipment is so widespread and the consequences of their general use are so far-reaching that many observers believe we are at the beginning of a revolutionary new era in administration. It is certainly apparent that the current study of public administration in the United States is largely the study of the impact of the new machines on large-scale organization and administration. Needless to say, for the moment at least, the machines are creating more problems in overall administration than they are solving, and there are certain to be many years of experimentation and adjustment before the new machines will have been fully mastered. Ironically, the very speed of change within the business-machine industry is itself a serious problem in administrative planning. A new electronic device has no sooner been placed on the market but what it has been made obsolete by the appearance of another machine of even greater speed or volume. All of this of course supports the need for the most careful and intensive research and analysis into all aspects of administration.

In the State of Minnesota, an extensive programme of installing computing equipment has been undertaken. Its highway department, for example, is now using an electronic computer for routine calculations that previously required thousands of expensive hours of time from our high-salaried force of engineers. This year for the first time they will have under machine operation the entire system of motor vehicle registration, involving nearly 2,000,000 automobiles, buses and trucks. In fact, the people of Minnesota pride themselves on the very substantial progress they are making in this crucial area of administration. However, they have learnt that they cannot make efficient use of the new machines until they have first completed an exhaustive analysis of all operations affected by the new installation. They have found that they must know everything they possibly can about all the related procedures, about the volume of the work involved, about the nature of particular operations to be machine-performed, about the skills and abilities of employees who will be expected to operate the machines, about the kind and amount of retraining that will be required, about the employees who will be displaced by the machines and the new opportunities that can be created for their re-employment, and about the physical space and electrical power that will be required. They have found it not only desirable, but essential, to delay further machine installations until they could complete a study that would gather such basic information. The study in itself is a formidable undertaking. It required enabling legislation and a special appropriation by the 1957 legislative session. As a result they now have under way what they call an Electronic Data Processing Feasibility Study. This is the first study to be undertaken by any of the 48 state governments in the United States. As the study proceeds they become more and more convinced of the necessity for further analysis and planning if they are to continue to improve their administrative operations.

The experience of the United States shows that there are no tricks or shortcuts to good administration. It can be achieved only if we know what our problems are and which of the various alternative methods will be the most effective for our purposes. Such insight and understanding cannot be acquired without systematic and continuous study by officials and employees specifically trained for that purpose.

Administration as a Process

Public administration obviously involves many complicated relationships. There are relationships between the top administrators and the descending levels of their subordinates. There are relationships between the government and the citizens it serves. There are very sensitive relationships between the personnel and the factors that affect their performance. The number and types of relationships within administration could be listed without end. Yet, despite its enormously complex character, administration remains essentially rational and systematic activity. Individual procedures relate to a larger complex of operations and the entire activity is governed by a single, inter-related set of objectives. Sometimes this fact is lost sight of by administrators who are caught up in their own limited operations; they often see administration as a series of separate and independent acts instead of as a continuous and integrated process.

Any effort at the improvement of an administrative procedure or group of procedures must be based upon a clear understanding of how such modifications will affect the larger system. It is essential, therefore, that administrators see their activity, however limited or specific it may be, as part of a continuous flow of activity. Each individual operation must be seen as part of a network of relationships; a slowdown or speedup in one sector will affect other sectors: a new machine operation at one point may break one bottleneck but create new ones. It is not always easy to see the larger aspects of the process; an administrator inevitably becomes preoccupied with the needs of his particular agency and he may become so intent upon fulfilling his immediate assignment that he may avoid any involvement in the activities or affairs of other agencies. This leads in the end to a segmented or fragmented government in which separate agencies are not part of an integrated process but virtually competing operations.

Thus it happens that in some governments individual procedures are treated as isolated operations, as a segmented series of administrative events. A moment's reflection tells us that this almost never should be the case. Take, for example, the matter of a government's payroll. At first glance the payroll appears to be nothing more than a specific instruments of getting the pay-cheque to the employee. Yet the payroll is a central feature of the accounting system and is closely related to budgeting methods and improved planning. A well-planned payroll system will provide data for improving the personnel system and it will help strengthen the system of accounting and internal audit. Similarly the budget system is often regarded as simply the preparation of a document that contains basic financial data. But, again, a well-planned budget system will be an invaluable instrument for the intelligent allocation of the government's resources, for the systematic control of its expenditures, and for the comparative analysis of the needs and operations of different agencies, and will serve as a central means for developing basic and long-term programmes for measuring the effectiveness of particular methods and particular programmes. The procurement system likewise is not exclusively the obtaining of materials and supplies. If properly planned, it will assist in the controlling, measuring, and strengthening of all administrative activity.

All of this is by way of supporting the central point that administration is one continuous interrelated process. It is a process that has flow and movement. Policy decision and administrative acts move up and down from the top levels of management to the many other components of the organization. The administrative process is, in many respects, like a living organism that has separate but related functioning parts. The directing or policy-making level in government bears to the subordinate levels of personnel and machines the same relationship that the mind in the human body bears to its arms and legs; central financial and accounting agencies are not unlike a blood-stream or circulatory system. The analogy could be expanded at great length. But this is perhaps sufficient to suggest that successful procedures do not operate in isolated context. They all combine to form one system serving one ultimate objective, namely, the purposes for which the government has been established.

The healthy organism has vitality and agency. Its mind or directing agency has clarity of purpose and effective means for communicating the nature of that purpose to all its separate but interrelated parts. Thus a healthy government will have a top management that clearly understands the purposes that the government seeks to serve and it will achieve uninterrupted communication, from the top, where policies are made, to the bottom, where they are executed, and, again, from the bottom up. Its operating members – the supervisors, the clerks, the inspectors, the accountants – will have clear directives upon which to act and effective tools with which to work. The pathways of activity will be clear and coordinated, just as are the nervous system, the circulatory system, and the respiratory system in the human body.

Administrative Leadership

The above analogy has been drawn at some length because improvement in administrative procedures requires a special kind of governmental leadership. The first need for any government is to define its purposes with clarity and in a fashion that all who are engaged in the process will have an understanding of the goals and objectives that are being sought. This burden falls heaviest, of course, upon the top levels of administration. The success of any organization is dependent upon its leadership; if there is at the top levels vitality, force, direction, clarity, and a willingness to make administration a co-operative operation, such spirit will permeate the entire organization. It is a leadership that succeeds in infusing the organization with an understanding of its purposes and in extracting from those who make up the organization not only dedicated service but also the application of their creative abilities. It is a leadership that fully senses its close connection with the other operating parts just as in the human organism mental health and physical health require clarity of mind and soundness of body, and, as modern science shows, the two are inescapably dependent upon each other.

If the leaders exercise imagination and originality, and if they encourage their subordinates to participate openly and freely in the decision-making process, the orgnization will soon be alive with excitement and purpose. When such spirit is present one need never doubt that the organization will grow and that it will fashion for itself methods and procedures that are adequate for its purposes.

Note

*This project required that all officials and all employees make a complete and systematic review of their own work in order to determine the points of strength and weakness in their operations. Administrators, employees and technicians, with the assistance of legislators, were asked to examine with complete honesty and objectivity their own administrative programmes and to make appropriate suggestions for improvement.

PART II
SELECTED ADDRESSES OF L.P. SINGH

10

Training of Civil Servants: The Wider Perspective

L.P. Singh

I must first correct the impression that I have agreed to address this gathering; I have only consented to talk to you. I had gone through the papers that have been circulated and I wondered if anything useful could be added to what had already been brought out. Yet, as I had been called upon to speak to you, I thought I might take this opportunity to put forward my views on certain aspects of the problem of training.

My considered judgement is that during the last 21 years since India became independent, the most critical deficiency has been on the managerial side. To some extent, the top Civil Service has neglected its management responsibilities. This is particularly regrettable as the Indian administration had a long and unique tradition of attention to management. You find that in the old manuals practically every little detail of management was put down. There was a tradition of choosing every individual for every little job with the utmost care. I have noticed in the old records the meticulous manner in which assessment was made of the weaknesses and strength of an officer's personality. Training was treated as an important function of management and apart from the institutional training that could be provided, great emphasis was laid on attaching young officers to experienced seniors who would give to the young officers generously, from the large reservoir of their experience. The itinerary was worked out with great care and practical training was provided in a number of items, including operations such as land survey and settlement.

Concluding Address delivered on February 25, 1969, at the Conference on Training sponsored by the Training Division of the Ministry of Home Affairs and organized by the Indian Institute of Public Administration at New Delhi.

The Second World War, to some extent, brought a disruption in this system since the overriding consideration of winning the War superseded activities like training, which though useful in themselves, had not a direct bearing on the War effort. The preoccupation with the immediate objectives resulted in the neglect of the instruments; but this was perhaps inherent in the situation. When Independence came soon after the Second World War, the country was again faced with gigantic economic, social and security problems and management functions and training continued to be neglected. It is necessary that this missing link with the past should be forged again and adequate attention given to training.

I need not dwell at length on the philosophy behind recruitment to the higher Services in the British days. Under the influence of Macaulay and others who thought like him, the practice developed of recruiting men of high intellectual ability and academic accomplishments at young age through a competitive method. The subjects studied by recruits were of no importance; what mattered was the quality of the mind as shown by academic performance. Naturally, in such a system of recruitment, post-entry training was of great consequence. During the 19th century, excellent training institutions grew at Fort William in Calcutta and later on, at Haileybury in England. In addition, training schedules in detail were framed after an officer joined his new post in the district. Our system of recruitment on general merit followed by a well-planned training stood the test of time, and occasionally one found a distinguished civil servant with a background of Zoology and a passion for Sanskrit poetry, distinguishing himself as an expert in the field of finance and banking. But the point on which I wish to lay stress is that with our system of choosing civil servants systematic training immediately after entry is essential. If you have a civil servant who enters upon his duties without any knowledge of the Constitution of India, the economic and social framework within which he has to function, or who is not aware of our cultural traditions or the cultural conditions in which he has to work, the consequences may be disastrous.

While it is true that there can be no substitute for training on-the-job and some sort of apprenticeship is necessary, the emphasis in India has always been on supplementing apprenticeship with institutional training. In this respect, I feel we have made a major departure from British thinking at least such as it was in the past. When the two All India Services, viz., the I.A.S. and the I.P.S., were constituted under the inspiration of Sardar Patel, good arrangements for their training were devised. The emphasis in the post-Independence training institutions was obviously different; instead of producing good agents of the Empire, the aim was to produce good patriotic Indians who could shoulder the burdens of higher administration.

With the growing professionalism all round, I feel a stage has arrived when civil servants will have to be trained for particular groups of specializations. The administrative functions have become so difficult and complicated that a generalist while possessing common sense and understanding of public affairs and management, must have a greater or lesser degree of specialization in some field or other. I do not believe that everybody is capable of framing a good budget, much less a performance budget, or of managing personnel, or planning the lay-out and equipment of an office, or dealing competently with political, social or economic problems of the country, or managing public enterprises. A greater or lesser degree of specialization has become necessary. Naturally, specialized training will be in diverse fields and the Training Division of the Home Ministry should devote attention to this complex problem. The initial post-entry training has to be widely conceived; and at the middle stage different groups have to be given specialized training. For topmost administrative jobs at levels where administration becomes something akin to statesmanship, the net has to be cast wide to get from the specialized groups men with conspicuous managerial ability and wide understanding of problems. At this stage one would look for the wider man rather than the specialist. In other words, for the first 5 or 6 years, it is all right for a generalist to have a wide grounding; for the next 15 or 20 years, he should cultivate a measure of specialization in one of the various fields; thereafter, while some may continue to rise in the specialized lines, others may be considered for wider managerial responsibilities, as far as possible, in not wholly unrelated fields.

On the question of perspective for training, I might suggest that in a rapidly changing technological and social environment, it would, perhaps, not be enough to train a man on the basis of his job requirements at the moment; a forward look is also necessary. The problem is indeed a little complicated: it is to determine the measure in which the job requirements of today and those of tomorrow, and perhaps, the day-after, should be blended.

I might illustrate this point with an example from a recent case. The other day, I had a discussion with senior police officers on the question of training of the higher police. We recognized that the police must be trained for the tasks which it shall have to face in the seventies, when there will be more urbanization, more industrialization, more science and technology, a changed pattern of living and a changed system of transport. The road pattern would change and the scheme of lighting, and what is more significant, the pattern and techniques of crime will change. We are already noticing that the style of violence is changing and it is a moot point whether equipping the police with long batons is at all worthwhile when violent mob have a tendency to engage the force from long distances through missiles of all kinds. What I am trying to emphasize is that as in the police, so in other professions, the job requirements will have a tendency to change rapidly and the planners of training will have to keep pace with this phenomenon.

While it is desirable to keep constant touch with the advances made in training techniques abroad, I might caution against adoption of these in our country without suitable adaptations. At the same time we should not be content with adapted application of current practices in advanced countries; we should know and take into consideration what people are thinking about training in future. I happened to read some years ago the report of the Police Commission in England and I found myself in enthusiastic agreement, not with the majority report, but with the dissenting note of Dr. Goodhart. Dr. Goodhart did not accept the current doctrines and was more exercised about the future. One should not stop after taking into account the current practices and institutional arrangements and techniques in other countries; one should also take note of the ideas that are fermenting, or ideas that are still at a formative stage. We should have a sufficiently sensitive antenna to catch the new ideas that are coming up. I am conscious that I am complicating the task of the Training Division in the Home Ministry, but it is precisely problems of this nature which it will have to grapple with, in order to keep up with changing conditions.

I have noted that in the current thinking, great emphasis is being put on Mid-Career Training. This is all right; but training should be a continuous process and should not come to an end somewhere near half way through a man's career. Even at the senior-most levels, there is need for a freshness of outlook and acquaintance with the latest developments. Indeed I have sometimes felt that older men, with their tendency to fall into a rut or to remain rooted in the past, require the stimulation of training even more than younger people. Of course, the programmes at this level need not be of a long duration and short appreciation courses may suffice.

Then there is the question of the total period in a public servant's career-span which should be devoted to training. When I was working out schemes for establishing an Academy of Public Administration and the creation of a Training Division in the Home Ministry, I had consultations with the Director of Training at the Army Headquarters and I discovered that when an army officer became a Lt. Colonel or a Colonel after putting an average service of about 17 years, the best among them had already spent some 7 years in various kinds of training. On the civil side, for a proportionate length of service, there might be nothing to show by way of training except the first year or so of initial post-entry training. I made the flippant remark that such disproportion between training for killing and that for serving the community constructively was hardly defensible. This ratio of 7 to 1 ought to be changed radically by increasing the total period of training in the Civil Service.

I might also suggest a slight modification in nomenclature. Instead of using the word 'training', the wider concept of 'training and education' would be desirable. A focus on training alone would remain confined to the study of job skills and knowledge related to a trainee's immediate functions. In our setting, there is need even for programmes which may not have a direct bearing on one's job, but which are calculated to develop a wider understanding of social and economic problems, and of society and public affairs generally. In this context, self-education programmes have their own place. One of the recommendations of the Second Pay Commission was that the study leave terms should be very considerably liberalized; that there should be no insistence on a man taking study leave only to pursue a subject which is clearly related to his own work; and that he should also be enabled to go to good institutions and spend six months or a year to educate and re-educate himself.

There is another small point which I would like to mention and this is about paying greater attention to imparting managerial and administrative skills to those who enter the public service on the basis of their professional qualifications. The need for training engineers, doctors and other professional groups in managerial skills, rules and regulations, canons of financial propriety, and the tenets of the Constitution, etc., is imperative. Occasionally, blunders are committed by people with professional backgrounds in their administrative functions, in the absence of knowledge of these basic principles. It could happen that an expert inducted to an administrative job may lose his professional competence in the process of administering financial, accounting and personnel matters; or he may perform these duties unsatisfactorily for want of proper training. There can, of course, be exceptions who would feel equally at home in their technical and managerial functions even without formal training; but for the bulk of them, some sort of induction to administration is necessary.

I might in the end invite your attention to an important aspect of personnel policy in the present-day setting. Although the need for specialization is accepted, the rotation of officers of the All India Services between the Union and the States should not be given up. This system of rotation has stood the test of time, and in the federal set-up which we have given to ourselves in the Constitution, interchangeability of personnel between the States and the Union is necessary for strengthening the unity of the country. The fact that the All India Service officers have been manning posts both in the Union and the States has, to some extent, helped the political leaders to sustain a spirit of cooperation and understanding between the Centre and the States. It would be desirable to evolve the functional doctrines of personnel management keeping in tact the framework of the All India Services. Perhaps, with a slight modification, a system of rotation will have to be evolved in broadly related fields, so that while the requirements of specialization are met, the historical compulsions behind the evolution of our administrative structure are not ignored.

11

Morality in Public Affairs

L.P. Singh

I express my deep gratitude for the honour done to me by inviting me to deliver the inaugural series of Dr. Amaranatha Jha Memoraial Lectures at the L.N. Mithila University. It is for me an undertaking of devotion to one who, as Professor of English Language and Literature, was my teacher while I was studying for Bachelor and Master's degrees; and he inspired me, as he inspired a whole generation of students, with love of literature, and learning. He set before us a rare example of pursuit of excellence; of a standard of meticulous precision in thought, and in expression combined with limpid felicity, which one could strive to attain but which I at least have found beyond my reach. Externally, he was a picture of academic gravitas and reserve; but his heart was full of kindness and compassion, and his dealings with all his students were always marked by patience, tolerance and generosity. He did not view his students in the mass; he knew and remembered, upto the end of his life, the name and personal traits of every student he had taught during more than two decades. When any of the students he had taught even in the early twenties had a chance meeting with him, he would give an agreeable surprise to his old student by addressing him by name. He had a prodigious memory, but coupled with it was his deep interest in every individual, which explained this remarkable phenomenon. He was an embodiment of rectitude and fairness, and one could, under all circumstances, count on getting from him ones just dues. He was a patron of various cultural and artistic activities, and of sports and athletics as well as of intellectual pursuits, exemplifying the Greek idea of developing the body along with the mind and aesthetic

---

Dr. Amarnatha Jha Memorial Lectures delivered on February 14-16, 1983 at L.M. Mithila University, Darbhanga (Bihar).

sensibilities. During the Vice-Chancellorship of two great sons of Mithila, Ganganatha Jha and Amarantha Jha, father and son, the Allahabad University became the premier institution of higher learning for about two decades, attracting eminent teachers and talented students from different parts of the country. Pedagogic infallibility as a dogma is clearly untenable in present conditions, but it can be readily accepted as a living reality when the student community faces great scholars and educators, such as Ganganatha Jha and Amaranatha Jha. I should like to believe that with its splendid tradition going back to the period of the Upanishads, and to Gautama, Mandan Misra, Sureswar and Vachaspati, and continued through the many following centuries, Mithila is still capable of providing to the country teachers in the mould of its two modern illustrious sons. My association with Amaranatha Jha, as a student ended in 1934. Renewed after some twenty years, when he honoured us in Bihar by becoming the Chairman of our Public Service Commission, it finally ended in 1955 when he passed away. But so deep has been the impress of his personality on me that I continue to have a vivid recollection of every detail of my cherished association with him.

I have chosen Morality in Public Affairs as the subject of my lectures because looking at the national scene in the perspective of some forty five years experience of public service I feel that the subject, encompassing politics, administration, economic activity and academic life, is of crucial importance to our democratic system, to the future of our country, and generally to the quality of life of our people. It is also, I think particularly appropriate that the subject of morality in public affairs should be discussed at this centre of learning in Mithila – the land of Janak. The concept of philosopher – king was developed in Plato's Republic only in the 4th century B.C., and that too as a utopian vision, not as a realized or realizable ideal, as Plato himself discovered in Syracuse. Janak, king of Vedeha, on the other hand, appears to have been a much older historical figure; he is a major character not only in Valmiki's Ramayana, but figures prominently also in a long dialogue with Yagna Valkya in the Brihad – Aranyaka Upanishad, which is one of the most ancient, pre-Budhist Upanishads composed not later than the 7th century B.C. He represents the ideal of a ruler combining sovereign temporal powers with high spiritual attainments; one who performed the duties of a ruler with philosophic detachment, remaining above the allurements of power or wealth and following always the moral path. Even if the historical identity of Janak were questioned, the value of a most ancient tradition of a king ruling with spiritual enlightenment, and on righteous principles, remains a beacon light. And so also the story of Rama banishing his queen, the Princess of Mithila, because of a base slander by the citizens. It may be an idealized and romanticised view of the extent of the obligations of a ruler to honour public opinion, however ill-informed and wrong it may be. But there is an element of practical value in the story. Those in power have to so conduct themselves, and require their relatives to so conduct themselves, that charges of dishonest or unethical conduct may not be levelled against them with any conviction or credibility, even in an atmosphere of wide-spread distrust and suspicion, in which calumnies can get currency.

Now let us look at the present scene. There is a yawning and continuously widening gap between the uniquely noble ideals and values bequeathed to us by Mahatma Gandhi, the vision and aspirations of the Founding Fathers of the Constitution and the standards set by Jawahar Lal Nehru during the first seventeen years of our Independence, and the state of affairs that has come into being.

Inaugurating a conference of officers of the Central Bureau of Investigation in 1981, the Prime Minister said, with the authority of her great office, and with all the information available to her, that increasing corruption at various levels, not only of the bureaucracy and of political life but also in trade and commerce was a matter of major concern; that there was feeling amongst the people that persons known to be corrupt escaped the clutches of the law because of their position and influence while the small fry are caught in the net. Such an impression, the Prime Minister observed, was detrimental to the credibility of the Government as a whole. The occasion of her address did not call for a reference to the wider ambit of morality in public affairs, for instance, unprincipled change of party loyalty, which has been occurring so extensively.

In an article published on the last Independence Day, the Editor of a daily newspaper of national standing, known for his sense of responsibility and balanced judgement, wrote: "The State is now in peril. As the saying goes, if the fence begins to devour the field no one can possibly protect the crop. This is happening to the Indian State. Many of those incharge of its machinery have begun to use it to advance their petty interests at the cost of the future of the country. To say that corruption has become a way of life is to understate the magnitude of the problem. There was corruption before. It has now become loot. One of the well-known practitioners of this no longer fine art used to boast to business magnates, 'my predecessors were fools. They were content with a ten per cent share in your profits. I believe in taking 90 per cent leaving only 10 per cent for you'. The others are not so boastful but are equally venal and rapacious".

By all accounts, there has been a frightening growth of corruption in high places during the last decade. In the early seventies it is the corrupt who were singled out. Now it is the honest. Some degree of corruption always existed, and was considered unavoidable, combination of human nature with power being what it is. But it was unacceptable; it was not only deplored but denounced, and at least during the sixties there was a sincere effort to deal with corruption and the corrupt. There is now a resigned and cynical acceptance of corruption at all levels. A feeling of helplessness has permeated the public mind. There is a growing feeling that the malady is too far advanced to be curable; that the whole system has been contaminated and has got beyond redemption. Corruption has lately been institutionalized, and a new political culture has developed which considers fund raising an inescapable political necessity and even legitimate. Individual leaders and parties, and factions within parties, have been going about this business, uninhibited by moral restraints or external checks. The purposes are ostensibly political, but to quote the picturesque language of a leading industrialist "God alone knows what proportion of the funds go to the privy purse of the individuals making the collections". As a rule, no proper accounts are kept; there is no known accountability to the party, and there is, of course, no audit, and no public disclosure. The transactions are almost always covert, known only to those who pay and those who receive. Politics in US may not be a shining example of unfailing adherence to ethical principles, but, following the Watergate scandals, a number of reforms were introduced in election campaign practices. In addition to public financing of federal elections limitations were imposed on the amounts of private contributions, and public disclosure of the names of substantial contributors was required. New codes of ethics were passed by both Houses of Congress, which limit a Congressman's external income and require almost complete disclosure of personal assets. Specific prohibitions were prescribed, replacing loosely worded ones. A Code of Conduct was adopted in India too, and was placed on the table of the two Houses of Parliament in 1964. But it was applicable only to Ministers and was not extended to Legislators. Being associated with the drafting of the Code, I had the feeling at the time that it was not rigorous enough; but the Ministers who had to take the final decision had a better understanding of what was attainable in our political environment, for even the Code as it stands has in its essentials, been practically inoperative. The Code provides that no Minister should personally or through a member of his family accept a contribution for any purpose whether political or otherwise; if any purse or cheque intended for charitable body etc. or a political party is presented to him he should pass it on as soon as possible to the organization for which it is intended. It further provides that no Minister should associate himself with the raising of funds, except for the benefit of a registered society or charitable body or an institution or a political party. He should however ensure that such contributions are sent to a specified office bearer etc., of the organization and not to him. The basic objective is that a Minister should not keep with himself any contributions voluntarily sent to him, and that when he associates himself with a general appeal for funds he should not himself receive the contributions. It is a matter of common knowledge that the prevailing practice is the opposite of what the Code sought to achieve. The Code requires that a Minister shall disclose in detail his assets and liabilities to the Prime Minster or the Chief Minister as the case may be. I do not know how regularly and truthfully this is being done, but I have some reason to believe that this has not always been done and could not be done without self-incrimination, in many cases.

Within a few months of Independence, which it was hoped would usher Ram Rajya, a regime of high virtue, morality, and well-being of all, reports of serious abuse of power and corruption among political persons in some parts of the country began to reach Gandhiji. At this prayer meeting on 11th January, 1948, Gandhiji read extracts from a letter from Andhra in which the following, among other statements occurred: "People's representatives take money from the people to get licences – indulge in black marketing – corrupt the sources of justice and force the administrative machinery to get transfers of administrative personnel". The next day, Gandhiji quoted from a letter from an old friend, which painted an equally lurid picture of corrupt and larcenous conduct of those in whom the people had placed their confidence. Gandhiji's anguished reactions and warnings went unheeded, and corruption continued to grow though slowly and inconspicuously. In 1963, D. Sanjivaiyya, who was then President of the Indian National Congress, complained publicly at Indore that Congressmen who were paupers in 1947 had become millionaires and multi-millionaires and own palatial buildings and factories.....without having any ostensible sources of such income. This may have an exaggeration and a generalization from a few notorious instances. However, even the Santhanam Committee on Prevention of Corruption, recognised, though in more cautious language, the prevalence of corruption at the political level. That was in 1964. Since then, the scale of public expenditure and investment and the size of the government regulated economy have increased enormously, and with these, the opportunities to those with power or political influence for making illicit gains. Other political parties too, singly or in combination, have held office in several States, and for three years also at the Centre, and criticism earlier levelled mainly against the Congress Party has become applicable to political functionaries generally. In the meantime, the enforcement of anti-corruption laws against holders of high offices has become so feeble as to be hardly in evidence. At the same time so untrammelled by moral values has politics become that there are instances of the importance and claim to high office of a politician being measured not in terms of what he can contribute to the state or public weal, but the size of the funds he can covertly raise. In the circumstances, is it at all surprising that things have reached the pass they have? To the general debasement of the standard of political morality there are no doubt exceptions, and that provides ground for a hope that in spite of the prevailing feeling of cynicism and despondency all is not lost; that given an upsurge of public indignation and courageous resistance, and resolute action by those with the ultimate authority and power, we can break through the tangled web of corruption, influence peddling and use of official position and power for self-enrichment. I shall return to this point later.

There are unethical political practices, which are related to, but are distinct from criminal corruption. Members of the Legislatures changing their party affiliations without seeking legitimization by going back to the electorate has not been a new phenomenon in Indian politics; the one notable exception during the past decades, was Narendra Dev's decision to have his socialist followers seek fresh mandate when they broke away from the Congress Party. But after the 1967 elections, which resulted in no single party getting a majority in several States, defections began to occur with a frequency, and on a scale, which undermined political stability and started under-mining people's respect for politicians and confidence in the political process. A study made in the Ministry of Home Affairs in 1967 showed that in a substantial proportion of the cases, lure of office, and not any ideological inspiration, had been the motive for the defection. An all party Committee on Defections, including also Jaya Prakash Narain and Hridaynath Kunzru, and with the Union Home Minister, Y.B. Chavan, as Chairman, made a number of recommendations of a not too radical character; and the Committee's report was placed before Parliament and taken into consideration. Thereafter a Bill was drafted in 1970, and its provisions were discussed by the Prime Minister with leaders of political parties, but the views expressed showed considerable divergence.

With the dissolution of the Fourth Lok Sabha, this first attempt to curb defections by legislation came to an end. But in May, 1973, the Constitution (Thirty Seventh) Amendment Bill, with the same object, was introduced by the Home Minister and referred to a Joint Select Committee of the two Houses. But before the Committee could submit its report, Emergency was declared, and with it this second attempt at legislation also proved abortive, the Bill lapsing with the dissolution of the Fifth Lok Sabha in January, 1977. However, defections continued; for instance in one of the North-Eastern States, the Congress Party, which had come to command an overwhelming majority by accretion of strength through defections, changed over wholesale to the Janata Party. In 1978, yet another anti-defection (48th Constitutional Amendment) Bill was sought to be introduced but because of strong opposition within the Janata Party itself, the proposed legislation was withdrawn. So Janata became even with the Congress.

After 1978, there has been no concrete move to introduce legislation, though there has been some talk about the initiative by two successive Election Commissions to have such legislation introduced. During all these years, defections have gone on unabashedly. There have been instances of members of the Assembly defecting and redefecting several times; and I had the bizarre experience of swearing in some such defectors in successive Ministries. What happened a few months ago in a northern state is too well-known, and too fresh in public memory, to require detailed mention in this lecture. All I would say is that it has shown the abysmal depth to which political standards have sunk. Right from the deliberations of the Committee on Defections in 1967-68, the arguments advanced against stringent legislation have been the importance of the individual members, freedom of association, and the need to allow healthy polarization of political forces. In fact, defections have had little to do with either, and have continued to be patently unprincipled and self-serving. To ask for a perfect legislation in such a matter is to ask for the impossible; even an imperfect legislation would be preferable to total absence of regulation.

In the vicious chain of corruption, unethical politicking and administrative degradation, defections are an exceedingly important link. Support is bought and sold; a large proportion of members of the Legislature, sometimes even a half, are appointed to Ministerial offices; and many others are given offices of profit in corporate State undertakings. The Committee on Defections had recommended that the size of a Ministry should be limited to ten per cent of the strength of the Assembly, and to eleven per cent where there is a bicameral Legislature, or fifteen per cent where membership of the Assembly does not exceed a hundred. But the recommendation has remained on paper and ministries of totally disproportionate sizes and wholly unjustified in terms of public interest or sound government continue to be formed. No parliamentary democracy has witnessed such a phenomenon, which is bound to bring the whole political system into ill-repute and to create a feeling of revulsion towards the manner in which it is being operated.

I am not in a position to give the authoritative up-to-date figures of defections and of the offices with which the defectors were rewarded. However, I quote from Dr. Subhash C. Kashyap's book "Ministers and Legislators": According to some studies on the subject during 1967-73 some 45 State Governments, were toppled in quick succession with as many as 2700 cases of defections by legislators. Over 60 per cent legislators all over the country were involved, many of them as changing their affiliation more than once, and some of them as many as four or five times within a year. On an average more than one legislator changed his label each day, and for sometime, again on an average, one Government collapsed each month. It is significant that some 212 defectors reached, Ministerial gaddis and some fifteen became Chief Ministers". These figures would be much higher if the statistics for the last 9 years were also available, but even the old figures give a clear enough idea of the dimension of defections and their destructive effect on political stability and morality, and even on a modicum of decency.

Leaving aside the question of legislation, the question of professional ethics for politicians – legislators and others – is worth some comment. There is a code of professional ethics for doctors and lawyers, but none for politicians, who after all, largely determine the conditions which vitally affect all sections of society. In the older parliamentary democracies norms of political behaviour have come to be accepted as conventions, evolved through experience, and carrying the sanction of public opinion. But the position in India is so markedly different, that it would perhaps be an act of self-deception if at this stage a code of conduct were framed for politicians generally, when we know of the fate of the Code of Conduct for Ministers. In the circumstances, the failure after 1978 to resume efforts to enact legislation must be a cause for concern. Is it that while defections are disapproved in principle they are welcome in practice notwithstanding the damage they have been causing to the parliamentary system and political ethics?

A discussion of morality in public affairs has, obviously to cover the public services, whose moral standards as much as, if not more than efficiency affect the lives of the people. In fact, integrity is an essential ingredient of true efficiency. Corruption in the bureaucracy is not of post-Independence origin. Kautilya's Arthasastra – which may not have been composed or compiled in the 4th century B.C., but which, according to the judgement of most competent scholars certainly dates to the pre-Gupta period – deals in detail with corruption amongst government servants and even mentions about forty ways of embezzlement, some of them with a very modern rings: "raw materials that are not paid for are entered;......prices of commodities enhanced; ... misrepresentation of the source of income; incongruity in representing the work turned out; misrepresentation of prices of commodities; making use of false weights and measures" etc. However, the Arthashastra also recommends effective steps for prevention and punishment of corruption. Skipping over the intervening centuries, one may refer to the prevalence of oppressing corruption and extortion by the British in India during the 18th century, and the emergency of "English Nabobs" with enormous fortunes collected in India. However, reform started during the regime of Cornwallis, and in the 19th century there came into existence higher civil services which were professionally irreproachable and maintained the highest degree of integrity. With some little erosion during the Second World War this standard was maintained well into the present century. After the departure of the British personnel in 1947, the Indians in these services, and the members of the successor services, continued the pre-Independence standards of integrity and probity; but during the last 15 years or so, the standards have fallen progressively, and one now hears from responsible persons stories of corruption even amongst a section of senior civil servants, and of general laxity in the matter of acceptance of gifts, other favours, and lavish hospitality from industrialist, businessmen, contractors and others who seek favours from the administration. The majority, I believe, are still uncorrupted, but the general weakening of the moral fibre has led to a growing reluctance to function, and to advise the political executive, with independence and objectivity even when issues of integrity or justice are involved. There are still civil servants who have the courage and integrity of mind to act and advise fearlessly; but this is a dwindling section of the services. The Prime Minister is reported recently to have asked civil servants to tender honest advice, fearlessly. It may have effect at the Centre; but in the political and administrative culture that has developed, it is doubtful if many in the States would do so, or if they did, they would not in many cases incur the displeasure of Ministers or other influential persons, and might have to face unpleasant consequences – which, in my view they should face rather than compromise. We have travelled far from the time when, speaking in the Constituent Assembly, Sardar Patel could say: "I have told them (Secretaries to the Government) that if you do not give your honest opinion for fear that it will displease your Minister then you had better go. I will bring another Secretary".

In the political environment to which I have referred, and with the decline in the standards of the senior civil services, corruption in the bureaucracy at the lower levels has assumed such proportions that there is now an almost universal belief that nothing can be had without giving some kind of illegal gratification. I have been told by a middle-level manufacturer that he has to pay bribes at eighteen stages to get through a perfectly unexceptionable proposal. A businessman has told me that his legal agents find it far cheaper, and quicker, to have his income-tax return cleared through payment of a bribe, than to go in appeal against an unfair assessment. Corruption in the lower, and even middle levels of the bureaucracy is not a new malady; but its scale and ubiquitousness certainly are.

How has this state of affairs come about? Prolonged inflation, which has drastically reduced the real income of the salaried classes has been one cause: the insidious effect of such inflation on social behaviour and personal morality is well-known. But the effect has been aggravated by the phenomenal rise in professional incomes, and the vast incomes earned by those operating the "black" economy. It is unrealistic to expect the salariat to accept austere living in an atmosphere in which other comparable sections of society are in a position to amass large fortunes and indulge in ostentatious consumption. The effect of decline of moral standards in political life has been another important factor. Once the tracks are made by leaders of society, the "big people", others always tend to follow. This has been the age-long tradition of India; as the Bhagwadgita says:

Yad-Yad acarati sresthas, tad-tad eve taro janah
Sa yat pramanam kurute, lokas tad anuvartate

(Verse 21, Chapter 3)

Whatsoever a high placed person does the same is done by others as well. Whatever standards he sets the people follow.

Looking at the impunity with which those with power and influence can disregard not only the expected standards of conduct, but even the laws of the land, the lower level public servants may well be reminded of Swift's remarks that laws and regulations are like a spider's web, which catches the small insects, but which the big ones always break through. Not that the web now is strong enough to catch even the bulk of the small creatures. The real point, however, is that even petty corruption cannot be effectively checked unless there is unquestionable integrity at the political and higher civil service levels, and there is improvement in the moral tone of society.

At the root of a great deal of corruption, and as a major factor in the awesome dimensions of the flourishing black economy, is the way the electoral mechanism has been functioning. Elections to the Lok Sabha and to the State Assemblies have been allowed to become too expensive; and the expenditure has gone on increasing from one election to another. I remember that while on an official visit in 1961, to a State in the grip of a mid-term election fever, the then Home Minister, Lal Bahadur Shastri, remarked that, with numerous jeeps churning the dust-tracks, and the peace of the country-side destroyed by the incessant blare of loudspeakers, the style of electioneering appeared to be following the American model, and had become totally discordant with Indian conditions, and the lives of our poverty-stricken masses. Indeed Gandhiji himself had said in 1946, that congressmen should not have to spend money on elections; and it may be remembered that it is from Congress that most of the democratic and secular parties have sprung. Election campaigns have, since 1961, become far more extravagant, and have begun to take recourse to new devices, such as those of commercial advertising. May I, by the way, mention that while flying by helicopter over certain areas of North

Assam, Shri Fakhruddin Ali Ahmed, as President of India, used to point out to me, with some degree of nostalgia, certain roads on which, he said, he used to travel on a bicycle to campaign for Congress candidates during the pre-Independence elections. One cannot, it has to be recognized, put the clock back in such matters; we have many more roads and automobiles, and conditions and style of life generally have changed. This would necessarily be reflected in the way election campaigns are conducted. And yet there is a great deal in the current practices that is wrong, and subversive of political health and morality. I quote from President V.V. Giri's message to the nation on the eve of Independence Day in 1974:

"It has been a most regrettable development in recent years that money power has come to play such a dominant role in the elections to legislatures. This, to my mind is at the root of corruption and corrupt influences in our public life. People may lose faith in cherished democratic values if leaders of all political parties do not take prompt corrective measures to remedy the situation by joint consultations".

Leaders of political parties have taken no such action; there have been two more general elections, and the evils to which President Giri had drawn attention have, if anything, got aggravated. Estimates of costs of elections vary, but it is generally agreed that the expenses run into several lakhs for a Lok Sabha seat, and those for an Assembly seat are in proportion. The prescribed statutory limits do not result in limiting the expenses, but only in an illegal and unethical act, as in most cases, the returns filed grossly underestimate the expenses incurred.

That there has been inflow of big, mostly black money, in elections during all these 30 years does not admit of the slightest doubt; nor does the fact that the amounts are now vastly bigger than they used to be in the 1950s and 60s. There is a matching of demand and supply; political parties and candidates need large, and at successive elections larger funds, and industrialists and businessmen, contractors and smugglers, tax-evaders, and unscrupulous fortune seekers – mostly operators of the black economy – are often only too willing to provide those funds. And more; for there is no public disclosure or audit of the funds received through these transactions, and personal greed may not unoften be coupled with electoral necessity.

On the other side, many of those who treat their contributions as investment; they expect, and get, a return in the form of "sympathetic consideration", if not as straight favour. They feel relatively secure in carrying on their dishonest activities; and they expect, not always without reason, to influence public policies and decisions. There are, fortunately, some who observe proper ethics in the conduct of their business or industry, and who make contributions to the election funds of a party with whose political ideology or programme they are in sympathy. But these are honourable exceptions, which do not alter the general picture.

When Ministers collect funds for elections or other political purposes some public servants may also get involved. At best they may refrain from advising against which they consider harmful or improper; at worst, they may actively facilitate such action. Thus governmental integrity is affected at different levels. I came across some cases in the North-eastern region in which Ministers, with the collusion of some civil servants, had sold, in eastern India, controlled commodities allotted to their States, in order, it was hinted, to meet urgent demands for funds for political purposes. But in fairness to the North-eastern region I must add that the illicit transactions there are, after all, rather modest compared to those in the more "advanced" parts of the country.

It would be beyond the scope of these lectures to discuss remedies for these grave ills, which are poisoning the political and governmental system. But I have myself no doubt that the circumstances call for urgent consideration of the whole problem of election expenses, including, in particular, the question of funding of Lok Sabha and State Assembly elections from the public exchequer. Other democratic countries have introduced such funding, and it should not be impossible to work out a practicable scheme in our country. Some intricate questions will, no doubt, arise, and any scheme that it evolved may not be free from one kind of objection or another. But unavailability of a perfect solution is often the hypocritical excuse of those interested in inaction and in maintaining the existing state of affairs. It has to be remembered that in a democracy the legitimacy of a government depends, to a large extent on the cleanness of elections, and if the elections are vitiated by the tainted sources of their financing, the faith of the people in the political system itself may be shaken, apart from perpetuating the baneful influence of ill-gotten wealth and politics and government.

II

A review of standards of conduct in public affairs, whether in the political or the administrative sphere, cannot be complete without looking into norms and patterns of behaviour in industrial and commercial life, and in the means and methods adopted generally in pursuit of material gains. There can be little doubt that the strong temptations that are offered to persons holding public offices, and to those in a position to influence such persons, are a crucial factor in the rampant corruption, and in lowering the moral tone of society. The Santhanam Committee had observed that the adoption of preventive measures against those who habitually corrupt public servants (and the committee was of the definite view that Ministers are and should be treated as public servants) would strike at the evil from the other end, it had unreservedly endorsed the view that the existence of large amounts of black money was a major source of corruption and it had proceeded to make certain suggestions, which were either not accepted, or having been accepted, were not put into effect with resolution. In the meantime, the growth, accumulation and power of black money, and the ramifications of the black economy have assumed far more disturbing proportions, widely debasing ethical norms, and eating into the vitals of our socio-economic and political systems. It would be unrealistic to expect any substantial improvement in public morality, so long as this state of affairs continues. It is primarily in this context that I propose to speak about the black or – to use an euphemistic word – the unofficial economy.

Different methodologies have been adopted to estimate the size of unaccounted incomes, and of the assets held clandestinely, and the estimates therefore vary considerably. Further, the estimates reflect changes in the scope and nature of economic activity and in fiscal and monetary policies over the years.

Kaldor's estimate of black income in 1953-54 was 6 per cent of the GNP, and in 1968-69 the figure was estimated as having risen to 9 per cent. The latest estimates vary within a very wide range, the uppermost figure being as high as 50 per cent of the GNP. According to the best judgement available to me, the figure is about 30 per cent, which with our present GNP would work out to an enormous sum – something of the order of thirty four thousand crores, at current prices. Leaving aside differences in quantification, a recent judgement of the Supreme Court provides a general indication of the magnitude, boldness and ingenuity of black money operations. This is what the Chief Justice of the Supreme Court had to say in the case of Sanchaita Investments (of Calcutta): "The partners of the firm have become millionaires overnight, clerks and chemists that they and some of their agents were in 1975, today they own properties which will put a prince to shame. 'Rags to riches' this is how one may justly describe the story of quick and easy enrichment. There is no question that this vast wealth has been acquired by the firm by generating and circulating black money". The firm was paying interest to investors at 48 per cent per annum, and the investors in turn were in all probability keeping the income from this source out of their income tax returns. Obviously, it is only through financing of illegal economic activities that a company can pay interest at such a high rate.

I need not speak at any length about the various devices adopted, and manipulations practiced for earning black incomes, or about the labyrinthine character of the unofficial economy. Tax evasion on a large scale both fuels this economy and makes its material fruits available to its operators, and their collaborators. With negligible exceptions, those engaged in business and industry resort to evasion of tax through concealment, falsification of accounts, and the like. There can be no doubt that a large part of taxable income annually escapes the tax net, if this could be prevented the bottom would be knocked out of the black economy. Evasion of tax is not a particularly Indian phenomenon, it occurs in most countries. As the English classicist and poet, A.E. Housman had said, "passion for truth is the feeblest in man", and many people in various parts of the world try to conceal their true taxable income, if they can. It is the scale and pervasive practice of concealment in India, its critical role in the black economy, and its linkage with black politics and bureaucratic corruption that are a cause for deep concern.

Gross under invoicing of exports, over-invoicing of imports, and incomes saved through these fraudulent devices, necessarily result in evasion of income tax and other applicable taxes. Further, as the Direct Taxes Enquiry Committee (headed by K.N. Wanchoo, a former judge of the Supreme Court) has pointed out, these processes lead to building up of illegal and clandestine foreign exchange held abroad in various forms; and this, as Dr. K.N. Kabra has pointed out in his recent, informative book "The Black Economy in India", results in "the oddity that a country, where capital, and more particularly foreign exchange reserves, are scarce, becomes a defacto lender of aid and capital to economically advanced, wealthier nations, with the concealed out-flow of funds". Exports by ghost firms and non-realisation of the price in India, and using the proceeds in a clandestine manner are another constituent of the black economy. There is smuggling of silver and narcotics out of India, and the smuggling of gold into India, and the latter particularly is an important factor in our black economy. Illegal transfers of antiques to foreign countries, and acquisition of foreign exchange from Indian residents abroad and making payment in India also contribute to the operations of the black economy.

There are unauthorized factories working in different parts of the country, there is extensive cornering of stocks, hoarding, and black marketing, adulteration and sale of spurious stuff, fakes and imitations, and ignoring of prescribed standards, all these activities generally violating or circumventing controls and regulations. The incomes earned by these dishonest means obviously do not enter the official accounts, they add to the sum of black money, and through reinvestment usually extend the ambit of the black economy. Most of these activities are carried on with minimal risk, if not virtual immunity from penal action, as the small number of criminal prosecutions show. It is often through corrupting public servants, or because of influential political support that this freedom from effective preventive or punitive action is secured.

There is an unofficial economy even in developed western countries, but not only is its size, except perhaps in Italy, much smaller, but its character also differs from that of ours. It is made up mostly of transactions in narcotic trade, gambling, "loansharking", drawing unemployment insurance benefits while having some income from unrecognized employment, and what is called "moonlighting", which consists of persons in regular but low-grade employment taking up a second job in off-duty hours. These activities do result in some loss of tax revenue and some underestimation of the GNP; but for the rest, their effect on the economy, or on the working of the political system, is not very significant. In India, on the other hand, we have, as the Direct Taxes Enquiry Committee had said, a dual economy, an official economy functioning overboard, and operating generally in conformity with laws and governmental regulations, and a parallel economy operating in competition with the official economy and at odds with it. Its repercussions are indeed multiple, and it affects in various ways the lives of the people. Large-scale tax evasion leads to a higher rate of tax, increasing the burden on the honest tax-payer, and reducing the revenue resources available to government for financing planned economic and social development. The objects of governmental controls and regulations, and or credit and fiscal policies are frustrated to a significant extent, inflationary pressures are increased, investment of black money in real estate pushes up land prices, in and around urban centres abnormally and efforts to reduce income disparities and gross inequalities in society through taxation are largely set at naught. In brief, the black economy in India has extremely harmful economic and social consequences, in addition to being the principal source of corruption, political and administrative, and generally lowering the moral tone of society.

Before I deal with government's reaction to the growth of the black economy, I shall touch briefly on the reasoning of its apologists. They argue that the evation of tax is the result of excessively high marginal rates of taxation, and that higher the rate of taxation the greater is the gain from evasion, and therefore the willingness to accept the risks of penal action. In short high taxation is an invitation to evasion. Further, they attribute to the incentives of black incomes the expansion of private investment, and therefore of acceleration of economic growth. And they blame the existence of numerous controls and regulations for the disposition to circumvent them. This is a warped line of reasoning, and one that a society with any ethical values, even apart from social commitments, cannot accept. If there were no taxes, there would, of course, be no evasion: if all controls were abolished the question of violating or circumventing them would not arise. Even if there were no laws there would be crime, laws only make crimes punishable, and act as a deterrent. We have opted for a mixed economy, and our economic affairs ought to be ordered with the rationality and imagination necessary to allow the private sector to function efficiently, without recourse to dishonest methods. This would apply to reasonable returns on investment and rewards for enterprise, to the rates of taxes, and to the determination of what controls on economic activities are essential socially and for planned development, and which controls hamper these activities without serving any public purpose. There are perhaps controls which cannot be justified by these tests, and the lowering of tax rates may decrease the temptation for evasion. However, these are matters for economic experts –and I have no pretension to any economic expertise-to advise on, and for the political executive and the legislature to decide on a view of the totality of legitimate political and social considerations. But, obviously, even by remote implication, dishonesty cannot be accepted as a permissible factor in achieving any economic goals.

In stating certain general propositions, I do not suggest that it is unsound economic or fiscal policies and excessive governmental regulation that are the principal causes of the growth of the parallel economy, or the true explanation of pursuit of black incomes.

While the bulk of our people remain abysmally poor and deprived, there has been, particularly among the privileged minority, a conspicuous growth of acquisitiveness, in many cases bordering on rapacity. There is feverish pursuit of wealth, untrammelled by moral considerations, or those of social responsibility. Part of the explanation may be sociological: to quote Prof. J.K. Galbraith, "As capitalism emerges from feudalism it is characterized by an anarchic rapacity that the people of advanced capitalist countries cannot understand". Money has increasingly become a major criterion of a person's social status, and many with illgotten wealth go about as leaders of society wielding power and influence, reminding one of Toqueville's observation about" an odious connection ... between the ideas of turpitude and power, unworthiness and success, utility and dishonour". How has such a situation come about? This country had become free under the leadership of Mahatma Gandhi, who incessantly emphasized the supreme importance of means, and preached the idea of trusteeship of wealth, and who symbolized in his own life the ancient Vedantic and Jain doctrines of aparigrah – the opposite of covetousness. But while remembering Gandhian ideals, one must accept that it would be unrealistic to expect the general run of humanity to be guided completely by those ideals in their practical life. Human beings, as they are, do seek material possessions, and need economic incentives, and altruism does not usually occupy the foreground of their mind. There is, in fact, a view that economic energy with political liberty tends to engender some immorality and selfish advancement of private good at the expense of public weal. Perhaps, this is what Nehru had in mind, when speaking in the Lok Sabha in 1961 he said "Corruption, if I may say so is a result of the democratic process, and I am a little afraid that as the process grows, corruption is going down to the village". (Incidentally Nehru had said at the Karachi Congress, some decades earlier, that if capital punishment were to be abolished, he would insist that an exception should be made in regard to corrupt public men and officers and that they be hanged by the nearest lamp post). But one could have reasonably hoped that the Gandhian legacy would have exercised a modicum of influence, especially on the affluent and the privileged, leading to some inner restraint and human decency, some regard for the larger interests of society, and respect for the laws of the land. Why is it that even between these modest expectations and the present reality there is such a wide gap? Why is it that among the functioning democracies, with capitalist or mixed economies, India should become notable for the size, extraordinary tentacles and influence of its black economy? Has this come about because of the state of our politics and administration, coupled with moral lethargy in society?

Since Independence there have been several inquiries into our system of taxation and tax administration, starting with the Taxation Enquiry Commission in 53-54: and ending with the Direct Taxes Enquiry Committee (presided over by K.N. Wanchoo, a former judge of the Supreme Court) which went into the problems of taxation, tax administration, evasion etc. in great depth, and made interim recommendations in 1971 and submitted its final report in 1978. In between, the Santhanam Committee had also made some recommendations in 1964. There has therefore been ample investigation of the system of taxation and tax administration, and there is a large body of well informed, well considered recommendations for action. And yet many of the recommendations have not been accepted, and action taken on others has so far has been inadequate and ineffective, and tax evasion, which is at the heart of the black economy, continues virtually unabated. In fact some of the measures taken by the government have legitimized black incomes and conduced to their perpetuation.

The Santhanam Committee had recommended that, as in some other countries, income tax returns and assessments should not be treated as secret; but they have, in effect, continued to be so treated, inspite of a guarded relaxation of the relevant provision of the law. In this matter, as in many others, a more open government would curb dishonest activities and improper administrative decisions. But as far as I know there is no disposition to withdraw the blanket of secrecy from a great deal that in a democracy need not be kept out of public view, that in fact, the people have the right to know. Incidentally, one does not know the esoteric reasoning that lies behind the practice of treating private lockers in banks as sacrosanct, even though it is well known that a great deal of black money and other assets dishonestly acquired and held, such as bullion and precious stones, are kept in such lockers.

Evasion of tax is a penal offence, and occasionally one reads about searches and seizures, and more rarely even of prosecutions. But in relation to the extent of evasion these operations are too few to have such deterrent effect, and they certainly fail to assure the public mind that a determined effort is being made to enforce the law. There are also reports that there are informal instructions that in certain classes of cases the officials concerned should obtain prior clearance from the Minister, which, if true, cannot but hamper the independent exercise of discretion by the officials empowered by the law, and would lend support to the widely held belief that when it comes to rich tax evaders, political and other improper considerations influence the decision. In certain other countries tax evasion is treated as a serious offence, and is punished with imprisonment in addition to the levy of a financial penalty. Our failure to deal sternly with an offence with such harmful social and economic consequences is only partly attributable to bureaucratic corruption; the real explanation lies deep in the country's politics.

The attempt to bring out black money after Independence started with a Voluntary Disclosure Scheme in 1951; and it was followed by another in 1965. There was yet another Voluntary Disclosure Scheme in 1975, as also a legislation in 1976 for the forfeiture of property acquired by smuggling and foreign exchange manipulations; but these measures could touch only the fringe of the problem of black money. The Direct Taxes Enquiry Committee has observed that, "These were more or less schemes for converting black money into white on payment of what turned out to be in most cases a small amount of conscience money. Disclosures made in the name of minors, ladies and benamidars have, on the other hand, contributed to perpetuating evasion... We were informed by the Central Board of Direct Taxes that there were several instances of the same set of persons taking advantage of all three schemes, which would belie the theory that such schemes help to rehabilitate the repentant tax-evader who is desirous of mending his ways". The Committee was therefore strongly opposed to schemes of voluntary disclosure, now or in future, observing that they "place a premium on fraud and are unfair to honest tax-payers". Incidentally, it is highly improbable that any political black incomes were expected to be, or were disclosed under any of the voluntary disclosure schemes.

The Special Bearer Bonds Scheme of 1981 was a new type of voluntary disclosure scheme, being in the nature of public borrowing from black money. It is reported to have yielded about a thousand crore rupees and to have helped in reducing the budgetary gap. It is also claimed to have the merit of transferring to government, for a period of ten years, control over the amount covered by the bonds. But it is open to all the objections, moral and those of ineffectuality, in curbing black incomes, that have been mentioned against earlier schemes of voluntary disclosures. It was in some ways even more attractive, to those with black money as no tax is payable on the money invested in the bonds, or on the interest (though at a low rate) earned on them.

The Direct Taxes Enquiry Committee had expressed itself as being firmly of the view that the malady of black money could be effectively checked only by drastic measures like demonetization, which would force the hoarders and tax evaders to disclose their ill-gotten gains. The value of demonetization as a powerful psychological deterrent is evident; and as 100 rupee notes account for about one half of the currency, and 50 rupee notes about one sixth, its practicability if confined to currency of these denominations should not be seriously doubted. But between demonetization, and schemes of voluntary disclosure and special Bearer Bonds, the Government had chosen these latter. This is likely to strengthen the cynical feeling that the black economy has come to stay, and that those with the power to curb it may not make genuine efforts to do so, as they are among the major beneficiaries.

Is the inadequate action to unearth black money and other black assets, and to curb generation of black incomes in future only the reflection of the personality of a "soft state", to use Gunnar Myrdal's words? To some extent it may be so. It is interesting that a small study group, composed mainly of British officials, set up by Lord Wavell to study India's likely post-war problems, had produced in 1944, a paper in which it had recorded the conclusion, while comparing the prospects of India and China, that China which had been through the fire of both internal revolution and external invasion was tougher and India was softer. What is more notable is the fact that Sir Ardeshir Dalal, then a Member of the Viceroy's Council had expressed agreement with that conclusion. The softness or toughness of a state however, is a cultural and political matter, not a moral issue. Moreover, a democratic, federal state is disinclined in normal times to take recourse to very harsh measures. In formulating policies and legislation in such a state there is an attempt to accommodate and reconcile the divergent groups and regional interests, and to govern on the basis of the attainable consensus and consent within the party in power, and in the country as a whole. But when a policy or its administration is influenced not by such a philosophy of democracy, or by the requirements of working a mixed economy, but even partially by considerations of personal gain, or illegitimate political profit, the question of public morality does obviously arise.

Prof. J.K. Galbraith has expressed the view that, "Between the modern corporation and the modern state there is a deeply symbiotic relationship based on shared power and shared reward". The tolerance and accommodation shown, all these years, to the operators of the parallel economy, and the periodic legitimisation of black incomes, do suggest the existence of some such relationship in India; in fact some of it exists in a far grosser form than in most other democratic countries. Those who are able to establish close links with the political and bureaucratic hierarchies are among the most flourishing operators of the parallel economy: the links are, as a rule, venal, and they affect economic decisions and administrations out of all proportion to the sums that are passed through these relationships. There is a wide-spread belief that in many economic transactions involving exercise of governmental or bureaucratic power – especially discretionary ones – there is some form of dishonesty, and that in foreign contracts the amounts involved in dishonest deals are in proportion to the value of the contracts. May I in this connection mention that while giving evidence before a Senate Committee in 1975, Haughton, Chairman of the Lockheed Aircraft Corporation had stated that "If you get the contract it is pretty good evidence that payments had to be made".

The Santhanam Committee was of the view that in Indian conditions, companies should not be allowed to participate in politics through their donations, and had concluded "that nothing but a total ban on all donations by incorporated bodies to political parties and purposes will clear the atmosphere". This view was eventually accepted and in the Companies (Amendment) Act, 1969, a provision (section 293-A) was made prohibiting any contribution to a political party, or for any political purposes to any individual or body, and making contravention punishable with fine and, in the case of individuals in default, with up to three years imprisonment. As things have developed, this attempt to close a small open inlet, has been followed by opening of flood-gates to unhampered and undisclosed flow of black money to political parties and for political purposes, without any public accountability.

I was a member of the Santhanam Committee, and I regret that we should have failed to recognize fully the strength, and unhealthy character, of the emerging economic and political forces that, in the coming years, were so completely to change the shape of things. We thought that the standards, and the general climate of the early sixties would be there for all times to come; and the earnest endeavours that were being made to eradicate such corruption and lack of probity as did exist, would be continued until the results aimed at were achieved. There were moral lapses in the conduct of public affairs but they were not considered at all acceptable, or even tolerable.

The 1950s were a period of relatively clean politics and administration. The momentum of the idealism that had marked the freedom struggle was still there; the light that had emanated from Gandhiji had not entirely faded out; there was the great authority and influence of Jawaharlal Nehru, and his inspiring example; and political parties were still concerned with ideologies, and had the discipline which goes with ideological politics. And when there was deviation from high standards, serious consequences followed. This is exemplified in the Mundra case. On certain allegations being made in Parliament, a Commission of Inquiry, with M.C. Chagla, the Chief Justice of the Bombay High Court as the sole member, was appointed, and on his holding the Union Finance Minister, T.T. Krishnamachari, "constitutionally" responsible for certain transactions of the L.I.C. with Mundra firms, Krishnamachari resigned from office. He was known for his ability and there was no doubt about his personal integrity; and yet it was considered proper for him to quit his high office.

The sixties about which I can speak from first hand knowledge, were a period when determined efforts were made to check corruption and unethical behaviour in public affairs. The appointment of the Santhanam Committee in 1962 was a major step in this direction, and its recommendations covered wide ground. I have already referred to some of the recommendations; there were many others, designed to promote integrity in administration, and among public servants. On many of these recommendations, action was taken; for instance, a Vigilance Commission for public employees was set up; the Central Bureau of Investigation was strengthened, and conduct rules for government servants made more stringent. A Code of Conduct for Ministers, as mentioned earlier, was laid down, even though the committee's recommendations regarding instituting a special procedure for inquiry into specific allegations against Ministers was not accepted.

A Commission of Inquiry with S.R. Das, a retired Chief Justice of the Supreme Court, was appointed to inquire into allegations of corruption against Pratap Singh Kairon, made in a memoranda submitted to the President, and following certain adverse findings of the Commission, Kairon had to resign. It is significant that the Commission had not held him directly guilty of abuse of power or of corruption; and it was his failure to prevent his sons and relatives from exploiting his position and influence that was held against him; and that was considered sufficient to call for his resignation.

In the course of investigation of a case against a mining

lessee, the Central Bureau of Investigation, came across entries in the lessee's book showing payment of Rs. 10,000/- to K.D. Malaviya, apparently for political purposes. S.K. Das, a judge of the Supreme Court was appointed to conduct an inquiry into the matter and his findings were adverse. Malaviya had to resign from the office of Cabinet Minister of the Union.

In 1964 on memoranda being received by the President containing allegations of abuse of office by the Chief Minister, Biju Patnaik, the Deputy Chief Minister, Biren Mitra and certain other ministers, the Central Bureau of Investigation was asked to make an informal scrutiny of the relevant records. The Bureau reported that there was need for further inquiries on a number of points. The matter was then examined by a sub-committee of the Union Cabinet, which held some of the orders and actions of the Chief Minister and Deputy Chief Minister as having been "improper, irregular, unwise, indiscreet or imprudent"; but on the material available it absolved Biju Patnaik of having derived any pecuniary benefits from the transactions in question. However the sub-committee proceeded to express "their profound concern at the picture emerging as a whole from the series of such individual transactions in many fields of activities of the State Government, of improper use of authority by leaders of the Government". The essence of the sub-committee's censure was that even if there had been no corruption in the commonly understood sense of the term the Ministers had shown themselves to be insensitive to problems of conflict of interests. The Prime Minister, Lal Bahadur Shastri, considered this sufficient for indicating, though obliquely, that Patnaik should resign from the office of Chairman of the State Planning Board and Mitra from that of Chief Minister in which he had succeeded Patnaik; and both did resign.

The most notable aspects of all the 3 cases I have cited are that when specific allegations were made by responsible public men in memoranda submitted to the Central authorities, serious notice was taken, and purposive action initiated; that all those who had to resign belonged to the party in power at the Centre; and the lapses were judged by very high ethical standards. There was yet another case in 1965 which conformed to the same pattern. Signed memoranda were received by the Prime Minister making certain specific complaints against a son of T.T. Krishnamachary, who had become Union Finance Minister again and casting reflections also on the conduct of the Minister. The Prime Minister proposed to send the papers to the Chief Justice of India for advice whether any action was called for; T.T. Krishnamachary was opposed to any such scrutiny and considered it more honourable to resign. Before I proceed further, may I say a word about the need to have a firm convention, if not a law against a person who had to demit office for unethical or improper conduct being appointed as a Minister again. K.D. Malaviya too was appointed as Minister after an interval of some years, as was Biju Patnaik though as a member of a different party.

During the Sixties and later, a number of Commissions were appointed by various State Governments to inquire into the conduct of former ministers during the period they had held office; and as far as I am aware those whose conduct was inquired into belonged to political parties other than those of the Ministers appointing the Commissions. In such cases, the question of political motivation is always raised, even though the Commissions themselves may be, and have in fact been, objective and fair and have also enunciated sound ethical principles for judging the actions of those holding high offices. It may be worthwhile evolving a procedure, applicable both to the Union and the States, which would free the appointment of a Commission from the suspicion or complaint of politically motivated harassment of a former Minister. I may add that the relevant recommendations of the Santhanam Committee and the Lok Pal scheme had sought to take care of this problem.

The crowning, but unsuccessful effort towards checking corruption and misconduct among Ministers and Central Civil servants was the introduction of legislation in 1969 to establish independent OMBUDSMAN type of authorities, under the designation of Lok Pal and Lok Ayukt. The legislation had been drafted broadly on the basis of recommendations made by the Administrative Reforms Commission but with a more restricted scope; and after it had been considered by Joint Select Committee, it was passed by the Lok Sabha. But while it was under consideration of the Rajya Sabha, the Lok Sabha was dissolved and the Bill lapsed. With some minor modifications, it was introduced in the Lok Sabha again in 1971, and it too lapsed on the dissolution of the 5th Lok Sabha at the beginning of 1977. Once again, legislation with much wider scope, bringing within its ambit, the Prime Minister, the Chief Ministers and Members of Parliament was introduced in the Lok Sabha in 1978, when the Janata Party was in power, and was referred to a Joint Select Committee, which recommended deletion or modification of some of its major provisions. The debate that followed the receipt of the Select Committee's recommendations had remained inconclusive when in July, 1979, the Janata Ministry resigned, and with the dissolution of the Lok Sabha soon after, this Bill too lapsed. Thus ended the move, initiated eleven years earlier, to set up an independent authority to deal with corruption and misconduct among the holders of the highest political and civil service offices; and since then the whole matter remains consigned to limbo. It would be a travesty of the truth to say that the need for an institution like that of Lokpal has disappeared, and too cynical to infer that the problem of corruption is now regarded as having become so intractable that it would be futile to attempt a remedy.

It would have been far more pleasant for me to present a picture of the country's impressive achievements in many spheres. Our external relations have been conducted with wisdom and vision, and are rooted in principles which have stood the test of time, and are now recognized practically all over the world as factors contributing to peace and evolution of a just international order. We have faced problems of security, external and internal, with courage and self-confidence. We have built a sound infrastructure through development of energy and communications and vast expansion of trained manpower, particularly scientific and technical. Our progress in agriculture is being cited as an example for others to follow. Also in the field of industries, including those requiring the use of modern technology, there has been notable advance; and we have developed managerial competence of a high order. We have a functioning secular democracy, and a pluralistic society, when many new nations have become totalitarian. Our governments at the Centre and in the States have coped, with a fair degree of success, with a multiplicity of problems rising from the religious, linguistic and cultural diversity of our population, and from regional pressures. It is in dealing with certain basic social problems that, in spite of a number of measures undertaken by the governments, the progress made so far has remained far short of the desired goals. Eradication of poverty may take long time, but there are inequalities so glaring and indefensible as to have a moral dimension. A small minority own the bulk of the country's wealth and account for about one-third of the total consumption, while the age-long deprived and under-privileged sections continue to suffer great hardships and disabilities. However, taken as a whole, there is no comparable example of a democratic and federal political system having had to face such enormous and extremely complex problems and of doing so with no small success within a span of just three decades and a half. No wonder that our country has, increasingly, begun to command respect throughout the world.

And yet, notwithstanding all these achievements, I have chosen to tell the sad story of the progressive decline of morality in public affairs and of our failure to act resolutely to stop the rot. In this concluding lecture, I propose to explain and emphasise the urgency and crucial importance of the problem. I believe that a nation which has responded so well to numerous other challenges has the capacity, and will have the will to respond also to this challenge of continuing decline in moral standards.

May I start with a quotation from the preface of one of Bernard Shaw's plays? This is what he has said: "The nation's morals are like its teeth; the more decayed they are, the more it hurts to touch them. Prevent dentists and dramatists from giving pain, and not only our morals become as carious as our teeth, but toothaches and the plagues that follow neglected morality will presently cause more agony than all the dentists and dramatists at their worst have caused since the world began". For 'dramatists' one has only to substitute 'those who comment on public affairs,' to see the complete relevance of the quotation.

More civilizations have been destroyed as a result of internal corruption than by external aggression, and regimes have collapsed on the erosion of their moral authority by deep-seated and prolonged corruption. There are number of instances even in modern times. During the last years of his Prime Ministership, Lloyd George collected funds by virtual auction of Honours; and the funds which should have been going to the Liberal Party coffers, had been diverted to his personal political fund. It is unlikely that he ever turned for his personal expenditure the money he received; but the stench of the Honours scandal had given rise to such strong repugnance that in spite of his great achievements as a war leader, and in domestic affairs, no chances were left of his becoming Prime Minister again. In the process, the Liberal Party too suffered grievous damage. The fall of the Kuominatang under Chiang Kashak provides another instance of the destructive effect of corruption. The Kuominatang government had international recognition; and it had an army four times the size of the Communist army. But corruption had attained gigantic proportions, and had pervaded all spheres of governmental and economic activity. Chiang Kaishek himself was known for the simplicity of his life, and he was never accused of personal corruption. But most of his officials and others who surrounded him were driven by insatiable greed; his brother-in-law HH King, was described as a "veritable financial octopus with tentacles over every business concern". In the words of a foreign observer, Vincent Sheean, "never in human history such large fortunes had been made by so few in such a short time in the midst of so much human misery, as in China during the war". The result was the destruction of the moral authority of Chiang Kaishek and the total loss of Kuomintang's credibility. These, along with the driving force of the communist ideology and the indomitable will of the communist leaders, were the principal causes of the fall of the Kuomintang. The defeat and disintegration of the government of South Vietnam, in spite not only of massive support from the USA but also their direct, prolonged military involvement, present yet another example of the fatal consequences of political corruption, and unbridled acquisition of wealth and privileges by those favoured by the regime. Nixon's case is a more recent instance of the disastrous consequences of adoption of totally unethical means, including outright lying, in pursuit of political ends. A powerful presidency had an ignominious and under the threat of impeachment and prosecution, and the pressure of a morally outraged public opinion; and partly as a reaction against Watergate; the Carter presidency that followed after the next election showed express concern for moral and human values.

However, Nixon's case shows also the inherent strength and resilience of a democracy. Always in a democracy there is, ultimately, the inescapable accountability of the rulers to the electorate, and to the people generally. There is also an awareness of the power of a free Press to mould public opinion, and fortunately our Press has played a salutary role in exposing corruption and misdemeanour. We have, further a source of moral sustenance in our higher judiciary which, on the whole, has been functioning so far as the custodian of legality, justice \and the rights of the individual-all of which have moral foundations. Above all, democracy presents periodically an opportunity for renewal, which can also be an opportunity for starting a process of regeneration, social and economic, but also moral.

In a democracy every individual, with his sense of right and wrong, matters, and while he can endure-and does endure in India-a great deal of injustice and wrong doing a stage comes when he gives expression to his feelings in a manner that matters, particularly by his choice at the polling booth. People can put up with a government unable to meet their needs and alleviate their hardships; it is against corruption and greed in high places, and extensive abuse of power that resentment and anger reach the boiling point, and a government is thrown out. Even the organized violence by sections of the rural poor that we have witnessed in some parts of the country is essentially a reaction against uncontrolled personal or sectional greed, not poverty as such. By the way, if poverty were the cause of violence and crime, history would be a continuous tale about these, for the great majority of people throughout history have lived in poverty.

Let us return from these general reflections about the destructive power of corruption, and the corrective potential of democratic process, to consider how the post-Independence decades have come to witness such progressive decline in public morality.

Times-morally-are so out of joint, that one hesitates to quote Gandhiji while discussing practical affairs, or to remind those conducting public affairs of his life and teachings. To do so causes boredom if not embarrassment, and is perhaps even regarded as exhibition of poor manners! I do, nevertheless, propose to quote what Gandhiji had to say on issues with which we are concerned in these lectures. The profoundly moral principles which he followed, and the supreme importance of means which he emphasized in leading the country's successful struggle for independence have not ceased to be valid in running the affairs of a free India. He has left us a unique legacy - a legacy of tremendous importance in human history, - of which we should not allow ourselves to be disinherited in the management of our national affairs.

I shall briefly mention the main elements of the Gandhian legacy relevant to the subject of my lectures. He rejected the traditional view that moral principles accepted in personal life need not guide the conduct of practical affairs, and observed, "It is generally believed that practical affairs or business and spiritual pursuits or Dharma are distinct from and incompatible with each other. If this belief is not false there is no hope for us at all. There is not a single concern or sphere of practical affairs from which Dharma can be kept out". He used Dharma in the sense of truth and righteousness, he declared that Truth is God, on another occasion that God is ethics and morality. He saw no conflict between the country's political and material interest and the fundamentals of morality, on the contrary, he believed that the moral decay of the people always preceded physical and material de-generation.

On the question of the relative importance of means and ends he was totally opposed to the view, held through the centuries – and now almost a part of our political and business creed – that the ends justify the means. Here are some of his observations on the subject: "It is absolutely wrong to say that if the motive is pure, the means are justified, whatever they may be. For realizing a pure end the means must be pure". Again, "Means are after all everything. As the means, so the end. Indeed the Creater has given us control (and that too very limited), over means, none over the end". To a person who argued that in the service of laudable ends any means would be justified, Gandhiji replied, "Your reasoning is the same as saying that we can get a rose through planting a noxious weed. If I want to cross the ocean, I can do so only by means of a vessel; if I were to use a cart for that purpose both the cart and I would soon find the bottom. The means may be likened to a seed, the end to a tree."

Addressing representatives of the business community Gandhiji had expressed the hope that "they would not resort to dubious trade practices and would not exploit 'Daridranarayan', and that the genuine Artha is that alone which includes 'Parmarth'".

During the last two years of his life his exhortations had an element of foreboding, even a note of tacit warning. In 1946 he said in one of his public speeches: "It could never be my wish that the Congress, the moment it comes to power, should discard the very ladder by which it has climbed so high", and again at a prayer meeting "the Congress leaders have to be true to their words and pure of heart. They must not be tempted by crores....". Obviously, with political leaders in mind, he observed that "the corruption of the best is the worst. A single drop of poison can convert a pot of nectar into a lethal draught".

In the context of the current feeling of resignation to corruption and unethical practices in politics and economic life, and the disposition to consider them as inevitable and, therefore, acceptable, it may be well to remember Gandhiji's observations that "Life is an aspiration... The ideal must not be lowered because of our weaknesses and imperfections", and the fact of his life-long resistance to evil in any form – from racialism and imperialism to untouchability.

I suppose, even those who are disposed to dismiss Gandhiji as a visionary cannot question the credentials of Jawaharlal Nehru and Rajendra Prasad as political leaders who carried high practical responsibilities, albeit, with respect for moral values, and they both not only found spiritual inspiration from Gandhiji but also accepted with deep sincerity and humility the validity of Gandhian principles in public affairs. While describing himself not as visionary but a practical idealist, Nehru considered Gandhiji's spiritualization of politics using the word not in a narrow religious sense, a fine idea, a worthy end, he said should have worthy means leading up to it, and that this was not only a good ethical doctrine, but sound practical politics, for the means that are not good often defeat the end and raise new problems and difficulties. Again, while speaking on the objectives Resolution in the Constituent Assembly, he referred to Gandhiji as the "architect of this Assembly and all that has gone before it and probably of much that will follow". These last few words expressed Nehru's belief that Gandhian principles will cointinue to govern the affairs of the Indian Republic, so do the words from his statement following Gandhiji's assassination:

"The light has gone out, I said and yet I was wrong ... the light that has illumined this country for these many years will illumine this country for many more years and a thousand years later that light will still be seen in this country and the world will see it and it will give solace to innumerable, hearts. For that light represented the living truth.... The eternal truths, reminding us of the right path, drawing us from error, taking this ancient country to freedom".

In a speech two weeks later he said – "what kind of triumph did Gandhiji wish for us? Not the triumph for which most people and countries strive through violence, treachery and evil means. That kind of victory is not stable. For the foundations of a lasting victory can only be laid on the rock of truth..." One does not have to stretch one's imagination to visualize what Gandhiji would have felt about the black economy, the corruption, the open unconcern for means, the unprincipled politics and all that have come with these, or how hollow in present conditions would his own eloquent words sound in Nehru's ears if he were to be here.

Rajendra Prasad, while speaking on the motion to adopt the Constitution, said, "Mahatma Gandhi laid stress on the purity of the methods, which had to be pursued for attaining our ends. Let us not forget that this teaching has eternal value and was not intended only for the period of stress and struggle, but has as much authority and value today as it ever had before. I shall only hope that all those whose good fortune it may be to work this Constitution in future will remember that it was a unique victory, which we achieved by the unique method taught to us by the Father of the Nation, and it is up to us ... to make it bear fruit for the man in the street. Let us launch on this new enterprise of running our independent Republic with confidence, with truth and non-violence..."

Dr. Radhakrishnan, a philosopher, no doubt, but also a person involved in public affairs, had, while seconding the Objectives Resolution in the Constituent Assembly, this to say, "much has been said about the sovereignty of the people. We have held that the ultimate sovereignty rests with the moral law ... People, as well as kings, are subordinate to that Dharma, righteousness is the king of kings – Dharaman kshatrasaya Kshatram – it is the sovereignty of this law which we have asserted". Incidentally, even Kautilya, whose Arthasastra is regarded as the classic exposition of a moral statecraft declared that, "in any matter where there is conflict between Dharmasastra and any secular transaction, the king shall decide the matter by relying on Dharma. If Shastra comes into conflict with any rational and equitable rule, then the latter shall be the deciding factor and the strict letter of the text to be nowhere".

Inspired by the country's spiritual heritage and Gandhiji's teachings, the Founding Fathers, conspicuous among them Jawaharlal Nehru, adopted the Sarnath Lion Capital of Asoka, as India's National Emblem, Symbolizing the ideas and values by which the new nation wished to be identified and to be guided in future. Adoption of an emblem associated with Asoka, the great philosopher-king of history, signified the nation's aspirations to conduct its temporal affairs on moral principles. The Dharmachakra of the Emblem, likened with Budha's first sermon represents the rotating Wheel of Law, which was considered to be supreme and whose message of righteousness was binding, even on the greatest of kings. The legend "Satyameva Jayate" taken from Mundaka Upanishad, links the National Emblem with our other great spiritual tradition, the Vedanta. Can we claim that our affairs are being moved by the wheel of righteousness? Can we say that we have been true to the aspirations and values embodied in our National Emblem, or even that we have been making endeavours in that direction? Can a nation escape paying a heavy price, sooner or later, if it weakens in its allegiance to its solemnly adopted ideals, and if it losses its soul?

I shall attempt to explore the reasons for the gap between the aspirations and dreams of the Independence decade, and the position today. There is a view, going back to Plato, that democracy promotes hedonism; that democracy, in the words of Tocqueville "encourages a taste for physical gratification; this may dispose men to believe that all is matter only; and materialism in its turn hurries them on with mad impatience to these same delights. Such is the fatal circle within which democratic nations are driven round". When a country, particularly a developing country, has to focus its attention on economic development the ambitious and enterprising members of the community take to the pursuit of economic goals without any moral restraints or regard for the wider interests of society; and economic competition aggravates this tendency. Thus consumerism among citizens, and commercialism, with all it involves, among the industrial and business classes combine to push into the background the moral and humans values of society. Such an analysis of what is apt to happen may have a degree of validity, but it cannot wholly explain and certainly not justify, the entire phenomenon of debasement of ethical standards that we witness.

Part of the explanation might be found in the nature of politics, and ultimately in the nature of men. Politics, it is said, is concerned with power: with acquiring and retaining power, and so using it that it is not lost at the next occasion for a possible change. These being the ends, whatever means are necessary for achieving them have to be adopted. It is a mistake, it is implied, to treat politics as an ethical pursuit, to be fastidiously guided by principles of personal or social morality; that politicians have to serve the interests of those sections of society which they represent; and they act primarily in pursuit of interests that are advantageous to them, materially or in terms of power. Pursuit of these personal and sectional or class interests is not admitted, for the obvious reason that it would damage, with the general public, the credibility of politicians or the party concerned. Policies and actions, however, selfishly motivated, are presented as intended to serve the public interest or designed to achieve widely accepted social goals, and they may, in some measure be actually so. These may be too cynical a view of politics, and too wide a generalization. There are instances in history, past and current, of noble ideals and ideologies providing the motive force for political action. It is only when poilitics becomes devoid of genuinely ideological divisions, when great intellectual, political or social issues give place to power blocks, each guided mainly by lust for power, that it may merit a cynical description. Regrettably, Indian politics, which was marked by high ideals, during the years following Independence has progressively lost much of its finer features and the growth of corruption in political life and administration and a dishonesty in economic life, which I have traced in my earlier lectures are undoubtedly attributable to this fact.

From what is called the realistic view of the nature of politics or economic activities, the argument shifts to the nature of man. It is argued that there is an ineradicable tendency towards selfishness and even evil in human nature, which has to be constantly kept in view in the conduct of public affairs, and that "if men were angels no government would be necessary". It is therefore futile to hark back to Gandhian doctrine of the supreme importance of the purity of means and of moral values generally, even though these had been accepted by the Founding Fathers of the Constitution. In brief, Machiavelli's and Hobbes' views of human nature, and their amoral or even immoral ideas about the nature of authority and statecraft are accepted, and our Kautilya, in spite of his statement about the supremacy of the Dharma, is regarded as lending indigenous support to those views, by most of the assumptions underlying his political theories and administrative prescriptions.

I do not think that Indian people, including those active in political and economic life, will consider these views to be sound or right, even when their conduct does not conform to moral principles or humane ideals. Our immemorial traditions, and the philosophies of our greatest modern thinkers, Mahatma Gandhi and Aurbindo Ghosh point in the opposite direction. Belief in high moral and spiritual potential of man, even to the extent of perfectibility, lies at the heart of Buddhism, Jainism and Vedanta. Ours is the only country which has experienced the impact of all the world religions: Hinduism, Buddhism, Islam and Christianity, and these latter two, as well as Hinduism and Buddhism, assume the existence in man of a moral consciousness, and an urge towards spiritual advancement. Aurbindo has written about the capacity of man to acquire a new supra-mental consciousness and living a higher life. It is, however, Gandhiji's thoughts that have direct relevance to the issues we are considering, for he stands out in human history, by example and precept for total adherence to truth, non-injuriousness and moral standards in politics, economic life and social relationships. He sought to break the chain of violence and wrong doing which have marked human history, by according primacy to means; without it men will continue, as in the past, to take to violence and other wrong courses for some and or other which they consider desirable, and the chain will continue. His thinking on all questions had its root in his view of the moral nature of man, and he was uncompromising in his opposition to any institution or practice which served to deny that nature. I have already quoted from his writings and speeches which bear out what I have just said. I have only to add one more: "Mankind would die if there were no exhibition any time and any where of the divine in man". I may conclude this part of my discussion with the affirmation that we must not accept the prevalence of corruption and dishonesty in public affairs as the uncontrollable products of human nature, or as being inseparable from politics, and that we have therefore to resign to their continuance.

The root of the matter lies in failure to take courageous action: failure to enact a law against defections; failure to curb the operations of the black economy by bold action rather than legitimize its fruits periodically: failure to break the nexus between electoral politics and those who have the economic resources, in most cases acquired by dishonest means, failure to observe the Code of Conduct for Ministers (which could have been embodied in law to avoid infringements): and failure to pass legislation to establish the institution of Lokpal. Many of the major recommendations of the various Committees and Commissions, set up by the Central and the State Governments, have not been acted upon; and the healthy processes set in motion during the sixties have been allowed, in recent years, to peter out, when with corruption and various kinds of abuses increasing alarmingly, they should have been pushed with great vigour. Behind all this story of inaction lies a general infirmity of the political will – an infirmity caused at least partly, by an unenlightened self – interest.

A vigilant and assertive public opinion could have countered this; but as it is, society has become so acquiescent that it has virtually ceased even to contemplate the prospect of any amelioration. There is a talk even among the intelligentsia that there is corruption all over the world. This may be true, but the scale, nature and level of corruption vary; and failure to take action is not a global phenomenon. Surely we should follow the example of the best-run democratic countries, with high standard of honest and probity. Even in these countries corruption and abuse of power do occur; but action is taken against the offenders, however high may be positions they hold. This was so in the sixties in our country too, as I have mentioned earlier. But do we all not know that many persons high placed in various spheres of life, have been going about their dishonest activities, with impunity, and moving in society in lordly style?

To the question what we as citizens can do for restoration of moral standards in public affairs and economic life, there is no simpler answer. I have mentioned the various legislative and other measures which were initiated during the sixties and early seventies, but were abandoned. An awakened social conscience and pressure of well-informed public opinion could have these measures revived and put through; for without institutional devices, and legislative sanction, there would be little hope of effective action. Individuals should resist corruption and abuse of power or economic opportunity, and not submit to these with a feeling of helplessness. Such resistance may have disagreeable consequences for the time being, but it can set in motion a powerful chain reaction. Men of character and integrity could come forward, or could be persuaded to offer themselves for election to legislatures, even though there may be heavy odds against such candidates with the present system of financing elections and the way parties select their candidates. After all, a fundamental question in democratic polity is, how to make it possible for the good to come into power. I confess, some of these suggestions would appear to be platitudinous or counsels of perfection; my justification for making them is that so sorry is the present state of affairs and so great are the stakes that any move for a change, however small and however beset with difficulties, is worth serious thought. Ultimately, the strength of a nation lies in the moral fibre of the people, and this is largely determined by the conditions which the state provides; a state which itself does not have respect for moral values cannot foster such values among its citizens. It is not the society of Gandhiji's dream that we can reasonably hope to establish in the present conditions; but we can ask for cleaner politics, a more honest administration, an economy free from gross and blatant abuses; and in general, respect for the principles and values embodied in our Constitution – which after all, is a political and legal document meant for regulating the conduct of public affairs, and not a spiritual or ethical treatise.

Is it too much to ask all those who take an oath of loyalty to the Constitution to respect that oath, or Ministers to be true to their oath of office? Is it an extravagant expectation that our rulers should have some active sense of moral costs, and moral limits, and those engaged in acquisition of wealth should have some sense of responsibility to society?

Before I conclude; I wish to speak about the matter which has been uppermost in my mind, namely the responsibility which institutions of higher learning generally, and the Universities in particular have for inculcating moral values among the youth, and through them, in raising the standards of conduct in society as a whole.

In the West, starting with the French philosophers of the Revolution, but specially from the beginning of the 19th century and in our own country during the last sixty years or so, culture has been profoundly dependent upon the Universities, and the set of values they embody. Earlier, society derived its values from religion, or from the mores and rigid conventions of a structured society; but from the time of the rationalistic revolt against the traditional system and beliefs, it is the Universities that became the nurturer of culture, and of intellectual and morel values in the west; and our Universities modeled, in their broad aims and concepts, on British Universities assumed a similar role. During the decades preceding Independence, and for some years thereafter, Universities had a strong commitment to intellectual pursuits; they fostered free inquiry and critical analysis; they welcomed innovative thought; and their ethos was marked by humanism and ideals of liberal democracy. To my mind, nothing has done greater harm than the ever-increasing politicization of our Universities. They have been forced by circumstances to drift away from their preoccupation with high intellectual purposes, and responsibility to society. Every now and then they have experienced disruptive turbulence: many of them are ridden with factionalism among the teachers and fatricidal strife among the students, and there are confrontations between the University authorities and teachers and between teachers and students. I have known a fine Vice-Chancellor, being hounded out in a manner that brought about his death; Vice-Chancellors have been subjected to physical violence; and just about a year ago one was murdered. Current politics has entered the Universities, not for the legitimate business of intellectual analysis and judgement, but to affect with all its rivalries and conflicts the lives of and mutual relations of the academic community. With such goings-on standards have inevitably declined, and by and large the Universities are no longer capable of functioning as institutions where the ills of our politics, economy and society can be fearlessly analysed, and from which healthy norms and values can be communicated to other spheres of life.

A University has the unique opportunity of imparting its values and discipline to the youth, who are potentially the most creative part of a society, and who are at the stage when the mind is most capable of imbibing the right ideas and principles. The number of boys and girls passing out of our Universities every year runs into several lakhs, and it is from these that our Ministers and most of our legislators, (compared to legislatures of many democratic countries the Lok Sabha has a higher percentage of members who are graduates or have higher degrees) are drawn. It is from the annually enlarging pool of educated youth that our civil services, learned professions, and business and industries at the higher levels, are manned. And what is of immense importance, it is graduates of Universities who, in vast numbers, become teachers in schools, where they can start the process of moulding the minds and character of our adolescents. The Universities have been and can again become radiating centres not only of knowledge, but also of values. They can provide to our talented scholars an environment in which they can realise their creative potentialities; they now do so in most cases only when they go out to work in foreign universities where they earn great distinction. A high standard of creative work can help our Universities to regain their soul.

Our Universities can, over a period, make a decisive contribution to the enlightenment of the public mind, and restoration of ethical standards. I believe that if we succeed in taking care of standards and values in our universities, the moral problems of the rest of society will take care of themselves. You members of the University community have a great challenge before you, and it is for you to respond to it.

12

Administrative Leadership

L.P. Singh

I am grateful to the Centre for Administrative Change for doing me the honour of inviting me to deliver the fifth B. Mehta Memorial Lecture. I am particularly happy to associate myself with the commemoration of the memory of a civil servant whom I knew well, both officially and personally, and for whose abilities and personal qualities I had great respect. In choosing the subject of my lecture, I have been influenced by that respect, and by the fact that in a period when the problem of administrative leadership has received scant attention, you in Rajasthan have recognized, in such a concrete and constructive manner, the role and contributions of an administrative leader of the sixties.

One hears a great deal about leaders in various learned professions, and those of the armed forces, and about captains of business and industry. Above all, so much is written and talked about political leadership. But while the common citizen is all the time made aware, painfully or with satisfaction, about the vices or virtues of individual administrators, there is little thought given to the place of administrative leadership in the management of public affairs; or to the study of qualities needed for, and the environment conducive to developing, such leadership. Some Indian civil servants have written autobiographies or memoirs; but I am not aware of any study of administrative leadership as such, or of those who were leaders of the civil services in their time. Political leadership is, undoubtedly of the highest importance; and there is truth in Thomas Carlyle's assertion that "the nation must be ruled by its best elements or perish" – I would only add "in the long run". The quality and character of political leadership undoubtedly

Fifth B. Mehta Memorial Lecture delivered on 19 December, 1983 at The Centre For Administrative Change, Jaipur, Rajasthan.

influence all spheres of life. But the administrator is the instrument through which the politically determined aims and objectives are translated into detailed policies and programmes, and through which the political will is ultimately executed. Administrative leadership, though lower in the scheme of things than political leadership, is an essential complement of political leadership and is therefore a worthy enough subject for a close study. France, before its present constitution came into force, provides an example of a state, through many years of political instability, retaining its vitality and making progress because of a strong structure of civil administration and competence of its higher civil servants. Indeed, one can reasonably take the view that the strength, and achievements – such as they were – of British Rule in India are attributable primarily to the higher quality of the men Britain sent out for about a hundred years to administer this country. While some of the finest products of their premier universities entered the Indian Civil Service, it was not often that the most talented of its politicians were sent to hold the highest political offices in India. It is in district administration, and not at the headquarters of government, that the wisdom of the British rulers found expression. Those wielding political authority in Whitehall or India greatly valued civil servants as their essential tools; as the saying goes, 'an ill workman quarrels with his tools'.

In regard to administrative reforms and adaptation of the administrative system and procedures to changing conditions, it is worth remembering that these are, in a large measure, professional matters, and it is only through a vigorous and imaginative administrative leadership that these objectives can be achieved. I was told by an eminent scholar closely associated with the work of the Hoover Commission in the nineteen-fifties that most of the important suggestions, which formed the basis of the Commission's recommendations, had come from within the civil services. Bureaucracy in general may tend to be inert and tradition-bound, but it has within it perceptive and forward-looking persons who recognize what is wrong and can think of practicable changes and innovations. But this "live" section of the bureaucracy needs leadership, which can articulate its thinking, and have it accepted by the political executive.

In 1980, I read a collection of writings on leaders of the armed forces during the two World Wars, edited by Field Marshal Lord Carver, and published under the title "The War Lords". I was struck by the fact that there is so much in common in the making of a "warlord" and a leader in civil administration: continuous and deep study of his profession; ability to look forward and to plan and prepare for future contingencies; capacity for quick adaptation to unforeseen circumstances; unflappability and resilience in an emergency or a crisis. Other common characteristics, it appeared to me, are an understanding of human beings; an eye for the significant detail, without getting immersed in the Minutia of his charge; and willingness to drive oneself hard while driving others to give of their best. Not all the "War Lords" had all these qualities, nor do leaders in civil administration have; but in both cases most of the qualities are essential components of leadership. There are, of course, differences to which I shall refer later. Incidentally, it is interesting how political masters everywhere – in Britain, France, Germany, and Soviet Union – thought rightly in some cases, but not in others, that replacing a military leader was the answer to a crisis. Are we in India not familiar with a similar phenomenon in the sphere of civil administration?

An administrative leader must have firm faith in the objectives he is pursuing, and in the means and methods by which he seeks to achieve the objectives. The firmness and sincerity of the faith are of such crucial importance that even when the objectives and methods are lacking in moral validity or wisdom they can, in favourable circumstances, and for a time, make for successful leadership. To take an example from political history, there can be no doubt that Hitler was a scourge on humanity and eventually proved a great malefactor even of his own nation. And yet by the strength of his faith in his own ideas and in the means by which he tried to realize them – thoroughly evil though these were – he became in the abnormal circumstances of Germany during the nineteen thirties, the supreme leader of a highly talented and educated people. Though the sincerity and firm faith in his aims and methods are necessary in a potential leader in civil administration, the aims and methods must be in harmony with the current political and social values of his country. In a totalitarian or authoritarian state the administrative leader will have goals and methods different from those of a leader in a democratic polity; the administrative leader in a country with a capitalist, laissez-faire economy will have objectives different from those in a country where the activities of the state extend over a wide field, and the emphasis is on pursuit of egalitarian ideals and the welfare of the people. One cannot become a leader of the civil services in India unless he has firm faith in the basic principles of our Constitution; in the Fundamental Rights, and the Directive Principles; in freedom, democracy, secularism and the rule of law.

And one who understands the problems, and respects the sensitivities of ordinary citizens. I may mention in passing that when a question was raised, in the context of recruitment to the Indian Civil Service, whether study of Greek and Latin classics had any relevance to practical administration, the answer was that to see human beings as the great masters had seen them was an invaluable asset to an administrator; for, ultimately it is human beings with whom all administration is concerned. An administrator may know all the laws and rules, but without an understanding of human beings, and genuine interest in them, he will not go far in his profession.

There are certain common factors in leadership in most fields, and I have mentioned many of these as between military and administrative leadership; and one can add to these, leadership in business and industry, with the proviso that in this case there is a deep, if not over-riding, concern for financial and economic results. For leadership in politics, capacity to project oneself and one's policies to the people, and to build and motivate a party organization, are essential requirements. A political leader has to seek popularity, in one way or another, for he has to seek a fresh mandate from the people, periodically. In contrast, any conscious effort to earn popularity might do more harm than good to an administrator. An administrative leader has so to conduct himself that he wins the confidence and respect of the general body of civil servants, and of the people in his jurisdiction; and in some cases popularity may also come to him, but it should be a sort of unasked for bonus. However, his sight has to be set on honest, firm and imaginative administration of his charge, on attainment of certain public goals by fair means and proper procedures, and if in the process he incurs some unpopularity, he should accept it with equanimity, as a price paid for his dedication, integrity and courage. In this respect, an administrative leader is akin to an academic, with single-minded devotion to acquisition and communication of knowledge, who accomplishes his best work, not in the glare of publicity but the quietness of a library or laboratory. It is through scholarly achievements and not self-advertisement that he earns fame, and becomes a source of inspiration to others. A civil servant who goes about receiving adulatory addresses, making exhortatory speeches, and courting popularity is not the stuff of which a true administrative leader is made. He is apt to arouse jealousy of politicians and to attract denigratory and sarcastic comments from his colleagues. Not by showmanship but by his intrinsic worth and accomplishments, expressed in action and conduct, that a civil servant becomes a leader in his profession.

An important element in the making of an administrative leader is his interest in and full knowledge of the organization over which he presides. He must know his tools, and keep them in good shape. The training and placement of personnel, their working and living conditions, their contentment and welfare, have to be his constant concern. The unglamorous housekeeping, and personnel management problems have to receive adequate attention from him. He is not a solo performer and has to ensure and accept responsibility for the efficient functioning of the whole organization, and all the services in his charge. Unfortunately in these matters the past traditions have not been maintained in recent years.

A leader has to know the qualities and limitations of individual officers working under him. He can trust some to act according to their own judgement and initiative; others may need detailed guidance and close supervision. Then there is the question of discipline; heading an undisciplined body is far removed from exercise of leadership. Maintenance of discipline in civil services, enjoying statutory protection and working in a free democratic society, is a complex and delicate business. Here there is marked difference from the armed forces, where there is a firm line of command and all lawful orders have to be obeyed without questioning, and quick punishment follows any breach of discipline. In civil administration rigid discipline requiring implicit, and unquestioning obedience to orders, cannot be imposed. Personal example, scrupulously fair dealings, exercise of moral influence and use of persuasion are ordinarily the appropriate means for ensuring discipline in a civil organization. It has to be brought home to officials that observance of discipline is right and proper and fully consistent with personal dignity, apart from being essential for the functioning of an organization, and serving the wider interests of society. A civil servant in authority who does not understand this, and thinks of punishment or threat of it as the best instrument of discipline, cannot become a true leader, however high may be the position he holds. On the contrary, one who condones minor faults with grace, who stands by a subordinate who commits an error of judgment and while acting in good faith, who even though not personally at fault is prepared to accept responsibility when things go wrong in his organization is readily accepted as a true leader. Conversely, one who withholds praise and encouragement from his subordinates, when these are due, and seeks to take credit for their good performance, forfeits their respect and any title to leadership. Sparing in censures, generous in praise and self-denial in the matter of credit are, I think among the marks of administrative leadership.

I have mentioned earlier how a country's constitutional and social system has to shape the values and out-look of an administrative leader. But while in a totalitarian or even authoritarian state, it is impossible for a civil servant to rise to a position of leadership unless he identifies himself completely with those wielding political power, democracy requires civil servants to remain detached from partisan politics. A civil servant, to quote Paul Appleby, is not a political eunuch; he has his own political views and beliefs. But he has to carry out faithfully the policies and lawful orders of the government of the day. This loyalty must not, however, extend to identification with the political party from which the government is drawn. Harmonious relations with the political executives of the day is an essential requirement for administrative leadership; indeed without such relations, which may require flexibility in approach while adhering to principles, an administrator cannot achieve a great deal. But a civil servant who allies himself with a political party or rises in the service hierarchy through political patronage can have no claim to administrative leadership. His colleagues and subordinates would treat him as an ambitious opportunist, whom they may fear, but would not respect or trust. It is character, and integrity in the widest sense, not personal ambition and hunger for self-advancement that are looked for in an administrative leader. I am told that ambition is a spur to high endeavour and as such a virtue. It may be so if kept within limits of decency and good sense. But to me ambition has always been suspect, for I have found in many cases distortion of values, and erosion of finer qualities caused by ambition. I have found ambitious men getting jealous of their talented colleagues, and trying to keep them down, when they should be making full use of them in the interest of the public service. It is unremitting pursuit of excellence in his work, and overriding dedication to public weal, rather than driving ambition, that, to my mind, are needed for developing administrative leadership. Human beings, whatever be the sphere of their activity, have self regarding concerns, but it is only those who subordinate these concerns to impersonal ends, who can make true leaders in administration as elsewhere. An administrative leader has also to have a personality which will impress itself on those he has to deal with: civil servants, political masters, and the public. Personality is not easy to define, but it is not difficult to recognize. An identical order or advice coming from two successive heads of an organization may evoke differing responses. Strength of character and conviction, sincerity and the cogency and clarity with which he expresses himself, are all components of personality. Advice, instruction or assurance from an administrator with a strong personality would be readily accepted when the same advice, instruction or assurance from an officer of weaker personality may be easily turned down, or disregarded.

I have been talking so far about the moral and human elements in the making of an administrative leader. His intellectual equipment and professional accomplishments are just as important. He must have a deep understanding of the constitutional and legal frame within which he has to function, and of the political and social forces at work in society. He has to have the skill to navigate between the rock of constitutionality and legality, and political exigencies and urgencies of economic and social development. He has to have intimate knowledge of the machinery of government, and of the procedures and practices according to which administration has to be carried on. He has to be a sort of specialist in the machinery and instrumentalities of government, in order to be able to act with speed, without making his actions vulnerable on the ground of irregularity or impropriety. His knowledge of the machinery and procedures has to be a part of his mental outfit, so that correct action becomes almost a reflex response. He has to have full knowledge of the substantive problems he has to deal with, and he has to know where and how additional knowledge can be had; for no one can always carry in his head, all the knowledge that is needed for dealing with a complex problem. He may create in his department a research unit on which he can draw, or he can seek help from a research or academic institution. We live in a complex and fast changing world, and an administrator who depends entirely on the store of knowledge available within his department, or who does not make full use of modern tools of management, particularly electronic devices, may find it difficult to rise to a position of leadership. A leader should have time to think, which is not easily available with the pressure of day-to-day work, and the "tyranny of the in-tray". If he can arrange his schedule in such a way that he has some time for thinking and original work, good and well. But in this context the support of a research organization and use of electronic devices assume exceptional importance. An administrative leader – indeed a leader in any field of activity – must lead in thinking as well as in action.

I have known civil servants holding the highest positions, who were totally barren in ideas. They were liked or disliked by those working with them, depending on their personal qualities; but they were not respected or regarded as dependable sources of inspiration, or guidance.

The general body of civil servants are too pre-occupied with their current tasks to be able to extend their sight to the future. But the leader must have, so to speak, bifocal vision. He has to attend to the day's work; but he has to look around for emerging forces, and problems on the horizon and to plan imaginatively for meeting future demands. And he has to prepare the administration by spotting and developing talented young officers, and other measures, for doing so. One only rarely comes across such vision and forethought; but when one does, one knows that there is a true leader.

Even the best of plans is not self-executing. There has to be skilful and vigorous implementation. Energy and unremitting exercise of will on the part of the leader are necessary, to bear down the inertia and slackness of individuals to be found in all organizations. Unforeseen difficulties arise in the course of implementation, which cannot be removed by a predetermined procedure, an innovative approach or quick improvisation is called for, which an experienced and enterprising leader provides. Under dynamic leadership, tasks can be accomplished ahead of the normal time schedule. An instance from the history of the Second World War will illustrate the point. Rommel has mentioned in his Diary, published soon after the war, that in his victorious campaigns he had surprised the allied forces by attacking earlier than his own staff had considered necessary for the preparations. Rommel had proceeded on the assumption that the allied staff must have made a similar estimate of the time that would be needed for mounting an attack, and the assumption had proved correct. In a review of a book on Rommel, published in London's Sunday Times in 1950, Wavell admitted that in the early part of 1941, when the British expedition went to Greece he had calculated that he would not be counter-attacked before the beginning of May – a calculation which was justified against any ordinary commander; but Rommel, who had been ordered by the German High Command to submit a plan by April 20th for a "cautious advance" actually attacked on March 31st, without ever submitting a plan, and caught Wavell unprepared. A bold and determined leader in civil administration can also drive an organization under him to complete even a major task well ahead of the time normally required for it. I know, for instance, that in a state some years ago all the headquarters buildings needed for a proposed new district were constructed in about six months, when they were supposed to take about a year, and an agricultural college was started, with improvised arrangements, and vigorous action, within six months of a decision being taken. I believe that some of you present here know of, and may even have been personally responsible for, similar achievements in your State. I have no doubt that wherever – whether under the Central Government or in the States – there is dynamic administrative leadership, tasks are being accomplished at a speed and efficiency far above the normal.

The question however, is whether such leadership exists, and is enabled to be developed in numbers which the magnitude and multiplicity of our problems require. Our administrative structure, both on the general and technical side, has a hierarchy of positions of leadership, beginning from the sub-Divisional level upto that of Chief Secretary/Development Commissioner, in the States and Secretaries to the Government of India, with the Cabinet Secretary at the apex. Our system of recruitment, based on competitive merit, ensures that the public services get a fair share of the top cream of the products of our institutions of higher education. We have well-designed training programmes and refresher courses, and there are deputations for study or training in foreign countries, to enable our civil servants to widen their mind and deepen their professional knowledge. In this matter things are far better than they used to be. Further our public services have had in the past a tradition of efficiency and integrity. And yet can we truthfully say that a majority of the positions of leadership are being manned today by persons with leadership qualities? Civil servants today have vastly wider opportunities and responsibilities in the field of economic development and welfare, than the young members of the I.C.S. and other higher services used to have, and leadership qualities are therefore needed now much more than they were before independence. There are still a number of civil servants at all levels, who exhibit leadership qualities; there will always be men and women with character, dedication and competence who show conspicuous performance even in an adverse environment. But one cannot go by such exceptions. One has to consider why a majority even of those who are expected to provide leadership to the general body of civil servants fail to come up to the desired standard.

Part of the explanation lies in the decline, in recent years, of moral standards in public life: in defections among legislators, widespread corruption, and frightening growth of the "black" economy. The general atmosphere of cynicism that has been created by all these has corroded idealism, and firm adherence to principles in the civil services. But there are other, more directly operating, factors. Tenures in particular appointments – even key appointments – are too short and uncertain, and that inhibits growth of self-confidence, and of the requisite knowledge and insight into problems of a district or a department. There were cases in the past of an officer holding charge of a district for many years, and a four year tenure was common enough even during the first few years after Independence. Now even a couple of years tenure has become uncommon. Heads of departments and Secretaries to Government are changed so frequently that few are able to acquire mastery over any subject. Then there is the decisive weight given to seniority, so much so that a sort of queue system has come into being; and every now and then, when there is a break from the system, the reason is not in every case outstanding merit, but intrusion of political or personal influence. In certain developed countries, of which I have some knowledge, advancement depends on superior merit, and younger civil servants, with outstanding ability, are put in key positions, which they are allowed to hold for several years. Even in our own country the average length of service which an I.C.S. officer had put in when he was selected for appointment to a post of Secretary to the Government of India, was 24 years; and some were selected when they had less than 20 years service. Merit, rather than seniority continued to be the main criterion for the highest appointments even in the fifties and sixties; but there has been a progressive increase in the emphasis on seniority. The rule of primogeniture may be appropriate in monarchical succession or in a feudal order, but in the civil services of a democracy the higher positions of leadership ought to be filled with civil servants with leadership qualities or potentials. However, I have been warned that unless the procedure for assessing merit is such as to ensure objectivity, shifting the emphasis from seniority would do more harm than good. This is undoubtedly true. Senior civil servants have, so to speak, a well-educated and highly perceptive constituency in the general body of civil servants, who have opportunities to watch, for many years, the abilities and character of their superiors. They would immediately recognize whether a person with or without true leadership qualities had been chosen for a key appointment; and an unfair selection may affect their morale. In the armed forces reputations can be won or lost in a single campaign or even a single major battle, and in every war many reputations, and high positions, are gained or lost. But in the civil administration there is no comparable risk of losing, or opportunity for gaining a quick reputation; both are long term affairs.

During the British regime the civil services were professionally very well managed; but they were not politically neutral; they had the over-riding aim of maintaining British rule. During the first twenty-five years or so after Independence the old system of professional management remained more or less intact, and the civil services were expected, by and large, to remain aloof from partisan politics. But thereafter notwithstanding avowed commitment to political neutrality, there has been a trend towards intrusion of political factors and personal influences in personnel matters, to the extent of some of the best civil servants being treated as persona non grata, by one regime or another and "officials on compulsory waiting for posting" becoming a recognized category. This combined with the decline in the standard of professional management of the civil services, has lead to a weakening of administrative leadership. There have been some cases of a post of Additional Chief Secretary being created and filled with a pliable and politically convenient person, to get round an able and upright Chief Secretary. In some States, several posts of Inspector General have been created for political or personal reasons; and in one or two States two or more posts even of Director General of Police have been created. A hydra-headed, uniformed force is something of an anathema, and incompatible with the concept of administrative leadership. Many officers, including those belonging to All India Services, are known to ingratiate themselves with local political leaders and to seek favourable treatment through their influence. There have been cases of officers in charge of police stations using political influence to get the District Superintendent of Police transferred out. In some cases notoriously corrupt officers enjoy immunity from punitive action if they are able to have influential political patrons. Such instances, even if they were not numerous would create an environment in which leadership potentialities cannot be fully realized. Those put in key positions for political or personal reasons may wield power and authority, and may be feared and obeyed, but they do not become administrative leaders. If the best are not put in a position to lead, and even when they are put, their authority and self-confidence are undermined bilateral political influence, there can be no effectrive administrative leadership.

I have so far dealt with administrative leadership at all levels, and in general terms. But the highest leadership can be judged only by performance, over a long period, in the top positions, carrying major, and diverse, responsibilities, and involving dealings with Ministers; by success in dealing with critical situations as well as normal problems; and by contributions to the making of new policies and programmes. Many administrators, successful in dealing with their current tasks pass into history without leaving behind any mark; the greatest are those who take up the initiative in building up new systems and institutions, and contribute to the shaping of legislation, which stand the test of time. These alone leave their mark on administrative history.

Before I conclude, I wish to say a few words on the question whether administrative leaders, like poets, are born. My answer is that they are in a large measure made rather than born, with the qualification, that unless a person has certain innate qualities of character and intellect and a strong personality, he cannot become a leader. But for the rest, it is a matter of nurture, and opportunities to develop administrative capacities and judgement, and keenness to make use of such opportunities, particularly at an early stage of the career. This is well exemplified by the Indian Civil Service. Young men recruited on the basis of their intellectual attainments, were early in life, put in charge of districts, where they had to deal with all sorts and conditions of men, and with diverse problems; their faculties were stretched and their minds enriched with experience. They made mistakes and learnt from them. And they developed self-confidence. It was out of such material that some first rate administrative leadership emerged. By way of an analogy I may mention the capabilities of a computer, and the quality of the programming. A crude, early generation computer cannot yield excellent results though fed with the best programme, but nor can even the most advanced computer produce excellent stuff from poor programming.

One more point, and I am done. There are certain basic elements in all leadership; but for the rest a leader has to adapt himself to the circumstances of the time and the tasks he is engaged in. Even apart from this, not every leader will have, in equal measure, all the components of leadership. I had the privilege of knowing personally two of the most distinguished Indian Civil Servants of the first half of this century, Chintamani Deshmukh and C.M. Trivedi, and I have seen papers left behind, and learnt a great deal from others, about a third, Girja Shankar Bajpai. Each had a distinctive excellence. The pre-eminence and extraordinary versatility of Deshmukh's intellect, and the luminous quality of his mind was recognized all round. But he functioned with effortless ease, and notable detachment. Trivedi did not have a comparable intellect, but he had infinite capacity for taking pains, and quite an extraordinary quality of practical judgement in dealing with a variety of problems. He was a sort of automatic pilot. Bajpai had a powerful and versatile intellect and a wide ranging mind, and he had power of expression of rare brilliance and elegance. So, administrative leadership cannot be put in rigid, standard mould.

I thank you for bearing for nearly an hour with my random reflections on administrative leadership.

13

Sardar Patel and Indian Administration

L.P. Singh

I consider it a great honour to be invited to inaugurate a lecture series on Sardar Patel, who has been without doubt, the greatest statesmen-administrator of independent India; indeed the greatest in my view that our country has produced during the last four centuries. He ranks with Asoka, and Akbar, as a unifier of the country. That is, the bulk of it, once the political forces set in motion towards the end of the last century, strengthened by imperial policies, and finally fed by urge towards power, had led inexorably to the creation of Pakistan. That the Sardar, already past seventy, should have had less than five years to accomplish his mission makes the achievement the more remarkable. Akbar, for instance, had ruled for more than four decades; and the British had taken a hundred years to extend their direct rule over India, and still with only paramountcy over a third of it. And never before in our history since the Mauryan bureaucracy, did we have a uniform system of administration, from which no part of the country was excluded. Nor was the country ever before unified as an unrestricted democracy. Even at the last election under British rule (1946) only about ten per cent of the population had the franchise.

To what the Sardar, the great statesman, achieved as a unifier, and as a principal contributor to the building up of the democratic constitutional structure, he added, as a superb administrator, signal contributions in meeting the formidable problems created by the violent upheaval accompanying the partition, and the extraordinary energy with which he attended to the complex and sensitive

---

Sardar Patel Memorial lecture delivered at South Gujarat University, Surat, on 15 December, 1986.

business of the partition council. While conserving the frame of the administration in British India built through the experience of a century and a half, he had the creative imagination and the will to extend it to the princely states, which had had diverse patterns of administration, far removed, in the vast majority of cases from the system in British India.

I have advisedly referred to Sardar Patel as statesman-administrator. Even an outstanding administrator may not have vision; absorption in the mechanics, procedure, and minutiae, and the achievement of immediate objectives tend to shackle the imagination and to limit projection of vision to the problems emerging on the horizon and requiring timely preparation for dealing with them. Curzon is an excellent example. Inspite of his exceptional administrative abilities he failed to see the progressive growth of Indian nationalism in a correct perspective, or to deal with Indian aspirations with sensitivity and imagination. Herbert Hoover is another example. He was perhaps the ablest administrator among the Presidents of the United States during the present century; but he failed to appreciate the dimensions of his country's unprecedented economic depression, or to deal with it. A statesman, in contrast, may have ideas and vision, understanding of a country's historical and cultural traditions, and the social forces current and developing. He may have all the right aims and perspectives; but he may not have mastery of the means, or a sound strategy of action; and he may not have the gift of getting the best out of his instruments – the bureaucracy. It is rare in history to have a combination of outstanding statesmanship with genius for administration. It was India's good fortune, at the most crucial stage of its modern history to have in Sardar Patel a combination of the vision of a statesman with the sagacity and practical outlook of an administrator, without which the Indian administrative system might not have been revitalized, and its standards might well have fallen below what the critical times and the new nation required.

Recruitment to the Indian Civil Service and the Indian Police had been first slowed down and then stopped because of the war and likelihood of constitutional changes, resulting in wide gaps in those services. In the meantime there had been considerable dilution of standards as a result of large numbers of ad-hoc appointments to the other services; and preoccupation with work connected with the war and civil supplies had caused neglect and dislocation of the normal activities of government. The administrative structure was there, but in weakened state, and the administration was generally in a rundown condition. Uncertainty about the picture that might emerge from the impending constitutional changes, and its effect on their own future had tended to affect the zest and self-confidence of the senior civil services. There was, further, the rising tide of communalism with ominous potential of violence. Such briefly was the background of the administrative situation which the Sardar as Home Minister in the interim government faced in 1946.

As the year 1946 advanced and the constitutional negotiations were taking their tortuous course, Sardar Patel started thinking of the future. The first momentous step he took was, in October of that year, to have a resolution adopted at a conference of the Congress Chief Ministers (inspite of opposition initially from some of them) authorizing the setting up of two all-India services, the IAS and the IPS, to succeed the ICS and I.P. The Muslim League's firm thinking was that if India was to remain united it could only be on the basis of a weak Centre, with its jurisdiction limited to External Affairs, Defence, and Communications, with no scope in such a constitutional arrangement for any all-India Administrative or Police Service. If there was partition the question of such services would obviously not arise. Going through the relevant documents of the period, one is left with the impression that by October 1946 Sardar Patel had come to the conclusion that with the intransigent attitude of the League partition was probably unavoidable, and that India must have new services, as successors to the ICS and IP, which, apart from filling the existing wide gaps in these services, would contribute to the unity of the country and the strength of the administrative structure, and make for a high standard of efficiency and uniformity.

The Sardar had a deep understanding of the lessons of Indian history. Regional and other narrow loyalties, leading to chronic divisiveness, had had free play in periods of absence of a central authority or its weakness. He was convinced that all-India services for general and law and order administration would be valuable adjuncts of a strong constitutional authority at the Centre, which however was to be consistent with the federalism of our Constitution, of which he was to be one of the main architects.

The contemporaneous documents also indicate that Sardar Patel was acutely conscious of the historical and cultural factors, and of the debilitating effect of a long period of subjection on the moral fibre of the Indian people, which were likely in combination to make India a "soft" state, prone to vacillation in critical situations or when faced with hard options. His experience of dealing with the Congress organization, and of the Provincial Ministries had strengthened his apprehensions. (I may mention, in passing, that a group of civil servants, asked by Wavell to study the relative prospects of India and China had reported even in 1944 that India would go for softer options; and as is well known many years later, Gunnar Myrdal categorized India as a "soft state"). The Sardar did therefore believe that it was essential for independent India's administrative machinery to have a strong frame, capable of withstanding stresses, and of maintaining discipline in administration and peace and order in society. For decdes the ICS and IP had been referred to pejoratively as the steel frame of imperil rule. This was a just enough description of their role as instruments for preserving British rule against the rising tide of Indian nationalism. But the Sardar conceived of the successor services in a role fundamentally different in objectives and style of functioning, but retaining the element of firmness. They were to be the servants of the Indian people, unfaltering in their loyalty to the country, and dedicated to executing with devotion the laws and policies of Indian governments. He laid down the broad principles on which entrants to the Administrative Service were to be trained. They were to be moulded into patriotic Indians, not as English country gentlemen oriented to working as agents of imperial rule as had been the aim even for Indians in the ICS. They were to have an all-India, and not a parochial outlook; and they were to have understanding of our past, and of Indian culture and social conditions. It was these basic ideas on which the IAS training institute was designed and later developed into the Academy of Public Administration.

The Sardar, as I shall amplify later, was no proponent of administrative authoritarianism; it needs to be remembered that he had a major role in the enactment of the Constitution including the articles dealing with the fundamental rights. However he did not believe that everything that had come down from the previous regime needed to be discarded any more than it was necessary to demolish every edifice erected in the past. Four years after Independence it was said, by way of criticism, that with the IAS and IPS the 'steel frame' had been continued and the administrative machinery had not been overhauled. Administrative machinery, unlike, for instance, an automobile, cannot be sent to a workshop for overhauling! Short of a violent revolution it can only be repaired and improved, adapted to perform new tasks and to serve changed purposes. The problems of peace and order had not disappeared with Independence; public order had still to be maintained and the laws enforced without fear or favour; extraneous influences and improper interference with administrative processes and in the execution of development and welfare programmes, from whatever quarters they came, had to be resisted, and only an administration with a strong frame could do so. To quote from Sardar Patel's own formulation in 1948: An "all-India service, efficient, disciplined and contented, assured of its prospects as a result of diligent and honest work, is a sine qua non of sound administration under a democratic regime even more than under an authoritarian rule. The service must be above party and we should ensure that political considerations either in its discipline or in its control are reduced to the minimum, if not eliminated altogether."

With the new all-India services, the strengthening of the police forces in the States as enjoined by the Sardar, and the reorganization of the Central Secretariat services carried through under his directions, the administration worked well enough during the difficult fifties. Communal peace was generally maintained, the gigantic task of rehabilitating millions of uprooted human beings was carried through, and two general elections on adult franchise were conducted fairly and peacefully. The dwindling remants of the ICS and IP, members of the IAS and IPS and of the Central services, worked with missionary zeal. Working, first in a State beset with problems, and from 1956 at the Centre, I can testify from personal knowledge, that many public servants felt the glow of a new dawn and strove to the limit of their capacity to prove worthy of the responsibility that had been placed on them. They worked with a passionate spirit, which went well beyond the normal call of duty and discipline; it fired the imagination and made for enterprise and creativity. One felt that it was rare good fortune to be alive and working in that momentous period of our history, and to be in a position after centuries to contribute to the realization of the country's great destiny.

There was, first, the inspiration from Gandhiji's life and work, which they shared with the rest of the population. His total commitment to truth and non-violence had, however, value transcending limits of a particular period and territory. Indeed his attempt to break the chain of violence which had plagued mankind throughout history, his emphasis on primacy of means in pursuit of any ends whatever, his precept of aparigrah, or non-acquisitiveness are bequests to entire humanity and were not meant particularly for the civil services. Pandit Nehru with his charismatic personality and liberal humanism, his world-outlook, and vision of a friendly and peaceful international order, his efforts to promote science and technology, and the scientific spirit, his commitment to planned economic and social development, was another immense source of inspiration, such as a people can rarely have.

However, it was Sardar Patel, who, so to speak was the patron-saint of the civil services, for it was he who had time and again publicly recognized their special importance in the new scheme of things, and explicitly placed trust in them. He had recognized them as patriotic Indians after they had been described for decades as mercenary careerists and lackeys of British imperialism; and he had made them feel wanted. The Sardar saw human beings as they are; he knew that whether it was the princes or public servants, men of property or humble workers, they had deep down their hearts patriotic feelings which many of them had in their material interests kept undisclosed during alien rule. With his open recognition of this fact he succeeded in releasing in them springs of patriotism. Many of those at the higher levels wanted to purge themselves, through exceptional endeavour, of the feeling of guilt they had as servants of a foreign power. They were not obsessed with question of their status, or driven by personal ambition; it was aspiration for the country that impelled them. Sardar Patel's public acknowledgement of the patriotism and dedication of public servants and his expression of trust in them, gave them the self-assurance and the élan without which they could not have given their best. It is significant that in a meeting held in the Central Secretariat to pay homage to Sardar Patel, a resolution was adopted by the gathering of civil servants to rededicate themselves to the service of the country and prove worthy of the confidence which the deceased leader had reposed in them.

Addressing the Constituent Assembly in 1949 the Sardar said "…. As a man of experience I tell you, do not quarrel with the instruments with which you want to work. It is a bad workman who quarrels with his instruments….Every man wants some sort of encouragement. Nobody wants to put in work when every day he is criticized and ridiculed in public….." Proceeding further he enunciated the doctrine of intellectual integrity of civil servants and their sharing responsibility with a sharpness which has not since been equaled. He said, "Today my Secretary can write a note opposed to my views. I have given that freedom to all my Secretaries". I have told them "If you do not give your honest opinion for fear that it will displease your Minister, please then you had better go. I will bring another Secretary….you have agreed to share responsibility". In course of the same speech he observed, "Many of them with whom I have worked, I have no hesitation in saying that they are as patriotic, as loyal and as sincere as myself". The compliment may have been over generous, but I have quoted it for the effect it had on the minds of civil servants. In his own life time, and in the two decades after his death the inspiration and animation received from his personality and achievements, his public statements and the principles he had laid down, had an effect on the spirit and outlook of civil servants, which is rarely recognized.

It may not be easy in the vastly changed atmosphere of recent years to appreciate the value of some of these intangibles or how decisive an element they were in Sardar Patel's contribution to Indian administration in those critical and formative years. One wonders whether these, and the rest of the Sardar's administrative credo and principles to which I refer later, were only transient influences. I do not myself think so. Any thing of real value which is put into an administrative system in a formative period becomes part of that administration's culture, which may be pushed into the background or obscured in an unfavourable political and social environment, but is not destroyed; with change of circumstances it reappears. Indeed, even today there are numerous men and women in the administration who function with rectitude and dedication similar to those of the years immediately following Independence. If their spirit of independence has been dampened, and there has been decline in courage and initiative, the causes are primarily political.

At the heart of administration, indeed of the entire business of governance lies the problem of power: its proper, skilled and timely use, and avoidance of misuse and abuse. Power is obviously not the personal property of the wielder, available for untrammeled use, as wielders of power not unoften persuade themselves to believe. This is the point of the dictum, that power corrupts. Viewed correctly, power is a trust, and like any trust it can be legitimately used only according to the rules and conditions governing it. In Administration, and the affairs of government generally, power has to be used according to the constitution and the laws of the land; and beyond these, according to the generally accepted norms of public conduct and, ideally also the unwritten moral laws of a society. Looking at our history during the last forty years, one is led to think that Sardar Patel stands out as the person who both made effective use of, and did not misuse or abuse state power. It is beyond the scope of this lecture to present a picture of the misuse and abuse of power, at different levels and in various spheres, and the grave damage these have done to the country, and the sufferings they have caused. We are all only too well, and most of us very painfully, aware of this. But I do wish to refer to the extensive failure to use the powers available to protect the interests of society and the innocent and the law-abiding, or to punish the evildoers. Who can honestly claim that powers that could be used to curb the growth of 'black money', and a host of economic offences, have been adequately used (though one is happy to note that they have begun to be used recently), or that action has been taken to check political corruption? So many powers, legal and administrative are available to check corruption in the administration, but they have certainly not been used on a scale and with the determination commensurate with the dimensions of the problem. Non-use of power is certainly not comparable in culpability to its misuse or abuse; nevertheless, it can do great harm. For it does involve failure to discharge a responsibility entrusted by the constitution or the laws, or, the mandate of the electorate. Apart from its directly harmful consequences non-use of state power sets the general tone, and encourages inaction at all levels of the administration. The Sardar never faltered in using the powers he had in the government, and, one could add, in the Congress organization. There were, for instance, cases in Bihar in which he took action undeterred by the temporary damage to the reputation of the Congress Ministry which the action was likely to cause. Civil servants, as well as others in high authority knew that no corruption or departure from the path of rectitude which the eagle-eyed Sardar noticed, would be condoned. I vividly remember the expression of relief on the face of a Minister, who was apt to misuse his powers for narrow political and even personal ends, on this day thirty six years ago when the sad news of the Sardar's passing away was received. Evidently, he felt that he no longer needed to live in fear of the Sardar's powerful hand coming down on him. Such was the just fear and awe of the Sardar, the vigilant moral censor of governmental and political ethics, among those disposed to depart from the straight path.

Reflecting over the developments in the conduct of affairs in subsequent years, and their cumulative effect today, one cannot help feeling that the country seem to have lost one of the valuable legacies of the Sardar. We have had for many years a generally 'soft' administration, reflecting the character of a "soft" state. The Sardar did not live long enough after Independence to endow the new state, and its administrative apparatus, with a durable toughness. We make laws and regulations in plenty but do not enforce them with rigour; they are often allowed to be transgressed with impunity. One notices among many of our public functionaries a tendency to move from passivity to over-reaction to situations, and to alternate between failure to use power and its abuse. In certain parts of the country the Arms Act is virtually a dead letter. Even grave offences against person and property often go unpunished. Energetic action in a crisis, followed by a period of complacence only leads to another crisis, when a steadily firm administration backed by a strong political will, and anticipation of likely developments are called for. That was the Sardar's way of doing things during those fateful, crisis-ridden five years. I have personal knowledge of a case when a political leader in eastern India who was organizing a separatist movement leading to acts of violence, was called by the Sardar and told that a more powerful leader in north India had been detained in similar circumstances, and given a stern warning. The leader, went back with the sobering knowledge that if he did not heed the warning unrelenting action would follow, and he stopped his disruptive activities. The point of the story is the importance of credibility of the strong will of the state, and effectiveness of its administrative machinery. A great deal is achieved by the moral authority of the government, and the influence that goes with it, often making action unnecessary. But moral authority is built over a period, and is lost if power is abused, and drained away if used only spasmodically. We have moved a long way from the Sardar Patel era and have over the years forgotten the experience that should have become an integral part of our governmental doctrine.

The idea of a "committed" civil service, committed to the current social philosophy of the party in power at the time, and not merely to carrying out loyally the government's progrmme, was the doctrine canvassed in the seventies. That idea has no open supporters now, but there is implicit in certain attitudes, and the desire that civil servants should identify themselves with their Ministers. Such an idea would have been an anathema to the Sardar. There certainly has to be commitment to the Constitution to which every civil servant has to swear loyalty, and to dedicated service to the people; but this is not the sense in which the word 'commitment' was used. There are some reports of a civil servant being expected, on the pain of a disagreeable transfer, or worse, to fashion his advice or action to suit the wishes or interest of a Minister or a Ministry; and one of the consequences is frequent changes of the incumbents of even key posts. A return to the Sardar's concept of the civil service – and I use the word in the broad sense which includes the police and those in the technical and professional branches – is necessary if the administration is to prove capable of coping with the multitude of problems which the country is facing. Considerations extraneous to the requirements of the law and the public interest ought not to be imported in the management of the civil services, or civil servants deflected from a non-partisan course. This certainly is not the position today.

May I pause here for a moment and refer to some instances which bring out two balancing elements in Sardar Patel's attitude towards the senior civil servants. He had a tussle with Lord Mountbatten in 1946 in the appointment of a particular Indian officer to the post of Home Secretary, but he did not hesitate to replace that officer after a couple of years, when he did not prove entirely equal to his responsibilities. In another case the Sardar as Minister of Information and Broadcasting sent away the Secretary, a talented Indian civil servant, who had procrastinated in giving effect to an order of the Sardar appointing a Muslim poet and litterateur to a key post under the Ministry. But on the other side, the Sardar's harmonious relations with civil servants and his sensitivity towards their feelings is exemplified by his distress when H.V.R. Iyengar, the Home Secretary, feeling hurt because of some mis-understanding, requested to be allowed to proceed on leave. The Sardar is reported to have remarked that never in his life had he come across an official working under him who had asked to be relieved out of dissatisfaction with his orders. In the event Iyengar was reassured. Also in the other two cases to which I have referred, the officers were moved out with due grace. The Sardar demanded efficient service and discipline from civil servants, but also treated them with courtesy and consideration. In this way he got the best out of them. Such a balanced attitude is as sound today as it was then, but is not generally in evidence.

The functions of the executive branch, being regulated by the Constitution, laws and statutory rules, are enmeshed with those of the judiciary. It has not only to deal with most of the cases under the laws made for administrative purposes including those for maintaining peace and order, but has also the function of reviewing the legality of executive actions. It will not therefore be out of place to touch upon the Sardar's attitude towards the judiciary. There can be no better testimony to his unqualified respect for the independence of the judiciary than what H.J. Kania, then Chief Justice, said in the course of his obituary tribute: "By his death the Judiciary has lost a great champion of its freedom and independence. It is within my personal knowledge, first as Chief Secretary of a State and later as Union Home Secretary, that the policy laid down firmly by the Sardar in the late forties continued to be followed till towards the later part of 1970, when there was indication of change in the attitude towards high judicial appointments. What happened during the seventies is only too well known. But even in recent speech before the Supreme Court Bar Association the present Chief Justice of India spoke about the inaction of the Government in making appointments to the High Courts and the Supreme Court, neglecting or not respecting the reactions of the Chief Justices of the High Courts and the Chief Justice of India, with the result that there were large numbers of vacancies in those courts, while the arrears were mounting. He proceeded to observe that the government not communicating the reasons for disagreement, "may conceivably give rise to suspicion that extraneous factors have played a part in the rejections....Moreover, if such practice is allowed to prevail, we might witness the sorry spectacle of those wishing to be appointed judges or promoted to the higher echelons of the judiciary running about the corridors of power and lobbying the executives."

The Sardar's aim was to establish a firm but just administration, and this required an independent judiciary manned by persons of ability and character. It is not enough that there should be no interference by the executive in judicial proceedings; independence of the judiciary requires a sense of security, self-respect and self assurance among judicial officers. The state of affairs described by the Chief Justice of India, and the feeling that a judge can be transferred from one High Court to another even if such transfer is not recommended by the Chief Justice of India in the interest of judicial administration, do not make for an ideal judiciary. Also, if there is unconscionable delay in disposal of cases, the effectiveness of the executive, for instance of the police is greatly reduced, and the citizen loses hope of getting redress against injustice. One can well imagine what the Sardar would have thought of situations as in Delhi and Gujarat in which the Bar felt called upon to go on strike to have a deserving person appointed as Chief Justice or a Judge. On the question of lobbying by aspirants to high judicial appointments, to which the Chief Justice of India referred, I am reminded of Sardar Patel's reaction to a senior judicial officer in Bihar having invoked the help of Minister in the Central Government in support of his representation. The Sardar not only turned down the representation, but asked the State government to convey to the officer that the way he had attempted to advance his claim had strengthened the Sardar's judgement about the officer's total unfitness for ever being elevated to the High Court.

His principles and methods of administration – the Sardar would not have approved of the words 'administrative philosophy' – were exemplified in his own way of conducting affairs, illumined occasionally by a pithy remark. H.V.R. Iyengar who had worked as Home Secretary with three successive Home Ministers described to me in a personal talk their diverse methods. One of them, with a subtle intellect, revelled in his dialectical skill and pointed out the flaws in every course of action that was proposed. But when requested to decide what should be done, he would tell Iyengar, "Do as you had initially proposed". Another Home Minister, with exceptional accomplishments in a learned profession, had such an open mind that he found it impossible in some cases to close it for months. Iyengar would return intellectually humbled, at the cost of some of his time, in the first case, and with a feeling of helplessness in the second. In contrast, the Sardar with whom he had worked earlier would listen intently, go to the root of the matter instantly, and either approve the proposed solution with just a nod, or give another, and a sounder solution, with the fewest words. And, to reproduce the substance of what Iyengar told me, he could then go forward to act with the feeling that the strength of the whole nation was behind him, and that the Sardar would stand by him whatever might come.

The Sardar's capacity for taking, what has been described by some who had close association with him as, lightning decisions was the product not only of the natural endowments of an administrator of genius, but also of the detailed knowledge of men and affairs, acquired by prodigious industry over the years and kept upto date by a variety of means. The Sardar lived in an age when computers were not in wide use; but the working of his mind is comparable to that of an advanced computer with access to first-rate software. In administration, decisions have often to be taken quickly; in Indian administration, with its extensive responsibilities in matters of development and economic management generally, and for providing social services, speedy decisions have particular importance. And yet, the decisions have to be sound. The lesson from the Sardar's life is that it is of vital importance for administrators, particularly at the higher levels, to systematically equip themselves with material relevant to their sphere of work, but develop the capacity to discriminate between the important and the unimportant. An eye for the significant detail, but not getting lost in the pursuit of minutiae for its own sake is the mark of an able administrator.

There was so much else in the Sardar's style of functioning which reflected his conceptions of how administration should be carried on, and which could well be treated as Sutras – to use an expressive Sanskrit word – to guide Indian administrators even today. The Sardar had a powerful, precise and piercing intellect with a capacity to take infinite pains in the pursuit of national tasks. But he was not an intellectual. It is far from my intention to under-estimate, in this academic community, the importance of intellectuals – of persons devoted to pursuit of knowledge and dealing in ideas. As in academic life, so in administration, one has to assemble and analyse the relevant facts, and be prepared to accept the conclusion to which the analysis leads. But there are some major differences between the two. A scholar has generally far more time to collect data than an administrator, who has often to take a decision on whatever material he can get within a short time, beyond which a decision cannot be postponed. There is also another significant difference: in academic work once the test of intellectual rigour and internal logic has been met, the matter ends; but in administration the tests of practicability and public acceptance have to be met, even if viewed from a purely logical angle the proposed decision is flawed. Critical situations had to be met and time was running out. More than any one else in that momentous period of our history the Sardar realized that there is, in the words of Shakespeare, "a tide in the affairs of men which taken at the flood leads to fortune". His decisions in the cases of Junagadh and Hyderabad are examples.

The Sardar's sight was set on action; time and again he emphasized the importance of implementation, without which even excellent plans and programmes could prove sterile. He had ideas, and was given to deep reflection on the country's problems, but he was not an ideologue – a trader in ideas for their own sake. He had a vision of India's future as a strong and stable nation, democratic and secular, with united and prosperous people. And he worked on the practical plane with passionate zeal towards the realization of that vision, but he was not a visionary. He was a realist, who looked at things with an eye unclouded by sentiment or illusive idealism. He is reported to have remarked. "It will be folly to ignore realities; facts take their revenge if they are not faced squarely....." He was rooted in principles, but flexible in the choice of methods, which he was prepared to adapt to the requirements of a situation. I shall presently provide some illustrations.

The Sardar was close to the people, as you gentlemen and ladies in Gujarat know very well. He was a son of the soil, who graduated into national politics through organizing movements of peasant resistance, and industrial labour, and as a municipal administrator. It is not widely known, in other parts of India, that having distinguished himself at the Bar examination in England, built up a very flourishing practice as a Barrister and adopted a western style of life, once he joined Gandhiji, he not only gave up his legal practice and discarded the western style of life but took a vow not to own any personal property - a vow that he kept to the end, dying without owning even a house. With such a background it was natural for him to be close to the people, sensitive to their needs and problems, and with deep concern for their wellbeing. But he was no believer in populism with all the spurious elements that go into it – a lesson for politicians and administrators.

Rhetoric in public speeches, and circumlocution, particularly in official writing are among our national characteristics. The Sardar was not an orator or a man of letters; at a university function he described himself as a graduate of the university of life. Both in speech and in writing he was brief, incisive and direct. And there could never be any doubt that he would stand by his word. Even Liaqat Ali Khan, a political antagonist before partition could say after his death that "...he always meant what he said and he said what he meant". It has been my experience that trust in his word is a far greater asset of an administrator than cleverness or elegant expression. Something of the Sardar's way of working rubbed off on the civil servants who had opportunities to see his mind at work. (I realize that I am holding out the Sardar's example of brevity in a lengthy speech! My only excuse is the embarrassment of riches, which his contributions to administration, accomplished and initiated and his many dimensional personality held).

'The Sardar has sometimes been described as a man of "blood and iron", and wholly inaptly compared to Bismarck. He was certainly a man of iron in the struggle for Independence, and its consolidation when it came. Watching the Sardar during the critical months of 1947-48, with the vast carnage, and movement of uprooted humanity in the western part of India, aggression in Kashmir and the problems of Hyderabad, General Bucher, the British Commander in Chief saw something "rock like in his demeanour" reminding him of "the pictures of Roman Emperors". He could not be deflected from his principles or pursuit of the basic national purposes. But he was wholly averse to blood-shedding unless the circumstances, such as the security of the country in Hyderabad or facing aggression in Kashmir, made use of the armed forces unavoidable. Save in the exceptional circumstances of Hyderabad and Junagadh, he secured integration, leading to merger, through persuasion, adroit handling and courteous dealings with the princes, appeal to their patriotism as Indians, and offer of generous and honourable treatment. He did not take recourse to intimidation, but if with the power of his personality and moral authority he was held in awe he could not help it. A cruder method of dealing with the princes might well have led to conflicts, with the danger of the country's Balkanisation in the still unsettled conditions.

He did not want government servants to be rigid or authoritarian in their relations with citizens; he wanted them to be imbued will sympathy and compassion. I quote his own words: "I shall now say a word to those government servants to whom has fallen and will continue to fall the implementation of the many measures of control and of regimentation of everyday affairs of the citizen which we have to enforce. The powers which they wield, if rightly used can bring the nation heavy dividends, but abused, can bring not only harm but disrepute. They will very often find that a kind word, a sympathetic gesture and an attitude of understanding, coupled with honesty and integrity, will enable them to do their work much quicker and much better than snobbery, a sense of superiority and such other departures from rectitude. No one has done more to see that the services get their just rights, due meed of credit, than myself. I therefore make a call upon them to do their part of national duty....If the legislature and government place such large powers in their hands, they also place on them responsibility for using them properly.....Let them, therefore, so conduct themselves that every action of theirs brings as much good to the nation as possible without injuring anyone except the evil doer". These are precepts of even greater validity in the present conditions than they were in 1950. In the course of the same address he had expressed his views about the need for compassion in these words, "we always speak of India's culture, of Indian civilization, but do we ever pause to think that the relief of the poor, natural among neighbours, charity to the helpless and kindness to the downtrodden have been the shining virtues of that culture and civilization? To describe a man who could offer such advice to government servants and talk so feelingly about compassion, as only a man of iron is a grossly unfair, and simplistic, delineation of a rich, many-faceted personality.

The Sardar had chosen to concentrate his energies on the country's internal affairs. But the clarity of his vision and uncanny foresight even in regard to external security are indeed remarkable. He advised against the Kashmir problem being referred to the United Nations or offer of a plebiscite under UN auspices. His fear of such course bringing in international politics into operation in a manner prejudicial to our interests, proved only too true. Sheikh Abdullah himself told me in November 1950, when I was on a private visit to Srinagar, that all his problems had their root in the uncertainty created by the reference to the United Nations and that while he had the greatest respect and affection for Mr. Nehru he would prefer Sardar Patel to handle Kashmir affairs and to cut the tangled knot by his direct methods such as those he had adopted in certain other cases. As recorded in V. Shankar's Reminiscences of Sardar Patel' the Sheikh had earlier spoken to the same effect to the Sardar himself. The Sardar had also cautioned the Prime Minister about the dangers which China's occupation of Tibet presaged. And on the policy adopted towards Nepal too the Sardar's advice, not accepted in 1950, was later proved to have been absolutely sound. He thought that no attempt should be made to export democracy to Nepal, that sponsoring a movement for democracy from Indian soil would be ill-advised, and that India ought to extend friendly help in promoting reconciliation of the main elements in Nepalese life, so that a government in keeping with that country's historical and cultural traditions, and suited to the existing conditions, could come into being. The policy followed in 1950 proved a failure within a few years and had to be reversed in the sixties, and completely changed in early seventies.

Time often provides a far better test of statesmanship and administrative genius, than contemporary judgement. In the Sardar's case his monumental achievements were acclaimed even in his life time. But in the cases I have just mentioned it was left to history to prove the wisdom of his views. I may also add an instance relating to internal affairs. Some twenty years after the Sardar's death Jayaprakash Narayan made a public statement as follows: "Rajaji once unburdened his heart by publicly confessing to a wrong he had done to Sardar Patel. I find myself in similar situation; the dominant feeling within me today is one of self-reproach because during his life I was not merely a critic but an opponent of the great Sardar".

It is only rarely in a country's history that a colossus, such as Vallabhbhai Patel makes his appearance; and it was our great good fortune that he was there at a crucial period in Indian life. How one wishes that we had today a leader, cast even in less heroic mould, who could turn the tide of corruption, indiscipline, violence and lawlessness, disunity and disruption, which now mark the national scene.

What I have said may be of little value, but in preparing this lecture I have myself derived great inspiration and felt immeasurably enriched.

PART III
EXTRACTS FROM GOVERNMENT REPORTS

14

Problems of Policing India

L.P. Singh

I am grateful to Shri Ali for inviting me to deliver this year's Sardar Vallabhbhai Patel Memorial Lecture. I was associated with the Academy project up to the stage of construction and I am happy to see this premier institution for training police officers in a fully developed state.

It was an imaginative and farsighted decision to associate Sardar Vallabhbhai Patel's name with this Academy. Not only now but even a hundred years hence those who enter the Academy would be reminded of the Sardar's immense contribution to the country's freedom and its consolidation and the relevance of what he stood for to the functions and responsibilities of the police. He was without doubt the greatest statesman – administrator of independent India, the greatest in my view during the last four hundred years. He stands with Asoka and Akbar as a unifier of the country. The historical and political circumstances and the policies of the imperial regime which led to the partition of the country were beyond his control. But the unification of the rest of the country accomplished within the five years of life left to him was a monumental achievement : even after more than a hundred years the British had only paramountcy and not direct rule over a third of the country. For the first time since the Mauryan bureaucracy there was established a uniform administration from which no part of the country was excluded. And never before had the country been unified as an unrestricted democracy in which all citizens had equal political and other rights.

In maintaining the unity of the country and its democratic and secular character the police have a crucial role. They have to deal not only with any overt threats to the unity of the country and to our constitutional system, but to maintain conditions in which the

---

Source: Sardar Vallabhbhai Patel Memorial Lectures (1984-2011). Sardar Vallabhbhai Patel National Police Academy, Hyderabad, Third Edition 2012.

process of national integration can go on smoothly. The political unity of a country can be secure only with a united and socially cohesive people. I hope that all those who pass through this Academy will always remember the responsibility they carry for preserving and sustaining the Sardar's legacy and will derive inspiration in their efforts from the example he set of courage and determination in facing heavy odds at a critical stage of our history.

It was a year ahead of independence that the Sardar got a resolution adopted by the Congress Chief Ministers authorizing the setting up of two All-India services : the IAS and IPS. He foresaw that these two services would contribute to the unity of the country and the strength of the administrative structure and make for a high standard of efficiency and uniformity. He had a deep understanding of the lessons of Indian history, which bore witness to regional and other narrow loyalties leading to chronic divisiveness, especially in periods of absence of a strong central authority. He was convinced that All-India services for general and law and order administration would be essential adjuncts of a strong constitutional authority at the Centre, operating in consonance with the functions to be assigned to the States in a quasi-federal Constitution of which he was one of the main architects. He believed that India could be governed only with firmness and could not be held together by adopting soft options or vacillation in critical situations. But it was not to be the sort of firmness which had characterized imperial rule. Members of the police and other services were to function as servants of the India people and not as their masters : and they were not to serve as instruments for promoting the political interests of those in power as they had been during the British rule but of the state and the laws. To quote from Sardar Patel's own formulation in 1948 : An "All India service, efficient, disciplined and contented, assured of its prospect as a result of diligent and honest work, is a sine quo non of sound administration under a democratic regime even more than under an authoritarian rule. The service must be above party and we should ensure that political considerations either in its discipline or in its control are reduced to the minimum if not eliminated altogether". In addition to creating the two All-India services, he initiated measures for strengthening the police forces in the States. But for these steps the administrative machinery might not have been able to cope effectively with the formidable problems which the country had to face following the upheaval of the partition and the sea-change which occurred with the advent of independence.

Sardar Patel's public acknowledgement of the patriotism and dedication of public servants and his expression of trust in them, gave them the self-assurance and the élan without which they could not have given their best. Addressing the Constituent Assembly the Sardar had said "..As a man of experience I tell you, do not quarrel with the instruments with which you want to work. It is a bad workman who quarrels with his instruments..... Every man wants some sort of encouragement. Nobody wants to put in work when every day he is criticized and ridiculed in public...." Proceeding further, he enunciated the doctrine of intellectual integrity of civil servants and their sharing responsibility with a sharpness which has not since been equalled. He said "Today my Secretary can write a note opposed to my views. I have given that freedom to all my Secretaries. I have told them, if you do not give your honest opinion for fear that it will displease your Minister, please then you had better go. I will bring another Secretary..... you have agreed to share responsibility". Though he specifically mentioned Secretaries to government, the principle he laid was obviously applicable to other officials as well. I have no doubt that he would have asked for similar independence for instance from heads of the police services.

No another occasion he said, "I spent a life time with Gandhiji, I am not a fool to forget his teachings. I also want village self-sufficiency. But what is the position in which you find yourself? Villagers are forsaking the villages for cities. If we do not have industries what will happen? Will villages equip the Army"? He did not question the validity of Gandhiji's non-violent philosophy as the ultimate deal. But he was a realist who saw human beings and the world as they are and society as it is constituted; and he was willing to deal with problems of security, peace and order through effective instruments under the authority of the state.

It was the Sardar's way to speak out sharply when the others in the same situation might have preferred to equivocate. In referring to the responsibility of political leaders and society in general, when there was a great deal of violence in West Bengal, he observed, "... Today when seventy percent of the policemen are Bengalies themselves, what is the sense of attacking them? They impose restrictions for our own good, not on orders from any foreigners. Any threat to civil liberties comes not from them but from those who foster the terrorist cult. You have to stop them if you want to keep your liberty. You cannot pass the buck to the police. No democracy can be run with the policemen's baton. It has become a habit with us to blame the police. We have to change this attitude. It was another police whom we criticized night and day. But if you do not have sympathy for them in the work they are doing today, you will regret it". Another observation of the Sardar will bear quotation : "It will be a folly to ignore realities. Facts take their revenge if they are not faced squarely and well". Can it be honestly claimed that all these years we have kept this in mind and have not allowed problems to get tangled because of failure to face facts in good time and with a clear vision and courage?

The Sardar had an iron will which would not bend under pressure : but he was always anxious to avoid blood-shed if the essential tasks could be accomplished through persuasion and accommodation of the legitimate interests and sensitivities of those concerned. This was exemplified in the way he brought about the merger of the princely States. He believed in firmness in administration in the sense that it should be impervious to considerations other than those of the public interest and fairness. He wanted powers available to government's agencies to be used when necessary without faltering : but he was totally against any abuse or misuse of power, which always erodes the moral authority of the government. His ideas about proper use of powers excluded ruthlessness or even authoritarianism. I quote one of his statements about the conduct of public servants, which is applicable to the police just as much as to other agencies of government.... "The powers which they wield, if rightly used can bring the nation heavy dividends, but abused, can bring not only harm but disrepute. They will often find that a kind word, a sympathetic gesture and an attitude of understanding coupled with honesty and integrity, will enable them to do their work much quicker and much better than snobbery, a sense of superiority and such other departures from rectitude... If the legislature and government place such large powers in their hands, they also place on them responsibility for using them properly... Let them, therefore, so conduct themselves that every action of theirs brings as much good to the nation as possible without injuring anyone except the evil doer". These are percepts of even greater validity in the present conditions than they were in 1950 for many more powers are now available, for instance, to the police. In the course of same statement he had expressed his views about the need for compassion in these words. "We always speak of India's culture, of Indian civilization, but do we ever pause to think that the relief of the poor, natural among neighbours, charity to the helpless and kindness to the downtrodden have been the shining virtues of that culture and civilization?" It may be occupationally difficult for the police to regard kindness and compassion as essential elements in their dealings: and yet they have to do so if they have to win the respect and have the co-operation of the people. The Sardar's idea in essence was : Make the virtuous and the law abiding feel secure, protect the weak and deal firmly with the evil doer. Could not this be an excellent motto for the police?

No branch of the administration in India has to face problem more formidable than those of the police. To begin with, policing any democratic country is a complex and sensitive affair requiring delicate balancing of divergent considerations. There is on one side the need to maintain order, to enforce the laws and to prevent and detect crime : on the other, the imperative of respecting the citizen's fundamental rights to freedom of speech, association, and peaceable assembly. There is in addition the expectation of citizens that under all circumstances their feelings and susceptibilities, as well as their rights, shall be respected ; but there is no general recognition that some restrictions on the rights of individuals and some inconvenience to them are the price to be paid for the good of society.

The police alone among the civil agencies of government have functions which can be broadly described as coercive, and they therefore, stand in the public mind as symbols ultimately of the brute power of the State. Moreover, in the nature of things those who have coercive power and the authority under legal sanction to use force are occasionally apt, particularly at the lower levels, to abuse or exceed their powers. These are not exclusively Indian phenomena. They occur for instance, in USA, UK and France, all well established democracies. In each of those countries, the actions of the police, especially in handling public order situations and interrogation of persons accused or suspected of crime are constantly subjected to criticism by political parties in opposition, citizens generally and in particular, groups engaged in protection of civil liberties.

Intelligence functions in our States are the exclusive responsibility of police officers and they are substantially so also in the Central Government, even though while engaged in intelligence duties the officers do not have police powers. In this matter too there is on the one side the need to collect intelligence in the interest of external and internal security, preservation of the constitutional system, and about plans and preparations for its subversion through violence or otherwise. On the other side, there is need to respect the rights of citizens including their right to privacy. We may leave aside the suspicion about intelligence officers engaging themselves in improper activities or being used for illegitimate purposes though under veil of secrecy the temptation to sin does exist in India as elsewhere. However, there is always the risk of an intelligence organization being accused of doing too much or too little. If things go wrong even because of the infirmity of political will or failure of the executive to take effective action, the intelligence organization usually comes in for unmerited criticism against which it cannot speak out. On the other hand, there is often the criticism that the "big brother" is casting his prying eyes on innocent citizens and adopting means, fair or foul, to get information. This creates the feeling that those opposed to government are being subjected to illegitimate surveillance. In this matter too, it is not only in India but also in other democracies that the intelligence organizations come under attack for what is regarded as their omissions or excessive and devious actions. But the difference is that while in those countries the intelligence personnel are not drawn usually from the police, in India all real or supposed failures and deviations get debited to the police.

In the matter of prevention and investigation of offences also, the police come under criticism, deserved or undeserved. There are charges of inaction, partisanship or corruption. Not unoften the police particularly in the lower ranks, are accused of applying third degree methods. The police do usually have the need to interrogate suspects and the only question is as to where the line is to be drawn between legitimate and humane interrogation, and interrogation involving mental cruelty. Use of physical force is of course, always impermissible, there is no question of a blurred line between its use and avoidance. The police are often accused of it and they always deny the charge. My own experience in different capacities have been that third-degree methods, even in the interrogation of insurgents and terrorists, is not only wholly wrong in itself, but often counter-productive, leading to false statements, and creating antagonism among the people. And whenever there is death in police custody it is assumed that it had been caused by torture.

Our quasi-federal system presents another set of unique problems. Public order and police are State subjects under the our Constitution, and yet questions about the alleged failure of the police to deal satisfactorily with a serious communal or agrarian situation or about commission of excesses are frequently raised in Parliament. Attempts to bar discussion on the ground of constitutional limitation do not always succeed, or satisfy the members raising the matter. For historical reasons, and our constitutional system under which certain general responsibilities are vested in the Union : the federal demarcations have not had the degree of clarity and general acceptance which, for instance, they have had in USA . There are occasions when the judgment at the Centre about the handling of a major public order problem by the police differs from that of the State Government's and it is not easy to satisfy two masters.

While on this subject may I invite attention to the fact that though 'police' is a State subject, we had, wisely a National Police Commission. The Commission's report is a monumental document of its recommendations. One may or may not agree with every recommendation made by the Commission ; but there is no recommendation which does not show deep thought and insight and a forward-look. But for constitutional reasons the bulk of the recommendations had to be sent to the States for consideration. I understand that the Central Government has taken decision on most of the recommendations which fall within its sphere. But from such fragmentary information as is available to me, it does not appear that on a substantial part of the recommendations the States generally have taken adequate action. In this matter, as in the standard of policing generally, there may, of course be variations. The Academy is perhaps in a position to examine the response of the States and at least to stimulate further interest in the recommendations through the police officers who after attending courses return to the States.

Apart from those of a democratic polity and our constitutional system, we have law and order problems arising out of our unparalleled diversity, the present stage of our historical development and certain other causes.

Our laws relating to fire arms and explosives though amended in recent years are still not commensurate with the requirements of the situation, and their enforcement far from so. We have international borders on our entire land mass, and some of our neighbouring countries have governments which are not friendly to us and some others even though friendly are not always able to prevent smuggling of arms and explosives or use of their territory for hostile activities against us. This has aggravated our law and order problems, especially those of serious dimensions. In practically all parts of north India, from east to west, there are illicitly held arms and explosives in the hands of the people, and in some parts of the country there are unlicensed factories manufacturing arms, or explosive devices. These are conditions in which no civil police can be fully effective, and the result has been that during the last

25 years or so we have gone on continuously increasing the strength of armed police in the States and under the Central Government. Part of the expansion of the latter was necessitated for effective policing of our land borders. But for the greatly expanded Assam Rifles, a semi-military organization, there would have been an even greater expansion of the armed police. I shall revert to the expansion of the police forces.

There are certain peculiar difficulties, reflecting the ambiguities and contradictions characterizing Indian life today. There is a view in certain quarters that the police should not enter a place of worship even if it harbours persons suspected to have committed grave offences. In fact, there is a strong feeling in sections of the Sikh community that even if an offence is committed within the premises of a gurudwara, the police should not enter the premises to investigate the offence, or to arrest the suspect. This has been amply exemplified in Punjab in recent years. This is a "doctrine" peculiar to India : though fortunately, objection to police entry in certain circumstances is not raised strongly in regard to Hindu temples, mosques and churches. There is no legal sanction behind the objection that is so emotionally raised by the Sikh community, but that does not alter the indignation that entry into a gurudwara arouses and not unoften leads to violent reprisals against the authorities. If certain places of worship are regarded as being, or to say, out of bounds for the police, the reason is that though we are avowedly a secular state the full implications of secularism, the separation of politics from religion, have not been clearly enunciated or have or had universal or unqualified acceptance. Otherwise, places of worship would be used only for religious and related social and cultural purposes; they would not be made centres of political activity including activity which violates the law of the land or pose a threat to the security and unity of the country.

It is also claimed that there is violation of the sanctity of an educational campus if the police enter it to enforce the law or to arrest suspects. It is certainly not desirable for the police to enter educational campuses unless there is a clear necessity for doing so. Beyond this, any objection that is raised has no rational basis. There have been cases in which an educational campus had been treated as a citadel from which students had gone out to commit acts of violence outside and then retreat to the safety of the campus. As far as I am aware except in Germany during the 19th Century no such claim of inviolability of educational premises has been made or is recognized in other countries. The claim of sanctity would be tenable if the premises were to be used only for intellectual pursuits. There could be no objection even to a most contentious political or socio-economic issue being freely discussed, and diverse ideologies and policies canvassed. In fact, even political activities would not be open to objection if they were kept within the limits of the law, or did not disturb the atmosphere of peace and social concord appropriate to educational institutions. But there is a misconceived notion that even if educational premises become centres of unlawful political activities or bases for unlawful acts outside the premises, the agencies of law and order should not intervene.

The Preamble of our Constitution declares India to be a secular republic, and yet outwardly or inwardly communal parties have been allowed to function in politics and even participate in Ministries formed by major secular political parties. This has been among the factors impelling national integration and even leading to communal strife. The police have thus to deal with the effect of causes over which they have no control. The causes can be removed only by legislatures and political parties, and through a change in the outlook of the people.

There has been a practice, if not an accepted doctrine, that following large-scale communal disturbances the criminal cases that are instituted should be withdrawn in order that inter-communal harmony could be restored. This in my view is an extremely pernicious practice. To begin with, there is difficulty about identifying most of the offenders when large numbers are involved. Secondly, independent evidence which could lead to submission of charge-sheets, or convictions in courts of law is not often available but to the extent the offenders can be identified, and direct or circumstantial evidence can be had, the cases must be prosecuted with utmost vigour. The law is respected, and has a deterrent effect, only when its processes are recognized as being inexorable and not subject to interruption on any extraneous considerations. To interrupt the processes of law for restoration of peace and harmony, shows a serious misconception and misjudgment about the consequences of such interruption. When expediency is given primacy over sound policies the long-term consequence is the opposite of what is desired. There has been far too much flabbiness in making full use of the law. If the powers available under the law are not steadily used, situations arise in which excessive use of force becomes necessary ; and spasmodic use of powers is unsatisfactory in more ways than one.

The unconscious delays that have been occurring in judicial proceedings have been a contributory factor in the growth of violence and lawlessness. The delays in disposal of cases not only take away much of the fear of the law, but are, like withdrawals, a distinct disincentive to the police. The diminution of faith in speedy action through the courts may even be a reason – indefensible though the action itself is – why the police some times feel tempted to resort to a short-cut, such as a fake encounter. Detailed comments on judicial delays would be outside the scope of this lecture : but there can be no doubt that they reduce the effectiveness and keenness of the police.

The question is sometimes raised whether the country is under-policed or whether if there is dissatisfaction with the police the reasons are to be sought elsewhere, such as their professional and ethical standards, certain imbalances in their composition and manning patterns, and their public relations. I mention certain statistics which a distinguished former police officer, Shri P.R. Rajagopal, has made available to me from the material collected by him for the third volume of his study of violence in Indian society.

While the population of the country had increased from 1951 to 1981 by 89.75%, the strength of the police in the States and Union Territories had increased from 4,67,770 to 8,97,830 that is by 91.95%. If the armed police battalions and paramilitary forces under the Central Government are added, the increase would work out to a much higher percentage, for the ITBP and BSF came into existence only in the sixties and the CRPF had been a tiny force in 1951. It is clear that increase in the strength of the police forces has more than kept pace with the growth of population, and also to some extent with the rise in the proportion of urban population, which requires a much higher scale of policing.

There has not doubt been increase in the total crime and the volume of crime per lakh of population, as the following figures will show :

	1951	*1961*	*1971*	*1981*	*% growth*
Murder	10,343	-	-	22727	+ 119.73
Volume	2.82	-	-	3.2	+ 4.3
Kidnapping	5157	-	-	13833	+ 168.24
Volume	1.40	-	-	2.02	+ 5.80
Dacoity	7301	-	-	14626	+ 100.33
Volume	1.99	-	-	2.13	+3.46
Robbery	9571	-	-	22996	+ 140.27
Volume	2.61	-	-	3.36	+ 4.84
Riots	20529	27199	64114	110361	+ 437.59
Volume	5.49	6.19	11.72	16.11	+ 15.63
Arms Act	N.A	10145	23908	69662	+ 586.66
V Volume	N.A	2.07	4.37	10.17	+ 39.11

Assuming that the reported figures of other crimes are close to the reality there may be no cause for alarm. What, however, is highly disturbing is the vast increase in the cases of rioting and offences under the Arms Act. In both these cases the increase was notably steep since 1971. It is the circumstances under which these increases had occurred, and the means and methods to be adopted by the police for dealing with those offences, posing as they do a serious threat to peace and security, that would require special attention during the present and the next decade. It may be beyond the powers of the police to deal with the deeper causes of the increases and certain other factors contributing to them; but the police could still curb these offences through an improved professional management, more imaginative and better planned approach backed by greater resolution.

A comparison of the increase in crime from 1971 to 1984 and its incidence per lakh of population in six other democratic countries, viz. USA, UK, West Germany, France, Australia, and Japan shows that both the extent of increase and incidence per lakh have been much lower in India. Our figures have been much lower even than those of Japan which is known for its orderly society and excellent crime control. The comparative figures may create a feeling of complacency. But it has to be remembered that all the other six countries are highly industrialized and urbanized, while India still remains an essentially rural country. There would be a valid basis for comparison if separate figures for our urban areas were available. There may also be a significant difference in the extent of registration of crime between those countries and India.

Looking at statistics one can perhaps reasonably make the observation that it is not so much the strength of the police forces but their quality, methods and techniques, and their equipment, which had fallen below the requisite standard. Briefly put, they point to the need for a radical qualitative improvement including some change in the structure of the police forces, with a higher complement of grades above that of constables and a corresponding reduction in the relative strength of the constabulary. A force so composed could perform better especially as there is a far higher standard of education in the force now. The National Police Commission too has recommended an increase in the complement of officers, giving cogent reasons for the recommendation.

I may mention in passing that creation of numerous posts of Director-General in the States, or increasing the number of Inspectors General to such an extent that the Deputy Inspectors

General and Superintendents of Police tend to lose their initiative and sense of responsibility is not the sort of restructuring that can improve things. I understand that Maharashtra and West Bengal have only one Director-General of Police. Can it be said that the police administration in these States is inferior to that in some of the northern and central States which have two or more Director-Generals? One could perhaps say with greater justification that the standard of policing tends to be in inverse ratio to the numerical strength of the apex organization. A uniformed force subject to strict discipline requires not a hydra-headed but unified control and direction. If the consideration is improvement of career prospects of senior officers other devices, such as higher scale of remuneration, could be considered, without affecting a sound professional administrative arrangement.

Whenever new problems or additional tasks arise the normal reaction of every department of government is to ask for additional personnel and usually to replicate the existing standard unit. It has been my own experience that often reallocation of the exiting men, a change in the manning pattern, and better equipment, in other words a qualitative improvement and adaptation to the new situation rather than a simple increase in number is a more productive approach. I believe that such an approach would be particularly appropriate in the case of the police services with increase in urbanization and the emergence of the middle classes as a substantial and still growing proportion of the population.

Once the view was taken that the pre-independence arrangemnt of the army holding a substantial strength of troops for internal security duties should be discontinued, the States and Union Territories had of necessity to increase their armed police forces. These forces had to be increased further with the growing feeling that the army ought not to be called in aid of civil authority for dealing with any but the most serious situations. In fact, there is now a clear recognition that even for dealing with serious communal disturbances, or terrorism as in Punjab, and excepting only insurgences, it is the armed police of the States and those of the centre which are not only the more appropriate but also the more effective instruments. The army is trained and oriented for its basic task of defence of the country. By the sixties it was realized that the burden of policing and country's international borders should also not be placed on the army. Moreover, as the policing of - international borders fell within the central sphere, and was a task which could not be effectively handled by the police forces of the States, creation of the Border Security Force and the Indo-

Tibetan Border Police, and expansion of the Assam Rifles became necessary. With increase in communal and other serious disturbances of the peace and of unlicensed firearms and explosives, it appeared that the armed police forces of the States would need to be frequently reinforced by central forces, and this led to a substantial expansion of the CRPF which had been a small force till then. The picture by the eighties was that the strength of armed police in the States and Union Territories had increased to about 2.6 lakhs including 221 battalions and that of the central armed police to about 200 battalions. But for these measures the demand of the army for aid to civil authority would have increased to an extent that might have affected the army's capability to face its legitimate task.

I am not aware of any democratic country where the armed police constitute such a large part of the total police force. Unavoidable in the circumstances as the increase in the armed police forces in the States has been so far it would not be desirable in my view to increase their strength any further. It has been my experience in different parts of the country that if the training, discipline and officering of the armed police battalions were raised to the standard of the CRPF, and their composition reflected better the various sections of the population, and in particular if they had adequate representation of the minority communities, and the backward classes, the armed police battalions could inspire greater confidence and be far more effective in dealing with communal and other major disturbances. I got an analysis made of the composition of armed police battalions, and of the police forces generally, in some of the States with which I was concerned in one capacity or another and I found that the minority communities and backward classes were in many cases under-represented. I have also found generally that the officering of the armed police battalion has been inadequate in strength and qualitatively unsatisfactory. Recruitment to the Indian Police Service, and to the Deputy Superintendent cadres in the States is made keeping in view the diverse nature of their duties and responsibilities. A large part of their duties falls in the sphere of control and supervision of the civil police, prevention and detection of the crime, and collection of intelligence. It is not every IPS officer or every Deputy Superintendent who has the aptitude, training and experience needed for commanding armed police battalions. And the problem does not end there. It is well-known that by and large able officers are kept in the general line or are deputed to the central police organizations, and not unoften the less competent ones are appointed to command the armed police battalions. These appointments sometimes have even a punitive purpose. It has been my feeling for a long time that IPS and also perhaps the State Police Services, should have separate branches for officering armed police battalions, with recruitment made by criteria related to the requirements of armed police. This branch of the IPS could also provide officers to the BSF, ITBP and CRPF, with a periodical interchange of officers between the States and the central police organizations. The recommendations made on this subject by the National Police Commission point in this direction but do not specifically provide that the armed police battalions in the States and Union territories, should be officered from the same branch of the IPS from which officers of the BSF, ITBP or CRPF would be drawn. This to my mind is one of the major problem which needs attention in the interest of better handling of major communal and other disturbances.

Once the standard of armed police battalions is improved and they are imaginatively located keeping in view the areas likely to have serious trouble, and they are equipped for rapid mobility, they should meet all reasonable requirements, supplemented when necessary by the central forces. There is in my view no justification for going on increasing the number of armed police battalions in the Sates. If expansion of the police forces is considered absolutedly necessary it should be made on the civil side.

One of the unfortunate results of the expansion of the armed police has been a radical change in the idea of policing, and a marked decline in the degree of reliance that could be placed on the civil police and on its purposive use. This has not been a deliberate decision, but an almost unnoticed process over the years. There is no situation in which the civil police, and in particular the personnel manning police stations, cannot have an important and productive role. Whether it is collection of information, taking timely precautions, and keeping higher authorities informed to enable them to intervene before things get out of hand, the officer in charge of a police station has a vital function. Prevention of ordinary crime and its investigation are of course the recognized functions of the civil police. To my mind, it is primarily through the improvement and reorganization of the civil police that the policing of the country can be raised to the desired standard.

The relative decline in the importance attached to the civil police has had yet another unfortunate consequence, and that is the increased hiatus between the police and the general body of citizens, especially in the urban and other areas with heavy deployment of armed police. It is through continuous contact with citizens that the police can win their good will, confidence and cooperation. And this would make a vast difference to the effective functioning of the police – in collection of intelligence, prevention of communal and other group clashes, detection of crime, maintenance of public order, and law enforcement generally. It appears to me that no single factor in police administration has had more unfortunate consequence than absence of good public relations and failure to have the willing cooperation of the people. There are several causes for this. There is often lack of courtesy in dealing with citizens. There is failure to use adequately the available powers for the safety, convenience and welfare of the people. There are, for instance, numerous traffic offences and cases of public nuisance and obstruction of which the police do not take notice. Sometimes no action is taken on information received from citizens about impending law and order situation The aged, the infirm and women, and the weaker sections of society generally do not get, or expect to get protection and timely succour from the police. Even specific complaints made to the police are in many cases not properly registered, or looked into, or are minimized.

Further, if because they are compelled by force of circumstances or if they choose for personal ends to forge links with persons with political power or influence the police will obviously not enjoy the trust or respect of the general population. Severance of such links, as also stoppage of any political interference, is an essential condition for establishing mutually beneficial relations between the public and the police, as it is for the discipline and efficiency of the police services. The National Police Commission was emphatic in its view that there should be no political interference with the police in the discharge of their duties. This is, obviously, an unexceptionable principle, but I understand that the recommendations of the Commission on this question have either not been accepted, or if accepted in principle have not been scrupulously followed. According to competent observers there has certainly been no abatement of political interference. However, the principle of non-interference with the police is sometimes expressed in absolutist terms. The Ministers are answerable to the legislature, and through the legislature to the people, for maintenance of law and order and honest and efficient functioning of the police. There should, therefore, be no objection to Ministers issuing such instructions as are in the public interest, and do not involve infringement of the law, or the principle of fairness and impartiality. After all, the police though functioning under statutory sanction are a part of the executive branch of government, and no society has accepted or, can accept the principle that the police should not be answerable except to their own departmental hierarchy. If we have had in recent years improper political interference with disturbing frequency, can it be claimed that when left to themselves, as they are most of the time, our police have generally distinguished themselves by wise and just use of their powers. If the police had so distinguished themselves, there would be far stronger public pressure to end political interference, and far greater readiness to accept their good faith even if they made a mistake in the exercise of their discretion.

There is, undoubtedly, great deal of corruption, particularly in the lower ranks of the police, eroding its efficiency and undermining public confidence in it. There may be various reasons for it. But the basic question is whether in an acquisitive society with widespread lack of integrity we can reasonably except a non acquisitive police service, unaffected by the maladies and standards of the society in which it function. In the prevailing atmosphere the task may be exceedingly difficult; and yet the senior officers have to make determined effort to curb corruption in the interest of the service itself, and the wider interest of society. The present situation ought not to be accepted with a feeling of helplessness or even complacency.

Resort to firing by the police is one of the central issues in India as in other democratic countries. It is obvious that the business of the police being to uphold the rule of law and to protect the humane values of a civilized society, they cannot act in a lawless manner or commit brutality, without forfeiting the good-will or confidence of the people. When a large CRP force was deputed to West Bengal in late sixties to deal with Naxalite violence they were instructed by the Central Government to act with utmost restraint and circumspection, which they did, and thereby avoided antagonizing the general population. I had the same experience in regard to the use of troops and para-military force while countering insurgency in Nagaland. The fact that the forces acted with evident restraint and even rendered social service to the disaffected population were among the factors which led eventually to the end of the insurgency.

There can be no doubt about the value of an essentially human orientation even of those entrusted with restoration of order and enforcement of laws.

From the period of the freedom struggle there was strong revulsion against use of violent methods by the police. This feeling continued after independence, partly as an ideological legacy of non-violent struggle, but also because of the admiration for the peaceful methods followed by the British Police in their own country. So whenever the police used force, and particularly when they opened fire on demonstrators there was public indignation and in the administration itself a feeling of embarrassment, and occasionally even of guilt. The result was that the police were always enjoined to avoid use of force to the farthest extent possible and always to act with conspicuous restraint in dealing with all law and order situation. There was a trend towards opening fire in the air, and Shri Shastry as Home Minister got orders issued that the police should use muskets and not 303 rifles if they had to open fire. But use of muskets have been found totally ineffective in dealing with communal violence that erupted in the tribal areas of Bihar in 1964, the rifles were back again. However, the general policy of restraint in dealing with law and order situations continued. But following certain serious communal riots in Maharashtra in the late sixties a deliberate decision was taken by the Central Government, in consultation with some of the Chief Ministers, that the policy should be a dual one; restraint in all other situations, but prompt and stern action, including firing, to curb communal violence.

It has to be remembered that repugnance to state violence is much greater than that to violence by individuals and groups, accept when it results in extensive loss of life. There is no doubt about abhorrence for a murder, but among large sections of thoughtful people there is greater abhorrence for capital punishment. The underlying idea is that the state and its agencies must 'function' as rational instruments and not be guided by passion or a retributive spirit. This is the reason why whenever the police use force, and especially if it results in loss of life, there is an out-cry for a judicial inquiry and for action against the officials concerned. It may appear odd to ask for a non-violent police force in a society surcharged with violence. But the state and its agencies are expected to, and ought to be guided by the higher values of a society, rather than reflect its unhealthy features and aberrations. Weighing all the relevant considerations the dual policy to which I have referred represents in my view the correct balance.

The police organization was initially designed for what was largely a rural society, and the process of urbanization going on since then has been accelerated during the last two decades. At the beginning of the century the urban population was only about 11% of the total population; it now exceeds 25% and may rise to about 33% by the end of the century. The problems of policing rural areas are essentially different from those of urban areas, and though there have been adaptations of the system to the changing situation it has often been more as adhoc responses rather than at fundamental reorganization of the system.

A five-year plan for modernization of the police was approved in 1970 at a cost of Rs. 50 crores, and it was intended that there should be successive such plans to meet changing conditions and requirements. I understand, further plans were sanctioned, though after an interruption. However, what is required is a fresh look at the whole problem of modernization and reorientation of the police services in the light of the greatly changed circumstances that have now come to exist and in the perspective of the further changes likely during the next 15 years. There has been not only notable politicization of the people during the last three decades, but also social, economic and technological developments which have altered, and will continue to alter further, the character of Indian Society. There has been phenomenal growth of the middle-class with different norms and expectations – who are estimated to constitute now about 15% of the total population. By the end of this century their proportion may well increase to 25% or even higher.

About 20% of the population at the top have income share of 50% of the gross domestic product, while the bottom 20% have less than 10%. The poorer sections with consciousness of their equal political rights but with a lower position in our traditional social structure and deprivation of a fair share of the products of economic development are understandably frustrated and restive. There is amongst them a thrust towards upward mobility in social and economic position. There are as a result social cleavages that have fragmented Indian society, with a fall-out in law and order problem.

There is vigorous assertion of their rights and identities by different ethnic groups, result in law and order problems, developing in some cases into insurgencies or terrorism as in the north-eastern parts of the country.

Laws providing for land reforms have been enacted but have not in many cases been effectively enforced : the political will is lacking when it comes to hurting powerful vested interests in the countryside. In such a situation agrarian tensions, frequently leading to violence are bound to occur. Even in the sixties the Union Home Minister had cautioned, in a speech in Parliament, that if land reforms were not effectively enforced the green revolution might turn red.

In all the three cases the remedy lies in the sphere of imaginative and resolute political action and social engineering. The basic problems are not such as would lend themselves to effective handling by the police; they can only deal with their law and order consequence. While the fault lies elsewhere the 'blame' is often attached to the police, even when they do their best, which unfortunately they do not in many cases.

The greatly extended economic activities have given rise to a variety of white collar crimes. There has been growth of organized crime, and Mafias have grown up in certain urban centres and coastal areas and even in some rural areas. The Mafias have not only economic strength, but in some cases even links with politicians and political groups. These are problems which require planned action at all levels of government. The police alone cannot cope with them, and they are sometimes even tempted to forge links with the controllers of organized crime and Mafia groups. At least these occasional links have to be broken by the higher police authorities even if it means incurring the displeasure of powerful people.

Economic interdependence and aspirations, a national educational system, cultural and social intercourse with a heritage of composite culture, the natural affinities between neighbours, and a shared consciousness of Indianness among all sections of our people are factors conducive to national integration and social cohesion. But every violent conflict between one religious, linguistic or ethnic group and another gives a jolt and interrupts the process of integration. Likewise, unchecked oppression of the deprived or outbreak of violence prevents or impedes resolution of social conflicts by an orderly procedure. It is here that the police have a crucial role. With intelligent anticipation, firm yet sympathetic handling and complete impartiality, they can in most cases prevent these interruptions.

Those charged with the governance of this country and certainly with its policing, have a task of exceptional complexity. A democratic polity, a quasi-federal constitutional system, an ancient people in the process of social transformation, historical legacies and diversities, conflict of traditional values with modern ones, of secularism with religious fundamentalism, and coexistence of rural with urban culture, make a formidable combination. There is no parallel in the world for such a complex situation.

If I have still made some critical comments and have even ventured to make some suggestions the justification is my long association with the affairs for the police, supplemented by an enlightening but also a chastening experience as a private citizen in recent years.

I thank you for the patient hearing you have given me.

15

Measures for Strengthening of Administration

Statement on "Administrative Procedure" laid on the Tables of the Lok Sabha by the Prime Minister on August 10, 1961 and the Rajya Sabha on August 24, 1961

Measures for improvement of administration are continuously under consideration. A review of the existing position was recently made particularly in connection with the formulation of the Third Five Year Plan.

The vigorous and punctual implementation of the Plan today forms the core of administrative activity.

The review of machinery of Government has, therefore, taken into consideration the difficulties of the Second Plan and the projected needs of the Third Five Year Plan.

2. The following principal objectives have been kept in view in taking decisions on measures necessary for administrative improvement:

(i) Individuals and organizations should be judged strictly by the test of results. For this purpose, they should be given a clear statement of tasks, means, obligations, time sequence of operations and the assumptions on which they are based. Attempt should be made to build reasonable challenge into each job and individuals and organizations should be given the necessary trust, responsibility and powers to achieve the results expected of them.

(ii) The present system of financial control should be reorganized. Itemised examination of financial proposals should be confined

From *The Indian Journal of Public Administration*, Vol. VII, 1961.

only to vital matters. Financial responsibility should be devolved, in liberal measure, on the administrative ministries and by them, in turn, on the implementing authorities. The control of the Ministry of Finance should be exercised through pre-budget scrutiny and by adequate reporting, random checks and work studies in such fields as may be considered necessary.

(iii) The responsibility of the Head of Department and the executive authority concerned with the implementation of programmes and policies will be substantially increased. This will be done both by giving additional powers and by the requirement that certain activities such as corruption and public relations should be dealt with on a more planned basis than before. The consideration of individual complaints as at present in these spheres will be supplemented by the drawing up of a programme of work at the beginning of the year by each Head of Department. This programme will be scrutinized by the Secretaries of the Ministries and progressed by them adequately.

(iv) The managerial skills of the public servants will be increased through a sustained progrmame of executive development by training and counselling. Powers will also be taken by Government for weeding out officials who are ineffective and against whom suspicion exists amounting to moral conviction.

(v) Simplification of procedures and work will be vigorously pursued by introducing work studies, by competently trained personnel, in all spheres of administration.

(vi) Relations with the public will receive special attention. A series of programmes will be initiated for inculcating courtesy and consideration and for changing the attitude of authority complex towards those who approach public offices for various purposes. Better arrangements will be made for dissemination of information to the public. It is also proposed to fix and publicise time limits for dealing with applications and requests made to Government offices by the public.

3. A number of concrete proposals have been worked out to give effect to these broad objectives. The important among them are mentioned below:

(i) Ministries need not conform to a standard pattern of organisation. They will be free to vary it, within broad limits, in order to introduce speed and quality of work suited to their circumstances.

(ii) Ministries should only concern themselves with matters of policy, general supervision and enforcement of standards. Executive agencies should consequently be made stronger and given greater responsibility.

(iii) Responsibility for financial management should be devolved in greater measure than before both on the Ministries and the executive agencies. The scheme now approved, which is about to be tried in the Ministries of Commerce and Industry, Information and Broadcasting and Community Development and Co-operation and the Department of Food includes: (a) formulation of a programme for intensive pre-budget scrutiny between the Ministry of Finance and administrative Ministry necessitating the preparation of budget estimates earlier than usual in cases in which actuals of the last year are not an important consideration, (b) further liberalization of financial powers to the Ministries in order to avoid references to Finance Ministry in the post-budget period except on vital matters, and (c) the exercise of control of important financial aspects by the Finance Ministry through an adequate reporting system and test checks. The Ministry of Finance is also simultaneously taking measures to strengthen its machinery for scrutiny of project estimates and their financial review. The details of the scheme are now being worked out. If it proves successful in the four Ministries selected, it will be introduced as a general system of financial management in other Ministries.

(iv) Control of the Ministry of Home Affairs on staff up to and including Section Officers should be transferred to the Ministries concerned. This will enable this staff being given training specially related to the Ministry in which they are employed and will also be conducive to better personnel management.

(v) Officials in key posts will be kept in their jobs for at least five years to enable them to produce the results expected of them. If there is any loss of prospects by their being kept in a particular post in the public interest, the loss should be adequately protected against.

(vi) Resort to committees, groups, conferences, etc., should be reduced drastically. Full responsibility should be given to agencies and to individuals and, with it, the necessary measure of support and trust.

(vii) Arrangements for technical preparation of projects and scheduling of work relating to them require to be strengthened, particularly as information relating to a large proportion of projects included in the Third Plan is still unsatisfactory. The concrete suggestion is that planning for the Fourth Plan should be started almost immediately and a comprehensive time-table may be worked out for completing studies for the Fourth Plan projects during the next three years.

(viii) The procedures relating to recruitment to scientific and technical posts will be studied by the Ministry of Home Affairs to introduce greater speed than hitherto in making such personnel available.

(ix) Continuous studies will be made with a view to simplification and improvement by the O & M Division and internal work study cells of Ministries of such procedures, identified by Secretaries of Ministries, as involve delay in decision-making and implementation.

(x) Follow up will be the responsibility of the normal line of supervision but agencies such as the Committee on Plan Projects and the Progrmame Evaluation Organization will continue their work of administrative research and evaluation.

(xi) It is proposed to appoint a small committee in each Ministry to locate officials who are ineffective or against whom suspicions exist regarding their integrity amounting to moral conviction. Measures will be taken to develop the ineffective persons by necessary counselling and training. In case persons are not capable of improvement and are in the age group of 45 to 50, they will be retired either on completion of 25 years of service or at the age of 50 years whichever is earlier. The retirement rules will be amended suitably. Persons lacking in integrity will be dealt with separately.

(xii) Work study will be introduced as a compulsory subject in the initial training curricula of all established services. Courses in work study for in-service personnel will also be expanded.

(xiii) Training in supervisory techniques will be stepped up for all types of personnel in service.

(xiv) Incentive schemes, based on systematically worked out standards, will be tried. Encouragement, through appropriate incentives, should also be given for achievement of specific objectives such as reduction in the costs of projects, reduction in the foreign exchange complement of projects, speeding up of the implementation of projects, etc.

(xv) Management of projects is a new and important part of administrative practice. Its special features are definite targets and schedules, costing, need for initiative and resourcefulness in execution and emphasis on technical efficiency and innovation. These demand adequate pre-planning and accurate estimating. Arrangements for technical preparation of projects and scheduling of work will be strengthened. Reporting from projects will be simplified and made more purposeful.

(xvi) Training arrangements will be undertaken to develop individual and group responsibility. Several measures are being devised under the following broad heads:

(a) techniques for fostering initiative, ability to programme and responsibility of individual officers (e.g., encouragement to officers to work out their own programme of work and to suggest criteria for judging their performance);

(b) increase in capacity for improvement in performance (e.g., by sampling activities to improve time distribution on various types of jobs, by organizing case studies and decision-making training).

(xvii) Heads of Departments should be made responsible for maintaining and improving relations with the public. They should prescribe, having regard to the limitations of staff and the nature of cases, time limits for disposal of letters, applications and petitions as far as practicable and should advertise them to the public. Endeavour should be made to adhere to them in all except cases requiring a greater degree of scrutiny than in normal circumstances.

(xviii) Each Head of Department should also draw up an annual confidential programme in advance indicating the types of corruption prevalent, the types of personnel involved and the measures he proposes to take to improve the situation. This programme should be forwarded to the Secretary of the Ministry concerned. Simultaneously the Special Police Establishment of the Ministry of Home Affairs should also send confidentially to the Secretary its own appreciation regarding corrupt practices in the charge of each Head of Department. The Secretary should, after a consideration of both the documents, approve of the final programme and indicate it to the Head of Department. He should also review periodically the implementation of this programme.

(xix) Similarly an annual programme should be drawn up by each Head of Department indicating the outstanding problems of public relations and the measures to be taken to improve them. This programme should also be progressed periodically by the Secretary of the Ministry concerned.

(xx) Where necessary, information counters should be established and they should be placed in charge of responsible officials who should be specially trained to cater to the needs of the public.

(xxi) National expressions for courtesy may be devised and opportunity should be taken of important national celebrations to emphasise the service aspect of public administration.

4. The administration of public enterprises is an intricate subject. The Report of the Krishna Menon Committee is separately under consideration affecting various organizational and management aspects of their working. Special features of their working insofar as they relate to their internal organisation and relationships were considered as a part of the general problem of strengthening administration. The decisions indicated above will be equally applicable to them; the details will be worked out according to the circumstances of each organisation concerned. The following additional decisions have been taken on improving the administrative functioning of the public enterprises:

(a) The Ministries concerned should have strong technical planning cells charged with responsibility for study of the broader technical and economic aspects of projects, defining stages of execution and ensuring co-ordination of all related measures.

(b) Within major state undertakings design and research units should be established and primary responsibility for preparing new projects placed on them.

(c) All major projects should have units for evaluation, review of progress, reduction of costs, raising productivity and checking of performance. These units should function under the control of top management authorities and without interfering in the direct line of supervision, but independently of day-to-day operations.

(d) The Ministry of Finance should strengthen their 'project co-ordination cell' so that it can (i) undertake thorough scrutiny of cost estimates and of the broader economic aspects of projects, and (ii) accept responsibility for presenting an annual report on financial and economic aspects of the Central Government's industrial undertakings as a whole.

(e) In view of the short time available for the formulation of the plans particularly in relation to industrial projects, the Ministries concerned are being directed to complete studies of the projects likely to be included in the Fourth Plan in the next three years.

5. The Planning Commission has, after a study of the references made to it by the Central Ministries and State Governments, decided to simplify the procedures for consultation with it. Variations in cost estimates up to 10% or Rs. one crore, whichever is less, will not be reported to the Planning Commission. Discussions regarding annual plans will be confined only to the more important projects and programmes. Procedures for Central assistance have already been considerably simplified. The list of Centrally-sponsored schemes has been drastically reduced as also the list of schemes in the plans of States for which assistance may have to be given according to certain prescribed patterns. These patterns are also being simplified. As regards progress reports on projects and programmes in the States, it is proposed that these should be received only at a single point within the Government of India, namely, the Ministry concerned, but the forms should be drawn up in consultation with the Planning Commission. The same principles will apply, mutatis mutandis, to schemes implemented by Central Ministries.

6. In spite of the effort to make the decisions taken on administrative improvements as detailed and comprehensive as possible, the above still remains a statement of general principles. A great deal of work is required to be done to give them concrete shape. It is a continuing task and cannot evidently be detailed at a point of time in a statement of this nature. A Committee on Administration has been established at the Centre headed by the Cabinet Secretary. It will be its special function to progress the implementation of these decisions and to report periodically to the Cabinet.

The steps outlined above are being brought to the notice of the State Governments. The Government of India will be glad to give such assistance to them as may be possible in implementing them.

16

Report of the Administrative Reforms Commission on the Machinery of the Government of India and its Procedures of Work, 1968

(I) Introduction

In its assessment of the existing machinery of Government and formulation of the proposals for its reform, the Commission has borne in mind "the new role which is expected of the Administration under the present conditions of growing enlightenment and rising expectations of the people". The Administration "must answer to the needs of the people and secure public response and cooperation". The Commission adds, "The Administration is also conditioned by the stage of social, economic and political development of the country and affected by the attitudes and motivations of those who run it. Viewing the problem in this perspective we (the Administrative Reforms Commission) found it necessary to take a realistic view of things and strike a balance between the needs of continuity and those of change. We have suggested a radical change of the existing structures or methods of work only where they have become totally outmoded. In other cases, we have tried to improve upon them. Even such balanced proposals for reorganization are likely to meet with resistance. Administrative practices and traditions which are no longer suited to new challenges of fast developing country must be overhauled and even weeded out. We need shed no tears over them".

Recommendations

(II) Machinery at Supra-Ministry Levels

(1) (i) (a) In order that the Cabinet may be able to provide

From *The Indian Journal of Public Administration*, Vol. XIV, 1968.

united leadership and overall directions, take policy decisions with expedition, oversee in a consistent manner the implementation of policies and programmes and in general to guide the administration on effective lines, it will have to be small in size and homogeneous in composition. The number of Ministers in the Union Cabinet should be 16, including the Prime Minister.

(b) Each Department/subject should be represented in the Cabinet by one or the other Cabinet Minister. There should not be any Ministers of State with independent charge of a department or departments.

(c) The size of the Council of Ministers and the Cabinet should be determined on a rational bases related to the needs of administration. The strength of the Council of Ministers should normally be 40. It may be increased in special circumstances but should in no case exceed 45.

(ii) The three-tier system in the ministerial set-up, comprising Cabinet Ministers, Ministers of State and Deputy Ministers, may continue. The office of Parliamentary Secretary, which has now fallen into desuetude need not be revived.

(iii) The functions and responsibilities of Ministers of State and Deputy Ministers and the powers which they may exercise within a Department or a Ministry should be clearly specified in the appropriate rules or orders.

(iv) The Prime Minister should consult the Cabinet Minister concerned before assigning a particular Minister of State or Deputy Minister to his Ministry.

(v) No more than two Ministers should be involved in the decision-making process in any Ministry.

(2) (i) The Prime Minister should be given institutional support, in the form of Deputy Prime Minister, for ensuring efficient and effective functioning of the governmental machinery. The Deputy Prime Minister should have the charge, in addition to his own portfolio, of such subjects and ad hoc assignments as the Prime Minister considers appropriate. The office of the Deputy Prime Minister should be recognized in the Transaction of Business Rules.

(ii) The Prime Minister should continue to be associated with key-appointments. He should periodically, say, once a month, meet, individually or in groups, the Secretaries of important Departments.

(iii) The Prime Minister should not ordinarily be in charge of a Ministry. His time should mostly be available for guidance, coordination and supervision. (In his note of dissent, one of the Members of the Commission, Shri H.V. Kamath, recommends that "the Prime Minister should be left free to have his own choice in the matter; to hold or not to hold a portfolio should be left entirely to his own discretion and judgment").

(3) (i) The existing Standing Cabinet Committee should be reconstituted into 11 committees, one each for Defence; Foreign Affairs; Economic Affairs; Parliamentary Affairs and Public Relations; Food and Rural Development; Transport, Tourism and Communications; Social Services (including Social Welfare and Family Planning); Commerce, Industry and Science; Internal Affairs (including Centre-State Relationships); Administration; and Appointments. The Committees should between them cover all important activities of Government. The membership of each Committee should not normally exceed six and should include all Ministers in charge of subjects covered by the Committee.

(ii) Every Standing Committee of Cabinet should be supported by a Committee of Secretaries which will consider in advance all matters to be taken up in the Cabinet Committee.

(4) (i) The role of the Cabinet Secretary should not be limited to that of a coordinator. He should also act as the principal staff adviser of the Prime Minister, the Cabinet and the Cabinet Committees on important policy matters.

(ii) The Cabinet Secretary should ordinarily have a tenure of three or four years.

(III) Relations between Ministers, Civil Servants and Parliament

(5) There is a growing feeling among the public that many of the Ministers lack interest in ensuring efficient administration and do not possess the acumen needed for the purpose. The Prime Minister should meet all Ministers individually or in group every month to discuss progress in implementation of policies and programmes and measures for improving the administrative efficiency. This should help promote a more active interest on the part of individual Ministers in improving the implementation process and the management of their Ministries.

(6) (i) In selecting his colleagues, the Prime Minister should give special attention to considerations of political stature, personal integrity, intellectual ability and capacity for taking decisions and sustained application to work.

(ii) In assigning a portfolio, due regard should be paid to the aptitude and capabilities of an incumbent.

(iii) A Minister should take a holiday of at least two weeks in a year which he should devote to reading, reflections and relaxation.

(7) The initial and annual statements of their financial assets and liabilities to be furnished by the Ministers under the Code of Conduct should be made available to the Lokpal. If any Minister fails to furnish such a statement the fact should be mentioned by the Lokpal in his annual report to Parliament. Suitable provision to this effect may be made in the Lokpal Bill which is now before Parliament. (Shri Kamath, in his note of dissent, adds that the Lokpal should be invested with the power to bring to the notice of Parliament not only the failure of a Minister including the Prime Minister to send him such a statement, but also those cases where he is satisfied that the statement before him is not quite correct or adequate).

(8) (i) All major decisions, with reasons therefore, should be briefly reduced to writing, particularly where the policy of Government is not clear or where some important departure from the policy is involved or where the Minister differs from the Secretary on an important issue.

(ii) There is a disinclination among quite a number of Ministers to welcome frank and impartial advice from the Secretary or his aides and an inclination to judge him by his willingness to do what they wish him to do. This has also bred a tendency on the part of an increasing number of civil servants to attempt to anticipate the Minister's wishes and proffer their advice accordingly. A further development of this unhealthy trend is the emergence of personal affiliations, leading to an element of 'politicalisation' among the civil servants. Ministers should try to develop a climate of fearlessness and fair play among the senior officers and encourage them to give frank and impartial advice. They should give the Secretaries the necessary guidance in carrying out their policies and orders.

(iii) The Prime Minister should, with the assistance of the Cabinet Secretary and the central personnel agency, take special interest to arrest the growth of unhealthy personal affiliations to individual Ministers among civil servants.

(iv) Minister should not intervene in the day-to-day administration except in cases of grave injustice, serious default or maladministration on the part of civil servants. Where a citizen's request or complaint calls for revision of a rule, procedure or policy, it should be met by effecting such revision, and not by relaxing the rules to accommodate an individual case.

(v) Secretaries and other civil servant need to show greater sensitivity to and a better appreciation of the Minister's difficulties, and to discriminate between minor adjustments on the one hand, and acts of political and other forms of accommodation compromising basic principles or likely to have substantial or lasting repercussions on efficiency and morale of the services, on the other. The official relationship of the Secretary to the Minister should be one of loyalty and that of the Minister to the Secretary one of confidence.

(9) (i) A Minister should be held accountable: (a) when he fails to formulate policy in respect of a major problem or when the policy formulated is found erroneous or suffers from major weaknesses; (b) when he neglects to pay personal attention on important issues other than those of policy where such attention is expected of him or wrongly handles such issues; (c) when there is a general or major mismanagement or maladministration in his Department/Ministry; and (d) when he commits some act of impropriety.

(ii) A Minister should not be held accountable for an act of a civil servant which is: (a) in express violation of a directive or order issued by him; or (b) by implication prohibited by policies already approved by him; or (c) is mala fide.

(iii) For reinforcing the principle of collective responsibility, it is essential that: (a) the Cabinet should be agreed on fundamentals and all important issues are discussed and settled by the Cabinet; (b) a Minister does not announce a new policy or a major departure from current policy with the approval of the Cabinet; and (c) a Minister should not ordinarily speak or make announcements on matters not within his portfolio. However, if the circumstances so require of him, he must get himself properly briefed by the Minister concerned.

(iv) Standing Committees of Parliament may be set up for reviewing the work of Departments grouped in five sectors, namely, Social Services, Economic Administration, Defence and Foreign Affairs, Food and Rural Development and Transport. These Committees should function on the lines of the Committee on Public Undertakings and without taking over the functions of the Public Accounts Committee. To begin with only two of the Committees need be set up. As the Estimates Committee is now doing for each Department the type of review which is proposed for the sectoral committees, it will be necessary to remove from the purview of the Estimates Committee the Departments which fall within the jurisdiction of the sectoral committee. Where a

Parliamentary Committee for a Department exists, it should not be necessary to have an Informal Consultative Committee.

(v) There appears to be among Members of Parliament a general distrust of civil servants and a feeling that the Government machinery is invariably inefficient. Such an attitude tends to demoralise civil servants. A balanced view should be taken of the working of a Government Department. Stray cases of bona fide default or shortcomings should be viewed against the background of overall achievement. (Shri Kamath, in his note of dissent, has taken the stand that "even where there are positive achievements to the credit of a department, its shortcomings and misdoings, whatever they may be, should be fully and ruthlessly exposed in the interest of administrative efficiency and integrity, while complimenting the Department for its good deeds").

(IV) Ministries and Departments

(10) The role of the Central Ministries and Departments in subjects falling within the State List should be largely that of a pioneer, guide, disseminater of information, overall planner and evaluator. An analysis should be made in the light of these criteria of the items of work now handled by the Central agencies and such items as do not fulfil the criteria should be transferred to the States.

(11) (i) Non-secretariat organizations engaged primarily in planning, implementation, coordination and review of a single development programme or several allied programmes, covering a substantial area of the activities of the Ministry and having a direct bearing on policy-making should be integrated with the Secretariat of the concerned Ministry. Such amalgamation, is especially significant in the case of activities of scientific and technical character and activities which call for a high degree of functional specialization.

(ii) The heads of non-secretariat organizations which are integrated with the Secretariat should function as the principal advisers to the Government in the respective areas and should enjoy a status appropriate to the nature of their duties and responsibilities. They may retain their present designations. It is not necessary to counter on them a formal ex-officio Secretariat Status.

(iii) In all other cases the present distinction between policy-making and executive organizations may be continued. Such distinction is vital for protecting the operational autonomy of the regulatory executive agencies and such developmental executive organizations as are mostly engaged in promotional activities, provision of a service or production and supply of commodity.

(iv) Executive functions at present performed by an administrative Ministry or Department which do not have a close bearing on policy-making should be transferred to an appropriate, existing non-secretariat agency or to a new executive organization specially created for the purpose, provided that the volume of the work justified its creation.

(v) Policy position in Departments and Ministries dealing with scientific and technical matters or with functions of highly specialized character should include persons having relevant specialized experience or expertise.

(12) (i) In non-staff Ministries other than those with board-type of top management, there should be set up three "staff" offices, namely: (a) an office of planning and policy; (b) a chief personnel office, and (c) a chief finance office. An administrative Department with a heavy charge or with functions which have no close affinity with the work of other department(s) may have a separate planning and policy office.

(ii) The office of planning and policy should include the planning cell recommended in the ARC report on Machinery for Planning. This office should continuously be engaged in formulating long-term policies, carrying out policy studies and evolving a series of well-articulated policy statements. It should also deal with the parliamentary work of the Department/Ministry.

(iii) The chief personnel office in a Ministry should serve as a focal point for the formulation and coordination of overall personnel policies, initiating measures for promoting personnel development and matters concerning discipline, appeals, memorials and service rules of cadres administered by the Ministry. It may also look after office management, O. & M. and general administration.

(iv) Each of the three "staff" offices should be manned by staff having specialized knowledge and experience. The head of each "staff" office should generally be of the rank of a Joint Secretary though in some cases he may even be a Deputy Secretary or an Additional Secretary depending on the quantum of work.

(v) In addition to the three staff offices, each Ministry should have a public relations office or unit.

(vi) The heads of the "substantive work" wings may deal directly with the chiefs of the three "staff" offices, as also with the Secretary and Minister on matters of technical or operational policy. Proposals having a bearing on long-term policy should, however, be processed through planning and policy office.

(13) (i) Distribution of work between the wings of a Ministry/ Administrative Department and within the divisions of a Secretariat

wing should be based on considerations of rationality, manageability of change and unity of command.

(ii) Each secretariat wing should have its separate identity and its budget should appear as a distinct unit in the budget of the Ministry. Its head should enjoy adequate administrative and financial powers.

(iii) The head of the wing should have the primary responsibility for good administration within the wing, effective supervision and control of staff and maintenance of high standards of discipline and conduct.

(iv) The head of the wing should have considerable say in formulation of the wing budget, creation of posts, subject to budget provision, spending of budgeted funds and appointment of personnel to the wing and their transfer therefrom. He should also have the necessary powers for effective day-to-day personnel management in the wing, e.g., powers to sponsor staff for training, to grant honorarium, to impose minor penalties and to fill short-term leave vacancies.

(14) (i) (a) There should be only two levels of consideration below the Minister, namely: (i) Under Secretary/Deputy Secretary, and (ii) Joint Secretary/Additional Secretary/Secretary. Work should be assigned to each of these two levels on the lines of "desk officer" system. Each level should be required and empowered to dispose off a substantial amount of work on its own and will be given the necessary staff assistance.

(b) The staffing pattern within a wing may be flexible to facilitate the employment of officers of various grades.

(c) The duties and requirements of various jobs in the Secretariat at each of the two levels should be defined clearly and in detail on the basis of scientific analysis of work content.

(ii) For smooth and effective working of the proposed "desk officer" system, the following measures will be necessary:

(a) introduction of a functional file index;

(b) maintenance of guard files or card indices which will contain all important precedents;

(c) adequate provision for "leave" reserve; and

(d) adequate stenographic and clerical aids.

(iii) (a) There should be set up in each Ministry or major administrative Department a Policy Advisory Committee to consider all important issues of long-term policy and to inject thinking inputs from different areas of specialization into problem solving. The Committee should be headed by the Secretary of the Ministry and should include the heads of the three staff offices (of planning and policy, finance and personnel) and heads of important substantive work wings (including those of the non-secretariat organizations integrated with the Ministry/Administrative Department). As and when necessary, the heads of governing bodies of important research and training institutions and boards and corporations outside the Government may be co-opted as members of the Policy Advisory Committee for such items of work as are of interest to them.

(iii) (b) Self-contained papers or memoranda, setting out problems, their various alternative solutions, merits and demerits of each alternative, etc., should be prepared for consideration by the Committee, and the decision arrived at should be duly recorded in minutes.

(V) Administrative Reforms – Formulation and Implementation

(15) (i) The Department of Administrative Reforms should confine itself mainly to: (a) studies on administrative reforms of a foundational character, (b) building up O. & M. expertise in Ministries/Departments and training the personnel of their O. & M. units in modern techniques of management, and (c) advice and guidance to these O. & M. units in effecting administrative improvements and reforms.

(ii) The existing O. & M. unit in different Ministries/ Departments should be reactivised.

(iii) A special cell on 'perspective reforms' should be set up in the central reforms agency.

(iv) In its methods of work, staffing pattern and organizational structure the central reforms agency should be 'research-oriented'.

(v) The Department of Administrative Reforms should be placed directly under the Deputy Prime Minister.

(vi) (a) It is necessary to develop strong, autonomous professional institutions which will promote original thinking on administrative reforms and innovations. Taking into account also the vast and diverse range of administrative reforms needed, external professional organizations are more favourably placed than internal O. & M. agencies for undertaking studies and investigations of the following types: (i) Streamlining the procedure and practices at points where private trade and industry and ordinary citizens come into contact with administration. (ii) Improvement of the machinery for redress of public grievances and for public relations. (iii) Studies in areas wherein it is important to inspire the confidence of the public in the objectivity of the findings. (iv) Studies on improvement of morale, motivation and attitude of public officials. (v) Problems of inter-action between the political and administrative processes which have an impact on the tone of the administration. (vi) Studies on the applicabilities of foreign administrative techniques and systems to local conditions in India. (vii) Problems of administrative reorganization and improvement in semi-government organizations and autonomous public sector undertakings. Studies on administrative reforms and improvements of the types mentioned above can be entrusted, with advantage, to autonomous professional institutions like the Indian Institute of Public Administration, Institute of Applied Manpower Research, Administrative Staff College (Hyderabad), and Institutes of Management at Calcutta and Ahmedabad and selected Universities.

(b) The Indian Institute of Public Administration has more recently undertaken some studies on contemporary problems of administration. It has serviced the Commission's Study Team on the Machinery for Planning and provided the Commission with background material on several problems of administration, prepared on the basis of special studies undertaken by it for the purpose. We are, however, not satisfied with the present limited role of the Institute in the field of administrative reforms and improvements. The Institute needs to develop specialized competence of a high order in various fields and tools of public administration. For development of such competence it would obviously need adequate support from Government.

(vii) There should be set up a council on administrative reforms to advise the central reforms agency on the planning of its programme of work, to review progress, to help induct fresh thinking into its working, and to coordinate the activities of the different professional organizations engaged in research on problems of public management. The Council should consist of eight members, drawn from Members of Parliament, experienced administrators and eminent scholars interested in public administration. It may be presided over by the Deputy Prime Minister.

(16) (i) The responsibility for overseeing the implementation of the recommendations of the Administrative Reforms Commission should rest with a senior Cabinet Minister enjoying high political prestige and possessing wide administrative experience, i.e., the Deputy Prime Minister.

(ii) Before the Cabinet takes up a report of the Commission, it should be considered by the Cabinet Committee on Administration which should consist of the Prime Minister (Chairman), the Deputy Prime Minister (if he holds a portfolio other than Finance). Finance

Minister and Minister of Home Affairs.

(iii) (a) A Special Cell should be set up in the Cabinet Secretariat under the over-all charge of the Deputy Prime Minister and the general supervision of the Cabinet Secretary, to process the Commission's reports. It should also assist the Deputy Prime Minister in over-seeing the implementation of the accepted recommendations.

(b) After the Ministry/Ministries have communicated their views, the Special Cell in the Cabinet Secretariat should, under the direction of the Deputy Prime Minister, prepare the necessary papers for the Cabinet Committee on Administration.

(c) Within a Ministry/Department the Commission's recommendations should be dealt with at a high level.

(iv) Within three months of the receipt of a report of the Commission, Government should place before Parliament a White Paper indicating their decisions on the basic recommendations contained in that report. (In his note of dissent, Shri Kamath has suggested that all decisions of Government on the recommendations of the ARC should be subject to approval, disapproval or modification by Parliament. He has further proposed the setting up in every State and Union Territory of a non-official, non-partisan people's committee or citizens' committee for awakening and strengthening public opinion in support of the implementation of ARC's recommendations).

(v) There should be set up an all-party parliamentary committee of both Houses whose functions will be to see that the recommendations accepted by the Government are implemented expeditiously.

(VI) A Central Personnel Agency

(17) (i) A separate Department of Personnel should be set up, with a full Secretary in charge who should work under the general guidance of the Cabinet Secretary.

(ii) This Department should have the following functions and responsibilities:

(a) formulation of personnel policies on all matters common to the Central and All-India Services, and inspection and review of their implementation;

(b) talent hunting, development of personnel for "senior management" and processing of appointments to senior posts;

(c) manpower planning, training and career development;

(d) foreign assistance programme in personnel administration;

(e) research in personnel administration;

(f) discipline and welfare of staff and machinery for redress of their grievances;

(g) liaison with the Union Public Service Commission, State Governments, Professional Institutions, etc.; and

(h) staffing of the middle-level positions in the Central Secretariat (of Under Secretaries and Deputy Secretaries) with the assistance of and on the advice of the Establishment Board.

(iii) (a) The Department of Personnel should not itself administer any service cadre. The administrative control of different service cadres should vest with individual Ministries and Departments concerned.

(b) The administration of the IAS, IPS and the centralized aspects of the Central Secretariat Service should be the responsibility of the Ministry of Home Affairs.

(c) The management of the Indian Economic Service and of the Indian Statistical Service should be transferred to the Department of Economic Affairs.

(iv) The Cabinet Secretary should, by convention, be regarded as Secretary-General of the new Department of Personnel, without being formally so designated. He should be actively involved in the development of and selection for "senior management" but not in appointments below that level.

(v) The new Department of Personnel should be placed directly under the Prime Minister. (Dissenting with this recommendation, Shri Kamath has pointed out that "in India with its federal democratic set-up, the Home Minister has to play a key role in so far as Centre-State relationships, and the millions of personnel employed at the Centre and in the States are concerned. The assignment of the Department of Personnel to the portfolio of the Prime Minister will probably weaken the position of the Home Minister without, in any way, adding to the strength of the Prime Minister's". Shri Kamath favours the location of the new Department of Personnel in the Ministry of Home Affairs and adds that "the placement of the Department, with a separate Secretary, in the Home Ministry rather than under the Prime Minister, will also obviate the possibility of any inroad in the position of the Cabinet Secretary as the head of the Civil Service").

(vi) An Advisory Council on Personnel Administration may be set up to act as a feeder line of new ideas and thinking on personnel administration. It should be composed of official and non-official experts in different aspects of personnel management, drawn from all over the country.

(vii) The Establishment Board should be located in the new Department of Personnel and the Secretary of this Department should be its Chairman. The Board should deal with appointments only up to and including Deputy Secretaries.

(VII) Grouping of Subjects

(18) (i) (A) Ministries and Departments in the Government of India as presently constituted should be reorganized into Ministries and Departments as follows:

Ministries	*Departments*
Ministries without departments	
1. Home Affairs	
2. External Affairs	
3. Irrigation and Power	
4. Railways	
5. Labour and Employment	
6. Defence	(1) Defence. (2) Defence Production. (3) Defence Supply.
7. Finance	(1) Economic Affairs (including Statistics and Insurance). (2) Revenue and Expenditure. (3) Company Affairs.
8. Works, Housing and Supply	(1) Works and Housing. (2) Supply.
9. Commerce and Industry	(1) Commerce. (2) Industrial Development.
10. Metals, Chemicals and Oil	(1) Iron and Steel. (2) Mines and Metals. (3) Petroleum. (4) Chemicals.
11. Transport and Tourism	(1) Transport and Shipping. (2) Tourism and Civil Aviation.
12. Communications, Information and Broadcasting	(1) Communication. (2) Information and Broadcasting.
13. Food and Rural Development	(1) Food. (2) Agriculture. (3) Community Development and Cooperation.

Ministries	*Departments*
14. Education, Health and Social Welfare	(1) Education. (2) Health and Urban Development. (3) Family Planning. (4) Social Welfare (including Rehabilitation.
15. Law and Justice	(1) Legal Affairs and Justice. (2) Legislative Department.
Others	
16. Prime Minister	(1) Department of Personnel. (2) Department of Atomic Energy, Planning as a Portfolio (without any department).
The Cabinet Minister who is also the Deputy Prime Minister	Department of Administrative Reforms
Leader of the House (Lok Sabha)	Department of Parliamentary Affairs, Cabinet Affairs.

(B) In particular:

(i) As recommended earlier:

(a) A new Department of Personnel should be created under the Prime Minister's charge with functions as indicated in recommendation 17 (ii) above.

(b) The Department of Administrative Reforms should be under the charge of the Deputy Prime Minister.

(ii) The Research and Development Organization of the Ministry of Defence should be located in the main Ministry and not in one of its Departments.

(iii) The Department of Revenue and Insurance should be reorganized as the Department of Revenue and Expenditure.

(iv) (a) "Insurance" should be transferred to the Department of Economic Affairs.

(b) The present functions of the Department of Statistics in the Cabinet Secretariat should be transferred to the Department of Economic Affairs in the Ministry of Finance.

(c) The Department of Economic Affairs should be responsible for coordination of all activities of Government in the economic field. The Commission for Prices, Cost and Tariff (the establishment of which has been recommended in the report on Economic Administration) should be administratively related to the Department of Economic Affairs.

(v) The Department of Company Affairs should be shifted from the Ministry of Industrial Development and Company Affairs to the Ministry of Finance.

(vi) External Publicity should be transferred to the Department of Information and Broadcasting (now a Ministry).

(vii) (a) The combined Ministry of Commerce and Industry should have two Departments: (a) Department of Commerce, and (b) Department of Industrial Development.

(b) The Council of Scientific and Industrial Research should be placed in the combined Ministry of Commerce and Industry in order to ensure a continuous dialogue between CSIR laboratories and their user industries.

(c) The Survey of India should be located in the Ministry of Irrigation and Power which accounts for about 30 per cent of its work. (Shri Kamath, however, feels that the cartography-oriented Survey of India should continue to be with the Education Ministry).

(viii) The Advisory Committee to the Cabinet on Science and Technology should serve as the central point for advising the Cabinet on science policy, setting priorities and planning and review of scientific and technological research. It should have a permanent secretariat to service it.

(ix) The Ministry of Transport and Shipping and the Ministry of Tourism and Civil Aviation should be combined into a single Ministry of Transport and Tourism.

(x) "Communications" should be transferred to the Ministry of Information and Broadcasting to form the Ministry of Communications, Information and Broadcasting.

(xi) The charge of the Department of Parliamentary Affairs should be held by a Cabinet Minister who is the Leader of the House (Lok Sabha).

(xii) A Directorate of Construction should be set up in the Department of Works and Housing.

(xiii) The Ministry of Steel, Mines and Metals and the Ministry of Petroleum and Chemicals should be integrated into a single Ministry of Metals, Chemicals and Oil.

(xiv) The Department of Community Development and the Department of Cooperation should be merged together to form the Department of Community Development and Cooperation.

(xv) The Department of Food, the Department of Agriculture and the combined new Department of Community Development and Co-operation should constitute together the Ministry of Food and Rural Development. (Shri H.V. Kamath, in his note of dissent, has recommended that Irrigation and Power should also be included in the proposed Ministry).

(xvi) (a) The Department of Rehabilitation should be merged into the Department of Social Welfare. (Shri Kamath, however, is opposed to the merger of "rehabilitation" into the Department of Social Welfare, and feels that it should continue to be looked after by the Ministry of Labour and Employment).

(b) The Ministry of Health, Family Planning and Urban Development, Department of Social Welfare and Ministry of Education should be amalgamated to form a new Ministry of Education, Health and Social Welfare.

(xvii) A Bureau of Youth Services should be set up in the Ministry of Education, Health and Social Welfare.

(xviii) The present functions of the Ministry of Home Affairs in judicial administration should be transferred to the Department of Legal Affairs in the Ministry of Law and this Ministry should be re-designated as Ministry of Law and Justice.

(In his note of dissent, Shri H.V. Kamath has pointed out that the haphazard development of Science and Technology in the country has been mainly due to the failure of the Government in setting up a strong and effective organization and machinery for directing and coordinating all activity in this field. He is of the view that there should be a separate Ministry of Science and Technology, and if necessary, the subject of "Power" may be transferred to this Ministry. Shri Kamath has also recommended that the Ministry of Finance may be re-designated as "Ministry of Finance and Economic Affairs" in order to focus attention on the work of the Ministry concerning positive and constructive aspects of economic development).

(xix) Responsibility for over-all coordination within a Ministry which has more than one Department/Secretary, should be specifically assigned to one of the Departments/Secretaries most appropriate for this purpose.

17

Report of the Fifth Central Pay Commission Restructuring the Government, 1997

Restructuring the Government

Introduction

Reinventing the Government

9.1 The entire machinery of Government has got to be reinvented. This is a mammoth task. It is not possible for us to go into the details of the restructuring exercise that such a reinvention would entail. In this chapter, we would like to take up the Ministries of the Central Government as an example and demonstrate how the restructuring could help.

Expansion in the Bureaucracy

9.2 We had 8 posts of Secretaries, 18 departments and a total workforce of 14.40 lakhs in 1948. Today, we have 92 Secretaries, 79 departments and a workforce of more than 41 lakhs. No doubt, the work has expanded, but the expansion of the Government is disproportionate to the increase of workload.

Earlier attempts at restructuring

9.3 There have been many attempts at reforming the Central Government. Some of these are:

- setting up of Organization and Methods Divisions in the Ministries
- setting up of a Department of Administrative Reforms
- setting up of a Department of Personnel, Public Grievances and Pensions
- setting up of Staff Inspection Unit

From the Report of the Fifth Central Pay Commission, 1997, pp. 127-36.

- introduction of Desk Officer system
- introduction of Financial Adviser system
- introduction of Annual Action Plans
- introduction of Performance Budgeting

Consultancy Studies

9.4 We had awarded two studies on restructuring of the Government to IIT, Delhi and Tata Consultancy Services.

IIT, Delhi

9.5 The IIT, Delhi identified the major objective of restructuring to be goal achievement and service orientation, through flexibility and efficiency. The restructuring options involved interventions at the level of situation, action and process. At the level of situation, the physical environment, the operating environment and the socio-cultural environment was to be changed. At the actor level, both systemic and attitudinal changes were required. At the process level, the interventions related to operational processes and strategic processes.

Interventions Suggested

9.6 For Phase I, the interventions found feasible at situation level were conducive physical working conditions; openness to environment; federalism; delayering; and decision-oriented system. At the actor level these were: training for multi-skilling; involvement in clarifying goals and objectives; quality and work consciousness; sense of dignity and individuality; promoting self-help; and receptivity to technology-based solutions. Process level options identified were: simplifying system of checks and balances; horizontal communication processes; minimal and appropriate reporting and documentation; upward feedback processes; privatized support services; reorienting strategically to liberalize; shedding functions to affiliated autonomous bodies; installing learning processes; reengineering work flows and continuous change in work processes.

The office of the Future

9.7 The findings of the study point towards a decision-oriented, facilitative, flatter, flexible, Information Technology supported, participative and elegant Government office effectively achieving goals with service and client orientation.

TCS Study 9.8 The TCS categorized various Government offices into three broad types – Core, Participatory and Auxiliary. Based on the decision-making matrices in these offices, the study concluded that one of the major changes in the organisational structure was to reduce the levels in the hierarchy from nine to seven. A flatter hierarchy would ensure speedy decision-making and be able to respond quickly to the demands of the environment.

9.9 The levels proposed were:

- Chief Executive
- Senior Executive
- Middle Executive
- Junior Executive
- Supervisory
- Assistant
- Support/attendant

Grades and Levels

9.10 Eighteen grades were proposed in these seven levels. The grades within a level would only be for promotional purposes and not form a hierarchy for reporting. The promotional channels were increased to provide career growth for the employees. Thus the hierarchial levels were delinked from promotional grades.

Decision-making more Important

9.11 The study laid emphasis on decision-makers rather than on assistants. It proposed that each section within a department should have just one Assistant – level position. Decisions should be hastened, and files and papers should be disposed off at the level to which they were addressed.

Utilisation of Redundant Staff

9.12 The support staff that would be rendered redundant could be utilized in the following manner:

- by training them in computer applications so that Government departments could redeploy them in those functions.
- by transferring them to new activities or projects, after giving them adequate training in the new skills.

Three Fold Restructuring

9.13 The TCS study considered restructuring in three streams. The first was organizational structure. The second was a comprehensive human resource development system to achieve greater efficiency, responsiveness and productivity, and to bring in sustainability in the organization. The third concentrated on the two major office systems –record management and dak system, office equipment, information technology and work environment.

9.14 In this chapter, we shall concentrate on the first stream viz. organizational restructuring in the context of the Ministries and Departments of the Central Government.

Our Proposals

The three basic questions

9.15 The first exercise we must have is to survey the entire gamut of Governmental functioning and ask the three usual basic questions:

- Does this need to be done?
- Does this need to be done in Government?
- Does this need to be in the Central Government?

Things that need not be done

9.16 The answers to these questions, if attempted in an objective and dispassionate manner, will show that some activities need not be undertaken at all. For example, we do not need the large and expensive memorials which have taken up so much of prime land and building space besides involving heavy recurring expenditure. The moment we identify this as an activity that should be stopped forthwith, a number of action points emerge.

Things that need not be done by Government

9.17 In the second category, we may conclude that bread, milk or condoms need not be manufactured in Government. In the third category, we may decide that 90% of our effort in education, health, agriculture, law and order etc. should be with the State Governments. Our honest replies to the basic questions will show us the areas in which restructuring can yield rich dividends.

Number of Ministries

9.18 One of the basic objectives of restructuring is reduction of staff. It is best to begin with the topmost category of Secretary. There is a general feeling that we have too many Secretaries to the Government of India. Health is a State subject. Do we really need three Secretaries in the Ministry of Health, looking after Health, Family Welfare and Indian System of Medicine? We would like to recommend that there should be just one Secretary for the whole Ministry.

Ministry of Industry

9.19 Similarly, industry is a State subject. We have separate departments of Industrial Policy and Promotion, Industrial Development, Public Enterprises, Heavy Industry, Small Scale Industries, Agro and Rural Industries and Textiles. With the reduced emphasis on licensing, one Secretary could look after all these subjects in a single Ministry.

Suggestions on Merger of Departments

9.20 Similarly, it does not seem necessary to deploy a Secretary each for Animal Husbandry, Interstate Council, Official Language,

Programme Implementation and the like. We have appended a small list at Annexe 9.1, suggesting some realignments of departments.

Size of a Ministry

9.21 The most major restructuring effort would be in determining the size of a Department or Ministry. The general formula that we would like to suggest in this regard is the following:

- If it is a Core Central subject, we may not take it up in the beginning.
- If it is a Core State subject, it cannot be a Core Central subject too. In that case it should be high on the list of Ministries to be reduced in size.
- As we move away from Core subjects to Participatory or Auxiliary subjects, the need for sizeable Ministries becomes more and more questionable. Such Ministries should be axed first of all.

Organizations Attached to Ministries

9.22 Ministries have certain organizations or activities, which may either be an integral part of the Ministry, or an attached or subordinate office. Very often, such organizations have no business to be in Government. They would be much better managed if they were in the public sector, the cooperative sector or as an autonomous body. Just one example of each type will suffice to clarify the point being made:

- Ordnance Factories would be better managed as PSUs
- Delhi Milk Scheme would be better off under the NDDB
- The Central Institute of English, at Mysore would be best managed if it were an autonomous body.

Delayering

9.23 Coming to the organization of a typical Department of a Central Ministry, we would like to recommend delayering as an antidote to delay. There should be a general rule that no file would be allowed to travel to more than three hierarchical levels before a decision is taken. The TCS study has hinted at the solution by delinking hierarchical levels from promotions. We have separately approved a modified version of the hierarchy suggested by

TCS as under:

- Top Executives
- Senior Executives
- Executives

- Supervisory Staff
- Supporting Staff
- Auxiliary Staff

ACP and Delayering

9.24 Thus there will be only six levels in the hierarchy. The TCS have suggested that promotions to grades within a level should be for purposes of financial benefit, but need not have any relationship with a higher decision-making level in the hierarchy. We have adapted the TCS recommendation to provide for the Assured Career Progression Scheme, by which all non-executive cadres will receive two financial upgradations on a time-bound basis while executives will benefit from three such financial upgradations. The ACP has been designed to delink hierarchy from financial upgradations, and should therefore help in delayering of the Governmental setup.

Level Jumping

9.25 Another method of quick disposal, which is quite related to delayering, is known as level jumping. Here there is conscious attempt to bypass rungs in the hierarchy. As early as September, 1968 the Administrative Reforms Commission recommended that there should be only two levels of consideration and decision below the Minister viz: (i) Under Secretary/Deputy Secretary and (ii) Joint Secretary/Additional Secretary/Secretary. This observation led to implementation of a scheme of direct submission of cases by senior Assistants to Branch Officers in 1974. In 1978, the scheme got a push when it was said that a case should either be seen by an Under Secretary or a Deputy Secretary/Director but not by both. The concept of level jumping, though known in Government, has not been effectively implemented so far. What is required is a firm guideline that at the executive level, the third level should be the last, where a decision is taken.

Desk Officer

9.26 A major piece of organizational restructuring was the enunciation of the Desk Officer concept. The attempt here was to convert the Central Secretariat into an officer-oriented system. The Desk Officer system was introduced in January, 1973 in selected wings of Ministries where at least 40% of the work related to strategic policy making, planning and problem solving. Each desk comprised two officers of the rank of Under Secretary or Section Officer or both. The Section Officer submitted cases directly to the Deputy Secretary, while the Under Secretary submitted his files direct to the Joint Secretary. The idea was to abolish the Section, which has too much of supporting staff in the shape of Assistants, UDCs, LDCs, Daftaris, Peons etc. The aim was to reduce the number of levels by at least two, to reduce the accent on noting and to lay stress on oral discussion, to foster greater participation in and commitment to organizational goals among officers at the base of the Secretariat structure. Each desk was given a well-defined area of functioning. SOs appointed as Desk Officers were allowed to authenticate orders and sanctions in the name of the President and to dispose cases on their own responsibility.

Why it has not made Headway

9.27 Currently, there are 1816 Sections and 427 Desks in the Government of India. The Desk Officer system has not made much headway due to the following reasons:

(a) Section Officers appointed as Desk Officers got all the responsibility but without much monetary incentive. They were allowed a special pay of Rs. 150/- p.m., which proved insufficient to motivate them.

(b) The staff unions saw the Desk Officer system as an attempt to reduce the dependence of the Secretariat on the supporting staff like Assistants, UDCs, LDCs etc. whose numbers are very large. They asserted their position in the JCM and forced the Government to slow down the implementation of the new system.

(c) There was just one desk attaché or P.A. attached to the desk, with the result that no memory could be built up, as in the case of the section. The working of a desk got disrupted even by the proceeding of one of its members on leave.

The New Desk Officer Concept

9.28 It is our considered view that no restructuring of the Secretariat can go very far unless the Desk Officer system is reintroduced in a highly effective manner. We propose to remove the defects in the earlier system by adopting the following strategy:

(a) The Desk Officer should be a separate and distinct post, not a mere honorific for a Section Officer, with a pittance as special pay. That is why we are suggesting that 25% of the posts of Section Officers be converted into Desk Officers in a higher pre-revised scale of Rs. 2500-4000.

(b) The percentage of 25% should gradually be increased to an optimum level, so that the bulk of the work, baring that pertaining to housekeeping and routine administration, is finally done in the desks and not in the sections.

(c) Each Desk should contain two officers and two Executive

Assistants. With a numerical strength of four, the absence of one or two members will not lead to a collapse of the Desk.

The Executive Assistant Concept

9.28 The next step that is necessary to restructure the supporting staff in the Central Secretariat is to create a multi-skilled position called Executive Assistant. He should replace the present posts of Assistant, UDC, LDC, PA and Stenographer. The qualifications prescribed for this functionary should include:

(a) graduation in any discipline
(b) the qualifications presently prescribed for a stenographer
(c) ability to work on computers.

Training to Executive Assistants

9.29 The training imparted to an Executive Assistant should be such as to enable him to discharge all the skills of noting, drafting, filing, stenography, typing, public relations, receiving telephone calls and visitors and so on. The idea is to have a multi-skilled employee capable of performing all the tasks required for a competent secretary in organizations other than the Government.

Multiskilling in Group 'D'

9.30 We have to inject the concept of multi-skilling at the Group 'D' level too. Here we may finally arrive at the ideal worker who may be called an Office Attendant and can really attend to all the auxiliary tasks in an office. But in the short run we are suggesting a rationalization into four occupational groups – office attendants, security attendants, cosmetic attendants and malis.

Office Systems

9.31 There is a whole area of office systems, about which the TCS study has thrown up a number of ideas. Restructuring of office systems has to make the office more efficient and effective. This can be done by:

- reducing unnecessary movement of files
- reducing the number of files with various officers at any given time
- preventing wastage of time in locating the files
- freeing officers from routine maintenance of records
- eliminating repetitive tasks
- making the dak system more efficient etc.

Coordinating Agencies

Planning Commission

9.32 Lastly, we come to the coordinating agencies in the

Government. The most gargantuan of these is the Planning Commission. There was probably some justification for its size and range of authority when our objective was a centrally controlled economy on the Soviet pattern. Now that such centralized planning models have been abandoned even in the country of their birth and we are moving towards an open, liberalized economy, we have to considerably reduce the size of the Planning Commission. Japan has a small Economic Planning Unit under the Prime Minister's Office. In our case, we can have the Planning Commission as a separate entity with much more reduced functions than at present. It should be an advisory body performing an idea generating role and providing alternatives before the national economy in a fast changing and technology-driven world.

Department of Programme Implementation

9.33 The Department of Programme Implementation also had a Programme coordinating and monitoring role at one time. Somewhere along the way, it has lost its mandate. It should be abolished.

PMO

9.34 The Prime Minister's Office has emerged as a coordinating office of sorts. It may be of advantage to have a less visible role for it.

Cabinet Secretariat

9.35 The Cabinet Secretariat is officially charged with the task of coordination and is geared for it. This position should be recognized and the Cabinet Secretary charged with the responsibility for ensuring coordination at the bureaucratic level. There may be need for some amendment in the Rules of Business to provide for certain matters to be resolved at the level of Secretaries through the intervention of the Cabinet Secretary, and at the level of Ministers through the intervention of the Prime Minster. This will impart the necessary edge to both the offices, in keeping a grip on the governmental machinery, so that all actions of Government are seen to move in the same general direction and in mutual harmony.

Conclusion

9.36 We have provided certain broad directions on the restructuring of the Central Secretariat. Similar solutions will also apply to attached and subordinate offices. It is our fervent hope that organizational restructuring of the Governmental machinery would lead to a more effective, more efficient and a service-oriented setup.

18

Ministry of Finance, Expenditure Reforms Commission, 2000

Summary of Recommendations

1. A cut of 10% of the staff as on 1.1.2000 to be carried out by the year 2004-2005.

2. A screening committee consisting of secretary of the concerned ministry, a representative of DOPT and a representative of Department of Expenditure should prepare annual direct recruitment plan for all cadres, with the approval in respect of group A posts, being accorded by a committee consisting of the Cabinet Secretary, concerned Secretary, Secretary (DOP&T) and Secretary (Expenditure).

3. There should be a total ban on creation of new posts for two years.

4. Staff declared surplus should be transferred to the Surplus Cell to be re-designated as the Division of Retraining and Deployment, who will pay their salary, retirement benefits etc. In these centres, where the number of surplus staff is quite small, the present practice of the parent organizations making these payments may be continued.

5. Surplus staff should be made eligible for a liberal Voluntary Retirement Scheme recommended by the Fifth Central Pay Commission with the exception that commutation entitlements will be as at present and the ex-gratia amount will be paid in monthly installments covering a five year period.

Ministry of Finance, Report of the Expenditure Reforms Commission, 2000, Vol. 1, p. 82.

6. Those who do not opt for Voluntary Retirement Scheme and are not redeployed within one year will be discharged from service.

7. Redeployment of Group D will be handled by DOPT and not DGET.

8. Group A official opting for Voluntary Retirement Scheme will not be required to seek approval for commercial employment after retirement.

Highlights of the Recommendations on Downsizing and Reorganisation by the Expenditure Reforms Commission

Ministries	*Directorate / offices*	*Sanctioned*	*Actual*	*Vacant*	*Surplus*	*To be abolished*
I and B		52319		8135		5603
I and B	AIR and DD	44540		7727		
I and B	Secretariat	85				56
Coal	Secretariat	171				
Coal	CMPF	1603	1346	257		
Coal	CIL	562071			19658	118414
Eco Aff	NSO	3404	1191	2213		
Eco Aff	Economic Division	51				42
Eco Aff	GIC	683				623
Eco Aff	Banking Division	220				
Eco Aff	IIC	126	87	39		106
Eco Aff	Mints and Presses	25000				16250
SSI and A and RI	Main Ministry	56				
SSI and A and RI	DC (SSI)	3586	3289	297		481
SSI and A and RI	NSIC	1451				602-849
SSI and A and RI	KVIC	4631				1349
SSI and A and RI	Coir Board	501	457	44		134
HI		214	210	4		
Posts		292672$				
Posts	Civil wing	1341				

Ministries	*Directorate/offices*	*Sanctioned*	*Actual*	*Vacant*	*Surplus*	*To be abolished*
Posts	Accounts organization	7859				5182
Supply		177	172	5		148
Supply	Finance wing	31	31	0		20
Supply	DGS and D	3540	2876	664		1194
Supply	CCA	1036				921
Supply	NTH	794		133		
Steel		642				40
Steel	JPC	265	205	60		
P and NG		314	296	13		
C and PC		257		25		
C and PC	Petrochemical Div (Secretariat)	16				11
C and PC	Chemicals Div (Secretariat)	14				8
C and PC	Office of Welfare Commission	1547		545		
C and PC	NPPA	60		13		
Fertilizers		272	255	17		
Fertilizers	Secretariat	59	56	3		29
Mines	Ministry	228				87
Mines	IBM	1743	1599	143		143

Ministries	*Directorate / offices*	*Sanctioned*	*Actual*	*Vacant*	*Surplus*	*To be abolished*
Mines	Coal Wing	1455	1455			1275
Mines	GSI	16310	13041	3269		
CA, F and PD						
CA, F and PD	NISST	155	21			
Cons Aff		215	204	11		
Sugar and Ed oils	BIS	2600	2100	500		
Sugar and Ed oils					20	16
NPC	NPC	651	530	121		150
Agr and Coop		7059				385
Agr and Coop	Economic Administration					41
Agr and Coop	NRMD	105				58
Agr and Coop	Rainfed Division	51				
Agr and Coop	All India Soil and Land Use Survey	511				254
Agr and Coop	Cooperation and Credit Div	105				52
Agr and Coop	Directorate of Plant Protection		1813			123
Agr and Coop	Direc. of Agriculture Marketing		1377			94
Agr and Coop	NCDC		798			82

Ministries	*Directorate / offices*	*Sanctioned*	*Actual*	*Vacant*	*Surplus*	*To be abolished*
Rural Dev			550			
Ex Aff			6640			
RT and H	Road Transport and Highways					57
RT and H	Road Wing					58
Shipping						16000
Shipping	main ministry	329		13		
Shipping	Secretariat	89				41
HRD	Secretariat	62	57	5		
Sec Edu	NCERT		2946			1834
Sec Edu	UGC		883			265
W and C Welfare		296	274	22		
YA and S		122	124	-2		
Sports		51	43	8		
E and F	Main Ministry	699	645	54	54	54
E and F	NRCD	117	126	-9		34
E and F	NAEB		91			30
E and F	ICFRE		2800			936
Culture		329	280	49		
Commerce			147			85
Commerce	MPEDA		428	28		

Ministries	*Directorate / offices*	*Sanctioned*	*Actual*	*Vacant*	*Surplus*	*To be abolished*
Commerce	Tea Board		150			37
Commerce	Cofee Board		1100			330
Commerce	Rubber Board					450
Commerce	dept proper		671			32
Commerce	sub offices		1560			67
UD and PA	Land and Dev Office					50% of C and D
UD and PA	Town and Country Planning Org					30% of C and D
Urban Dev	Directorate of Plant Protection					20
Urban Dev	Directorate of Printing	12764				6421
Pers and Pub Gr	documentation div					28
Civil Aviation		696			166	166
Civil Aviation	Commission of Railway Safety	162	162	0		50%
Tourism	DG, Tourism		242		28	28
Ind Pol and Prn		990				450
Ind Pol and Prn	Salt Commissioner office					800

List of Departments/ Division/offices that need to be wounded up

Ministry/Departments	*Recommended to be wounded up*	
Information and Broadcasting	NFDC	
Information and Broadcasting	DD and AIR	To be shifted to Prasar Bharti Corporation
Information and Broadcasting	Film Division	
Information and Broadcasting	Children's Film Society	
Information and Broadcasting	Directorate of Film Festivals	
Information and Broadcasting	Directorate of Field Publicity and Song and Drama Div	
Information and Broadcasting	Photo Div	Functions to be transferred to Press Information Bureau
Information and Broadcasting	Publication Division	
Coal	CIL	
Small Scale Industries	Small Industries Service Institutes	
Small Scale Industries	Production Centre (SIDO)	
Heavy Industries	BIFR	
Supply	Inst of Supply and Quality Mgt (DGS and D)	
Supply	DCI and S	
Economic Affairs	Board for Industrial and Financial Reconstruction	
Economic Affairs	Appellate Authority for Industrial finance Reconstruction	
Steel	Office of Devt Commissioner for Iron and Steel	
Mines	NIRM	
Mines	NIMH	
Mines	BGML	
Cons Affairs, Food and PD	Directorate of Vanaspati, Veg Oils and Fats	
Cons Affairs, Food and PD	Directorate of Sugar	

Ministry / Departments	*Recommended to be wounded up*	
Cons Affairs, Food and PD	Indian Grain Storage Mgt and Research Inst	
Cons Affairs, Food and PD	National Institute of Sugar and Sugar Tech (Mau)	Agriculture University or Training Centre
Cons Affairs, Food and PD	HVOC	
Cons Affairs, Food and PD	Tariff commission	
Agriculture and Cooperation	National Oil Seeds and Veg Oils Dev Board	
Agriculture and Cooperation	Coconut Board	
Agriculture and Cooperation	Directorate of Oilseeds	
Agriculture and Cooperation	Directorate of Pulses	
Environment and Forests	Environment wing	
Environment and Forests	ICFRE	
Culture	Centre for Cultural Resource and Training	
Urban Development and Poverty Alleviation	National Building Organisation	
Urban Development and Poverty Alleviation	Government of India Stationery office	
Urban Development and Poverty Alleviation	National Building Organisation	
Urban Development and Poverty Alleviation	HPL	
Industrial Policy and Promotion	Office of Salt Commissioner	
Road Transport and Highways	Indian Road Construction Corp Ltd.	
Shipping	Tariff Authority for Major Ports	
Human Resource Development	National Institute of Adult Education	
Women and Child Dev	CSWB	
Women and Child Dev	CSWD	
Personnel, PG and UPSC	Documentation and Dissemination Division	

19

Report of the Second Administrative Reforms Commission on Organizational Structure of Government of India, 2009

Summary of Recommendations*

1. Rationalizing the Functions of Government

(a) The Government of India should primarily focus on the core functions stated below:

(i) Defence, International Relations, Public Order, Justice and rule of law.

(ii) Human development through access to good quality education and healthcare to every citizen.

(iii) Infrastructure and sustained natural resource development

(iv) Social security and social justice.

(v) Macro-economic management and economic policy.

(vi) National policies in other sectors.

(b) Government at all levels should be guided by the principle of subsidiarity.

(c) There is need to carry out a detailed analysis of the functions/activities in each Ministry/Department in the light of (a) and (b) above. This should be followed by restructuring which may include decentralization/delegation or hiving off activities.

2. Rationalizing and reorganizing the Ministries and Departments.

---

*Extracts from the Report of the Second Administrative Reforms Commission on Organizational Structure of Government of India, Ministry of Personnel, Public Grievances and Pensions, Department of Administrative Reforms and Public Grievances, April 2009.

(a) The concept of a Ministry would have to be redefined. A Ministry would mean a group of departments whose functions and subjects are closely related and is assigned to a First or Coordinating Minister for the purpose of providing overall leadership and coordination. This concept of a Ministry and the Coordinating (or First) Minister may be explicitly laid down in the Allocation of Business Rules. Adequate delegation among the Ministers would have to be laid down in the Transaction of Business Rules. A consequence of this, rationalization of Secretary level posts wherever required may also need to be carried out.

(b) Individual departments or any combination of these could be headed by the Coordinating (or First) Minister, other Cabinet Ministers/Minister(s) of State.

(c) The structure of the Government of India should be rationalized by grouping together closely related subjects as illustrated in paragraph. Without going into the details of how the existing Ministries can be grouped based on how closely their subjects are inter-related, the Commission would like to demonstrate through the following examples how this can be achieved.

For example, the Ministry of Local Government could include the following Ministries/Departments:

(i) Rural Development.

(ii) Drinking Water Supply.

(iii) Housing and Urban Poverty Alleviation.

(iv) Urban Development.

(v) Panchayati Raj.

Further, the following Ministries/Departments could be clubbed under the Ministry of Transport:

(i) Shipping.

(ii) Road Transport and Highways.

(iii) Civil Aviation.

(iv) Railways.

Similarly, the Ministry of Energy would include the following Ministries/Departments:

(i) New and Renewable Energy.

(ii) Petroleum and Natural Gas.

(iii) Power.

As a consequence of this exercise, the Commission expects that the number of Ministries in Government of India could be reduced from about 55 at present to about 20-25.

3. Recasting the Allocation of Business Rules

(a) There is need to recast the Allocation of Business Rules to make them more focused on the goals and outcomes of each Ministry/Department in order to shift the emphasis from a detailed listing of activities/subjects of each Ministry/ Department to a broader perspective.

(b) The Allocation of Business Rules should first provide a Statement of the mission of the department followed by a list of subjects and functions.

(c) There is need to bring greater uniformity in the description of the roles and functions of various Ministries/Departments.

(d) Ministries/Departments should maintain a master list of all laws pertaining to the subjects dealt with in that Ministry/ Department instead of mentioning them in the Allocation of Business Rules. The underlying principle should be stated in the Rules that all laws relating to the subjects and functions allocated to a Ministry/Department would fall under its purview.

(e) Instead of naming the individual PSUs and autonomous organizations under each Ministry, the Rules should merely have a generic entry to the effect that all PSUs and Autonomous Organizations whose functioning is directly related to subject(s) of the concerned Ministry would be under its jurisdiction. However, in cases where activities of a PSU or an autonomous organization relates to more than one Ministry/Department, then it may be advisable to list out such PSUs under a particular Ministry/Department.

4. Focus on Policy Analysis

(a) In order to make them binding, the general principles to govern the extent of delegation from Departments to their attached and subordinate offices (executive agencies) may be incorporated in the Transaction of Business Rules. These principles may stipulate that the Ministries/Departments should concentrate on the following:

(i) Policy analysis, planning, policy making and strategic decisions.

(ii) Budgeting and Parliamentary work.

(iii) Monitoring of implementation through systems and procedures.

(iv) Appointments of key personnel.

(v) Coordination.

(vi) Evaluation.

(a) Attached and subordinate offices should serve as the executive agencies of the ministries and concentrate on the implementation of Government policies and programmes.

5. Policy Evaluation

(a) Each Department should introduce a system of policy evaluation to be carried out at the end of prescribed periods. All relevant policies should be updated in the light of the findings of such evaluations.

6. Creation of Effective Executive Agencies

(a) Each Union Government Ministry should scrutinize the functions/activities of the ministry to confirm whether these activities/functions are critical to the mission of the Department and can only be carried out by government agencies. This should be done with reference to core areas mentioned by the Commission in para 1.

(b) Only those functions/activities that are in line with the principles enunciated in paragraph above should be carried out directly by the Department/Ministries. Other functions/activities should be carried out by the executive agencies of the department.

(c) Each agency, whether a new body or an existing departmental undertaking/agency/board/special purpose body etc. that is to function as an executive agency, must be autonomous or semi-autonomous and professionally managed under a mandate. Such executive agencies could be structured as a department, board, commission, company, society etc.

(d) The right balance between autonomy and accountability needs to be struck while designing the institutional framework of executive agencies. This could be achieved through well-designed performance agreements, Memorandum of Understanding (MOU), contracts etc. However, preparing and enforcing such performance contracts requires considerable upgradation of capacity in the concerned government departments.

7. Reorganization of Ministries

(a) Each Department should lay down a detailed scheme of delegation at all levels so that the decision-making takes place at the most appropriate level. It should be laid down in the Manual of Office Procedure that every Ministry should prescribe a detailed scheme of delegation for its officers. This delegation should be arrived at on the basis of an analysis of the activities and functions of the Ministry/Department and the type of decisions that these entail which should be dovetailed with the decision-making units identified in that Department.

(b) The scheme of delegation should be updated periodically and should also be 'audited' at regular intervals. The audit should ensure that the delegated authority is actually exercised by the delegatee. The scheme of delegation should be placed in the public domain.

(c) The number of levels through which a file passes for a decision should not exceed three.

(i) In cases where the Minister's approval is required, the file should be initiated by the Deputy Secretary/Director concerned and should be moved through the Joint Secretary (or Additional Secretary/Special Secretary) and the Secretary (or Special Secretary) to the Minister.

(ii) Cases requiring approval of the Secretary should go through just two levels (e.g. either US and Director, US and JS or Director and JS).

(iii) Cases requiring approval of the JS/Director/DS should come through just one level. The exact combination of levels should be spelt out in the scheme of delegation for each Ministry/ Department whereas the number of levels as suggested above should be prescribed in the Manual of Office Procedure.

(iv) The Department dealing with administrative reforms in the Union Government should be entrusted with the task of ensuring compliance with this stipulation.

(d) For addressing cross cutting issues, the Secretary of the concerned Department should have the flexibility to create inter-disciplinary teams.

(e) The Manual of Office Procedure should be recast based on the principles that these issues can best be resolved by ensuring that each Ministry/Department lays down a detailed scheme of delegation at all levels so that the decision-making takes place at the most appropriate level.

(f) The Departments should build an electronic database of decisions that are likely to be used as precedents. Thereafter such database should be periodically reviewed and where necessary, changes in rules introduced in order to codify them. There may also be precedents that may be the result of wrong or arbitrary decision-making which the Department would prefer not to rely on for the future. In such cases the Department would have to appropriately change its policy/guidelines and if required even the rules to ensure that these precedents are not wrongly used.

8. Coordination Mechanisms

(a) There is need to ensure that the existing coordination mechanisms like the Group of Ministers and Committee of Secretaries function effectively and help in early resolution of issues as stated in Cabinet Committee and GoMs. Selective, but effective use of GoMs with clear mandate and prescribed time limits, would be helpful.

There is need for ensuring extensive horizontal coordination where policies are spread over a number of departments and where policy delivery mechanisms are distributed in different parts of the government. This issue of coordination among departments in the Government of India was also examined by the First Administrative Reforms Commission (First ARC). It observed as follows:

One of the major tasks of the Cabinet is to ensure coordination of all important policies, programmes and decisions of Government. There exist at present nine Standing Committees of the Cabinet as follows:

Internal Affairs;
Foreign Affairs;
Defence;
Prices, Production and Exports;
Family Planning;
Food and Agriculture;
Tourism and Transport;
Parliamentary Affairs; and
Appointments.

The Commission recognizes the importance of coordination amongst various Ministries/Departments, more so because of new and emerging challenges in many sectors, which require a coordinated national response. The Commission has already recommended re-grouping of government functions into inter-related categories to be assigned to a Coordinating Minister to improve such coordination. Besides, while examining the internal structures of the Ministries, the Commission has suggested a flexible, inter-disciplinary team based approach, which would inherently serve to improve coordination.

The need for inter-Ministerial coordination at the apex level would be reduced as a result of these measures. Nonetheless, there will always be issues and problems for which high level inter-Ministerial coordination would be required. In such cases, the extent and quality of coordination would depend on the skill of the coordinator and the spirit with which the members participate. To achieve the necessary coordination, a Secretary should function as a member of a team rather than as a spokesperson of his/her Department's stated position. Furthermore, effective functioning of the existing mechanism comprising the Cabinet Secretariat, Committee of Secretaries, Group of Ministers and Cabinet Committees should, therefore, be adequate to meet the requirement of inter-Ministerial coordination.

An area where the Commission feels the need for having a formal coordination mechanism relates to issues, which may arise between the States and the Union Government particularly in relation to sectors like power, transport, water etc. While, at present, such issues are often taken up for resolution by the Government of India through discussions between the concerned Ministry/Ministries and the States, there may be instances where resolution of such issues gets delayed in the absence of an inter-Ministerial mechanism. It should be possible to resolve such stalemates by the States bringing the matter before the Cabinet Secretary for consideration by the Committee of Secretaries based on which the Union Cabinet could take a final view. Secretary (Coordination) could play a key role in facilitating this coordination. Selective, but effective use of GoMs with clear mandate and prescribed time limits, would be helpful.

(b) Unresolved issues concerning States which require inter-Ministerial coordination in Government of India, should be placed before the Committee of Secretaries (CoSs) and then to the Union Cabinet for resolution.

9. Creating an Effective Regulatory Framework

(a) Setting up of a Regulator should be preceded by a detailed review to decide whether the policy regime in the concerned sector is such that a Regulator would be better placed to deliver the policy objectives of the department concerned.

(b) In addition to the statutory framework, which underpins the interface between the government and the regulator, each Ministry/Department should evolve a 'Management Statement' outlining the objectives and roles of each regulator and the guidelines governing their interaction with the government. This would guide both the government department and the Regulator.

(c) There is need for greater uniformity in the terms of appointment, tenure and removal of various regulatory authorities considering these have been set up with broadly similar objectives and functions and should enjoy the same degree of autonomy. The initial process of appointment of Chairman and Board Members should be transparent, credible and fair.

(d) The appointment of the Chairman and Board Members for all such regulatory authorities should be done by the Union/State Governments after an initial screening and recommendation of a panel of names by a Selection Committee. The composition of the Selection Committee should be defined in the respective Acts and may broadly follow the pattern laid down in the Electricity Regulatory Commission Act.

(e) The tenure of the Chairmen and Board Members could also be made uniform preferably three years or 65 years of age whichever is earlier.

(f) Legal provisions regarding removal of Board Members should be made uniform while at the same time ensuring sufficient safeguards against arbitrary removal. This could be achieved by allowing removal by the Union Government only on fulfillment of certain conditions as laid down in Section 6 of the IRDA Act with the additional safeguard that a removal for abuse of power shall be preceded by an enquiry and consultation with UPSC.

(g) Parliamentary oversight of regulators should be ensured through the respective Departmentally Related Standing Parliamentary Committees.

(h) A body of reputed outside experts should propose guidelines for periodic evaluation of the independent Regulators. Based on these guidelines, government in consultation with respective Departmentally related Standing Committee of the Parliament should fix the principles on which the Regulators should be evaluated. The annual reports of the regulators should include a report on their performance in the context of these principles. This report should be referred to the respective Parliamentary Committee for discussion.

(i) Each statute creating a regulator should include a provision for an impact assessment periodically by an external agency. Once the objective of creating a level playing field is achieved, the intervention of the Regulators could be reduced in a phased manner ultimately leading either to their abolition or to convergence with other Regulators.

(j) There is need to achieve greater uniformity in the structure of Regulators. The existing coordination mechanisms such as the Committee of Secretaries/Cabinet Committees, assisted by Secretary (Coordination) could easily ensure that the institutional framework for all Regulators follows, by and large, a uniform pattern.

Index